Farm Worker Futurism

DIFFERENCE INCORPORATED

Roderick A. Ferguson and Grace Kyungwon Hong, Series Editors

Farm Worker Futurism

Speculative Technologies of Resistance

Curtis Marez

DIFFERENCE INCORPORATED

 University of Minnesota Press
Minneapolis • London

An earlier version of chapter 2 was published digitally as "Cesar Chavez's Video Collection," *American Literature* 85, no. 4 (2013); http://americanliterature .dukejournals.org/content/85/4/811. Portions of chapter 3 were published as "Cesar Chavez, the United Farm Workers, and the History of Star Wars," in *Race after the Internet,* Lisa Nakamura and Peter Chow White, eds. (Abingdon, Oxon: Routledge, 2011), 85–106; copyright 2011 by Taylor and Francis; reprinted by permission of Taylor and Francis Group, LLC, a division of Informa plc.

Published by the University of Minnesota Press
111 Third Avenue South, Suite 290
Minneapolis, MN 55401-2520
http://www.upress.umn.edu

Printed in the United States of America on acid-free paper

The University of Minnesota is an equal-opportunity educator and employer.

22 21 20 19 18 17 16   10 9 8 7 6 5 4 3 2 1

Library of Congress Cataloging-in-Publication Data
Names: Marez, Curtis, author.
Title: Farm worker futurism : speculative technologies of resistance / Curtis Marez.
Description: Minneapolis : University of Minnesota Press, 2016. | Series: Difference incorporated | Includes bibliographical references and index.
Identifiers: LCCN 2015039885| ISBN 978-0-8166-7231-8 (hc) | ISBN 978-0-8166-9745-8 (pb)
Subjects: LCSH: Agricultural laborers—Effect of automation on—California—History—20th century. | Agricultural industries—California—Automation. | Agricultural laborers—Political activity—California—History—20th century. | Agricultural laborers—Labor unions—California—History—20th century. | Labor movement in motion pictures.
Classification: LCC HD1527.C2 M36 2016 | DDC 331.7/63097301—dc23
LC record available at http://lccn.loc.gov/2015039885

To Shelley

Contents

Preface and Acknowledgments

This book is an interdisciplinary study of the material and symbolic significance of technology in conflicts between agribusiness corporations and workers of color in California from the 1940s to the 1990s and beyond. An important practical and symbolic means of exploiting and disciplining labor, agribusiness technology also became the medium and object of struggle over the future of California agriculture and the larger cultural and political contexts supporting it. Farm workers have opposed mechanization in the fields, industrial work camps, and, perhaps most famously, pesticides. They have also responded to capitalist efforts to dominate the visual field by turning a critical gaze on agribusiness in numerous graphics, photos, films, and videos, decoupling technology from an exclusive connection to patriarchal white capitalism. Farm worker unions did not simply change *what* audiences saw but instead attempted to alter *how* they saw agribusiness, inverting the hierarchical relations of looking that structured the agribusiness-dominated mediascape, and promoting new kinds of activist spectatorship among farm workers and their supporters. Finally, farm workers have appropriated visual technologies to imagine better worlds and to project different, more egalitarian social orders. From this perspective, farm workers' visual technologies—including moving picture cameras, video cameras and players, and computer screens—constitute tools for speculative world-building.

One reason that scholars have not appreciated the political significance of what I call *farm worker futurism* is because they have not always attempted to understand and model farm worker visions of the world. Recalling the historical materialist method of research and analysis Walter Benjamin developed for his "Arcades Project," *Farm Worker Futurism* employs a method of reading and interpretation that juxtaposes often low, marginal, ephemeral, and seemingly "minor" cultural fragments to bring into relief historical relations of power otherwise occluded in more conventional historical accounts based in dominant archives and more familiar kinds of evidence.[1] The work of reconstructing a farm worker perspective is necessarily "speculative," but it reveals relations of power that remain invisible if we overlook farm worker views. So while *Farm Worker Futurism* draws on dominant state and capitalist sources, focusing in particular on agribusiness fantasies of a future where workers have been replaced with machines, it foregrounds forms of evidence generally rendered subaltern in more conventional histories, including not only examples of visual culture produced by farm worker movements but also farm worker practices of looking that bring into critical relief the limits of the present by imagining better futures.

I delivered talks drawn from this book at multiple venues, and I am especially grateful to audiences at the American Studies Association convention, the Modern Language Association convention, the Latina/o Studies Association convention, the Reimagining the Hemispheric South Conference at the University of California, Santa Barbara, and the University of California San Diego Ethnic Studies Colloquium. Portions of chapter 3 were published in *Race after the Internet,* and I am grateful to one of its editors, Lisa Nakamura, for her insightful suggestions.

I began this project while assistant professor in the American studies department at the University of California, Santa Cruz, where I benefited from working with Gabriela F. Arredondo, Pedro Castillo, Jim Clifford, Michael Cowan, Angela Davis, Dana Frank, Rosa Linda Fregoso, Susan Gillman, Herman Gray, Jennifer A. González, Kirsten Silva Gruesz, Lisbeth Haas, Amelie Hastie, Yvette Huginnie, Norma Klahn, Olga Najera-Ramírez, Eric Porter, Catherine Ramírez, Renya Ramírez, Russell Rodriguez, Shelley Stamp, Deborah Vargas, Judy Yung, and Patricia Zavella. During my joint time in the School of Cinematic Arts' critical studies department and in the Department of American Studies and Ethnicity at the University of Southern California I was lucky to know and learn from Adán Avalos, Anne Friedberg, Ruthie Gilmore, Mark Harris, Jane Iwamura, David James, Priya Jaikumar, Chera Kee, Kara Keeling, Marsha Kinder, Doe Mayer, Tara McPherson, Jaime Nasser, Sionne Neely, Veronica Paredes, Dana Polan, Laura Pulido, Howard Rodman, Luis Carlos Rodriguez, Jennifer Rosales, John Carlos Rowe, Noelia Saenz,

Marita Sturken, Janani Subramanian, and Bill Whittington. While at USC I served as the editor of *American Quarterly,* which directly and indirectly sustained this project, and I'm especially grateful to the journal's group of brilliant associate editors for their friendship and solidarity—Roderick Ferguson, Jim Lee, Lisa Lowe, and Dylan Rodriguez. Also during my tenure at *AQ* I was fortunate to work with the late Clyde Woods on a special issue titled *In the Wake of Hurricane Katrina.* He was a brilliant and generous thinker whose analysis of the neo-plantation South has informed my own understanding of "farm fascism" in the Southwest.

I want to thank Ester Hernández for giving me permission to reproduce *Sun Mad, Heroes and Saints,* and *The Beating of Dolores Huerta by the San Francisco Police.* While the first image has been widely circulated, according to Hernandez the other two are published here for the first time. I similarly thank Clara Cid and Ricardo Favela's children, Florentina, Margarita, F. Manuel, and Rosita Favela, for permission to reproduce Ricardo Favela's art, and Esteban Villa for giving me permission to reproduce one of his posters. I am grateful to Alex Rivera for making the brilliant film *Sleep Dealer* and for sharing ideas about it with me. We first met at USC, where I organized a weekend conference on borderland genre films in which he previewed *Sleep Dealer,* and our subsequent discussions at conferences and events at UCSD's Arthur C. Clarke Center for Human Imagination and elsewhere have been formative for this project.

While still at USC I was incredibly lucky to be part of an intellectual collective at the University of California, San Diego that included Luis Alvarez, Jody Blanco, Fatima El-Tayeb, Yen Espiritu, Ross Frank, Tak Fujitani, Rosemary George, Sara Johnson, Lisa Lowe, Nayan Shah, Stephanie Smallwood, Shelley Streeby, Danny Widener, and Lisa Yoneyama. I miss what was, and I know this book would not exist without you, my friends. Since joining the UCSD ethnic studies department I have found brilliant new friends and colleagues, and I especially want to thank Patrick Anderson, Ricardo Dominguez, Kirstie Dorr, Dayo Gore, Dave Gutiérrez, Adria Imada, Roshanak Kheshti, Sara Clarke Kaplan, Stevie Ruiz, Daphne Taylor-Garcia, Wayne Yang, Kalindi Vora, and Sal Zárate. I owe debts I can never repay to Beatrice Pita and Rosaura Sánchez, not only for their brilliant book *Lunar Braceros,* but also for their years *en la lucha.* I also want to thank the ethnic studies department staff whose work has helped make mine possible: Damarys Alicea-Santana, Samira Khazai, Christa Ludeking, and Daisy Rodriguez.

I'm grateful to the University of California's Humanities Research Institute for sponsoring the residential research group "Between Life and Death: Necropolitics in the Era of Late Capitalism" that enabled me to complete the book. I also want to thank the group's organizers, Grace Hong and Jody Kim, as well as its other participants: Alexander Hirsch, Christina Hong, Thu-Huong Nguyen-vo, Andy Smith, and Lindsay Smith. I am especially grateful to Grace Hong—most excellent organizer, interlocutor, editor, and friend.

I am especially thankful to former University of Minnesota Press editorial director Richard Morrison. Richard was confident about the project at a moment when I wasn't quite, and his support and encouragement renewed my faith in all tomorrow's parties. Thanks as well to UMP director Douglas Armato, who provided valuable advice as I prepared the final manuscript for publication, and to Erin Warholm-Wohlenhaus, Ana Bichanich, Mike Stoffel, and Nicholas Taylor for their editorial and production assistance.

Above all, I owe everything to my parents. My father, Paul Marez, was a hard and skilled worker whose laboring life began in the cotton and melon fields of California, but his love was making things out of wood. He was a master carpenter who built things both useful and beautiful with hands rough and strong but at the same time capable of great tenderness. My dad was also a world traveler, an organic intellectual, and a voracious reader. He died before it was completed, but I like to think Paul Marez would have enjoyed this book.

My mother, Linda Marez, gave me her keen sense of ethics and justice, teaching me the values of humility, equity, and compassion. She is perhaps the single most important influence on me as a student and intellectual. Without her encouragement and support—not to mention the hours and hours spent on the phone with admissions staff and filling out financial aid forms—I could never have become a professor.

In the end this book belongs to Shelley Streeby. It has been many years in the making, and in that time Shelley traveled with me to archives, read and advised me on every word, and gave me the encouragement and love I needed. I can honestly say she helped keep me alive during a particularly tough year of political work. Brilliant and beautiful, I would do anything to remain by her side.

Introduction
Farm Workers in the Machine

Set in Mexico, Alex Rivera's film *Sleep Dealer* (2008) speculates about the political economy of computer technologies through the eyes of migrant workers. As the director explains, he

> basically uses the genre of science fiction to flash forward five minutes or five years to look at the politics between the United States (and Mexico) if they keep going the way they're going today. I guess science fiction is always looking at political and economic realities shot into the future, but this is from a perspective we haven't seen before: the U.S. from the outside . . . In this future, the border is closed. Instead of physically coming to the United States, work-ers go to cities in Mexico and work in giant factories or sweatshops where they connect their bodies to high-speed, network-controlled robots that do their labor. So their pure labor crosses the border, but their bodies stay in Mexico. It's kind of a sick and twisted spin on the American dream.[1]

The film develops a scenario the director first presented in *Why Cybraceros?* (1997), a short work distributed on VHS cassettes and the Internet that combined archival film footage, TV news video, and computer anima-tion. A satirical response to the Internet utopianism of the late 1990s, *Why Cybraceros?* takes the form of a fictional corporate promotional film for a new computer technology that promises to address the social con-sequences of Mexican migration to the United States. It incorporated scenes from the 1959 agribusiness-made short film *Why Braceros?* which attempted to blunt opposition to the bracero guest worker program by describing it as a temporary measure that would be unnecessary in the

1

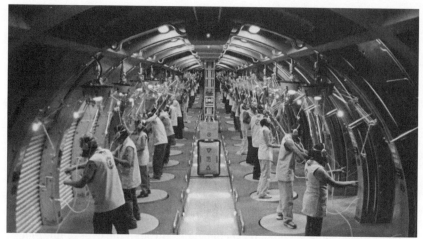

"Virtual" labor. *Sleep Dealer,* directed by Alex Rivera (2008).

Farm worker 'bots in *Sleep Dealer.*

future, when agriculture would be largely automated.[2] Reframing the footage as science fiction, Rivera raises critical questions about long-standing agribusiness fantasies of replacing migrant workers with machines. Extrapolating from Rivera's work as well as that of other artists, cultural producers, organizers, and activists, this book excavates historical formations of farm worker futurisms in California's agricultural valleys and beyond.

While often overlooked in academic studies or depicted in popular media as part of the primitive past, the San Joaquin Valley and other California agricultural regions emerge in this study as hubs of what I call farm worker futurism and its transformative speculative practices. Ernesto Galarza's 1977 study *Farm Workers and Agri-business in California, 1947–1960* anticipates *Sleep Dealer*'s near-future dystopia, narrating how agribusiness corporations mechanized production in order to discipline farm workers and destroy their unions, including the local of the National Farm Workers Union (NFWU) that Galarza helped to organize in the Valley. After World War II, he argues, automatic machines began "taking over" in the fields and orchards, using electronic "brains" and "eyes" to plant, tend, harvest, and sort produce. Particularly striking for Galarza were the mechanized cotton pickers and their "mechanical partners," the cotton "planter–cultivator" and "the scrapper that salvaged un-harvested bolls" that moved "in formation sweeping through hundreds of acres of cotton fluff like a rumbling herd of trunkless elephants." By 1950 there were over 1,400 mechanical cotton pickers in the Valley, which from Galarza's perspective looked like "'an assembly out of science fiction.'"[3] During the 1950s and 1960s, agribusiness machine manufacturers anticipated Galarza's simile, often comparing agricultural technology to "something out of science fiction."[4] Agricultural machines do indeed recall period visions of robots and space vehicles, and vice versa, suggesting that in its self-promotion agribusiness produced a futuristic visual culture of technological progress that overlapped with Cold War science fiction.[5]

The future projected by agribusiness failed to materialize, however, and with the hindsight of Walter Benjamin's last angel of history, Rivera's *Why Cybraceros?* represents agribusiness utopias in ruins. The film undermines corporate images of technological progress by incorporating scenes from a United Farm Workers (UFW) film called *Fighting for Our Lives* (*FFOL*, 1974) that shows police beating striking union members in the grape fields of the San Joaquin Valley. Cold War corporate claims that mechanization would ultimately make farm workers obsolete, we are reminded, were succeeded by the historic efforts of the UFW in the 1960s to foreground the vulnerability of workers to pesticides and other supposedly progressive tools of corporate agriculture and to organize workers to oppose agribusiness futurisms with other demands on the future.

In what follows I analyze struggles between agribusiness corporations[6] and farm workers over technology—especially visual technologies such as cameras—as means for projecting competing futures. From the

"An assembly out of science fiction." An experimental mechanical cotton picker, circa 1942. Photograph by International Harvester Company; courtesy of Wisconsin Historical Society.

late 1940s, when Galarza's NFLU went on strike in the San Joaquin Valley, to the early 1990s, when the UFW helped organize a rolling fast in solidarity with janitors at Apple Computer in the Santa Clara Valley, I study the dialectic between agribusiness and farm worker futurisms in visual culture. In opposition to forms of agribusiness sovereignty partly secured by domination of the visual field, farm workers have claimed what Nicholas Mirzoeff calls the "right to look"; thus, studying their visual culture enables the reconstruction of a subaltern "counterhistory of visuality."[7] Viewing agribusiness from below reveals how farm workers have appropriated visual technologies to imagine better worlds and project different, more egalitarian social orders.

Post–World War II farm worker unions used visual technologies to compress time and space, using photography, film, and video to respond immediately to strike conditions and to reach national and global audiences. Unions thereby attempted to produce effects of virtual co-presence, whereby farm workers, union volunteers, civic and religious groups, and consumers who existed in dramatically different and distant social spaces were brought into compelling mediated contact. Farm workers became

Futuristic farm vehicles. *(Above)* An International Harvester exhibit promoting a "Tractor of the Future" prototype, streamlined to resemble a jet plane, circa 1955. *(Below)* An agribusiness artist's rendering of the tractor of the future, remote controlled by satellite, circa 1960. Photography by International Harvester Company; courtesy of Wisconsin Historical Society.

particularly adept at employing technologies of time–space compression in part because of wider histories of transnational labor migration, especially between Mexico and the United States. Technology has long been central to the United States' relationship to Mexico, both materially, in terms of military and industrial power, and ideologically, in the form of influential discourses defining Mexico and Mexicans as backward and technologically inferior. At the same time, however, and in ways largely invisible to many contemporary U.S. Americans, Mexican migrant workers have taken up technology and formed complex techno-cultures. The novel historical uses of visual technologies by farm workers, including moving picture cameras, video cameras and players, and computer screens, thus anticipate the widely noted use of Spanish-language radio, mobile phones, and social networking Internet sites to organize the massive 2006 immigrants' rights protests.

In his famous study of California agriculture Carey McWilliams calls the agribusiness combination of public and private police violence and aggressive efforts to use the media to control public opinion "farm fascism."[8] Agribusiness farm fascism also included segregated carceral work camps which, like the agribusiness-dominated political economy more generally, prepared the way for the contemporary prison industrial complex in California, or what Ruth Wilson Gilmore calls the "Golden Gulag."[9] Visual technologies were an important component of corporate efforts to control labor and public opinion, and not only because big growers and the local police who supported them often used cameras to observe and harass farm workers.[10] The deployment of film and video cameras by agribusiness and the police as means of labor control and surveillance presupposed hierarchical relations of looking that practically and symbolically reproduced farm worker subordination, both directly, at the site of production, and indirectly, in a larger mass culture directed at non–farm worker audiences. In such contexts California farm worker unions have struggled to organize workers and produce their own media in opposition to the agribusiness monopoly over visual technology. Farm workers thus undermined agribusiness depictions of workers as mere machines of production by themselves mobilizing media technologies.

Which is to say that cameras and other visual technologies mediate the *visual field* and its attendant power effects. Despite their significant differences, the neuroscientific and psychoanalytic accounts of the visual field are generative for theorizing the significance of visual technologies in conflicts between capitalists and workers. In neuroscience "the term 'visual field' . . . refers to the spatial array of visual sensations available to (introspective) observation." In this sense the visual field is composed in response to external visual stimuli but is not its direct reflection, and dramatic differences can occur "between the exact form of the sensory stimulation and the final sensory experience." When a subject's sight is in part physically blocked, for example, perception will often fill in the blank as it were, imaginatively providing versions of what is visually missing, suggesting that the visual field presupposes subjective cognitive mapping.[11] I extrapolate from this model to theorize the heterogeneity of visual fields in particular times and places, arguing that visual fields are partially constituted by forms of socially and historically produced perceptual mapping that in turn shape the construction of historical social realities. The deployment of cameras, screens, and related kinds of visual prosthesis in the agricultural fields of California exemplify what W. T. J. Mitchell calls the chiasmatic relationship between the social construction of the visual and the visual construction of the social.[12]

The account of the visual field(s) suggested by Lacanian psychoanalysis foregrounds its constitution in social antagonisms. For Lacan the visual field is embedded in "imaginary" power dynamics of visual identification, mastery and domination, alienation and aggression. His analysis of the relationship between the visual field of the Imaginary and the Symbolic order suggests that the visual and the discursive often interact, combine, and reinforce each other in contests over power. Of particular significance for the present study is Lacan's lecture about visual perspective. The "geometrical dimension of vision," according to Lacan, represented by artistic illusions of perspective and depth, presupposes a "subjectifying relation" that produces the Cartesian subject of Western modernity. The commonsense realism of geometric perspective presupposes a particular "mapping of space" that "does not exhaust . . . what the field of vision as such offers us."[13] As an example of that which exceeds the Cartesian subject in the visual field, Lacan analyzes the use of *anamorphosis* in a famous Renaissance painting by Hans Holbein titled *The Ambassadors.* Anamorphosis refers to a visual trick in which artists include a distorted image in a painting that can only be recognized when the viewer adopts an oblique perspective. *The Ambassadors,* one of the most famous examples of the technique, presents a "realist" geometric image of two powerful men combined with the distorted image of a skull in the bottom center that is perceptible only when seen in a sidelong glance:

The two figures are frozen, stiffened in their showy adornments. Between them is a series of objects that represent in the painting of the period the symbols of *vanitas* . . . and these objects are all symbolic of sciences and arts . . . What, then, before this display of the domain of appearance in all its most fascinating forms is this object, which from some angles appears to be flying through the air, at others to be tilted? . . . Begin by walking out of the room in which it has long held your attention. It is then that, turning round as you leave . . . you apprehend in this form. What? A skull . . . All this shows that at the very heart of the period in which the subject emerged and geometrical optics was an object of research, Holbein makes visible for us there something that is simply the subject as annihilated.[14]

Here modern relations of looking produce subjectivities subtended by the skull, harbinger of death and conflict that undermines the commonsense perspectives of power and authority. Recalling Ester Hernandez's famous antipesticide print titled *Sun Mad* (chapter 3), in which the smiling face of the Sun Maid advertising icon is replaced with a skull, farm worker visual culture could be described as "anamorphic" in that it probes the blind spots in corporate imagery and promotes oblique farm worker vantage points on social reality that effectively "annihilate" privileged agribusiness perspectives.

In addition to Lacan, the work of Frantz Fanon and Judith Butler suggests that, on the one hand, the visual is structured by intersecting hierarchies of race, gender, and other axes of difference; and, on the other, that the organization of visual fields in domination tends to reproduce and extend domination.[15] Historical social constructions, the high-tech agribusiness visual field, and the farm worker visual field simultaneously mediate and enact struggles over power.

As part of battles over the future of social reality, farm worker futurism recalls recent theorizations of "speculative fiction." Afrofuturist cultural critic and artist Kodwo Eshun, for example, contrasts dominant forms of financial speculation with African diasporic speculation, or "the appeals that black artists, musicians, critics, and writers have made to the future, in moments where any future was made difficult for them to imagine."[16] Similarly, Catherine S. Ramirez has analyzed examples of "Chicanafuturism" in art and literature that explore how "new and everyday technologies, including their detritus, transform Mexican American life and culture"; that raise questions about "the promises of science, technology, and humanism for Chicanas, Chicanos, and other people of color"; and that make claims on futures from which people of color are generally excluded.[17] Most recently, in their introduction to the Internet-based collection "Speculative Life," Jayna Brown and Alexis Lothian juxtapose dominant "speculation"—"an epistemology of greed, a sanctioned terrorism, and a neo-imperialism organized around the capture of abstract futures and the subjugation of transnational labor forces"—with critical forms of "speculation" that refuse logics of "power and profit" in order "to play, to invent, to engage in the practice of imagining."[18]

Farm Worker Futurism is thus concerned, in the words of Eshun, with "the possibilities for intervention within the dimension of the predictive, the projected, the proleptic, the envisioned, the virtual, the anticipatory and the future conditional."[19] I draw a distinction, however, between futurism—the projection of a particular, determinant future social order—and futurity as open-ended desire for a world beyond the limits of the present. In the first instance I analyze agribusiness and farm worker futurisms—visual discourses and practices that promote "utopian" images of distinct yet overlapping future worlds. Farm worker futurisms, I argue, were simultaneously antagonistic to and in sympathy with elements of agribusiness futurisms, and this contradictory convergence of otherwise opposed formations is the result of a partly shared model of linear, progressive time characteristic of the forms of "historicism" criticized by Benjamin but directed at imagining the future rather than narrating the past. Like historicism, the linear, progressive temporality of "futurism" tends to displace discontinuities, contradictions, exclusions, and violence, in favor of a celebratory, monumental future time, or what José Muñoz and others theorize as "straight time" and what I would call "reproductive futurism."[20]

While in subsequent chapters I analyze in detail the important critical edge of farm worker futurisms, I also foreground their limitations and contradictions. The latter were well represented recently when plans for naming a U.S. Navy cargo and ammunition ship after Cesar Chavez were realized and the vessel was launched to fireworks and the sounds of the "Marines' Hymn," which begins with the "Halls of Montezuma" and the U.S.–Mexican War. Chavez was famously a proponent of nonviolent protest, opposed to the Vietnam War and, as we shall see, conflicted about his own World War II naval service, and so it is tempting to read the *USNS Cesar Chavez* as a sign of the UFW's nationalist co-optation. But against narratives of decline—the inverse of the linear, progressive time of historicism that similarly tends to displace contradiction, exclusion, and violence—I conclude that the farm worker movement was always from the start characterized by visions of future worlds that were both critical *and* conservative.[21]

By contrast with "futurism," I use "futurity" to capture the expectation of the future as possibility, not guaranteed but also not foreclosed. I build on Muñoz's *Cruising Utopia: The Then and the There of Queer Futurity,* where he defines "queer futurity" as "not an end but an opening or horizon." For Muñoz, futurity describes a kind of "utopian" thinking and action that is "not prescriptive" but that "renders potential blueprints of a world not quite here, a horizon of possibility, not a fixed schema." Futurity means desire for something beyond the here and now, "desire for both larger semiabstractions such as a better world or freedom but also, more immediately, better relations within the social that include better sex and more pleasure."[22] Queer futurity, in other words, represents a collective historical materialist critique of the present and its limits.

Muñoz suggestively develops his theory of futurity out of an examination of labor. In "The Future Is in the Present: Sexual Avant-Gardes and the Performance of Utopia," he analyzes queer performances containing "an anticipatory illumination of a queer world, a sign of an actually existing queer reality, a kernel of political possibility within a stultifying heterosexual present." Following C. L. R. James he calls such performances "the enactment of . . . a future in the present." The title of James's volume, *The Future in the Present,* according to Muñoz, "riffs on an aspect of Hegelian dialectics suggesting that the affirmation known as the future is contained within its negation, the present." One of James's examples is "an actually existing socialist reality in the present": "In one department of a certain plant in the U.S there is a worker who is physically incapable of carrying out his duties. But he is a man with wife and children and his condition is due to the strain of previous work in the plant. The workers have organized their work so that for ten years he has had practically nothing to do." This shop floor where workers partly socialize their labor in support of one another resembles the collectivist, mutual aid orientations and organizations of farm worker unions, including cooperative medical clinics, auto mechanics, food banks, and of course film and other media-making. Muñoz draws on James's account of factory workers as "social performers" in order to "read the world-making potentialities contained in the performances of minoritarian citizen subjects who contest the majoritarian public sphere." Partly based on labor contexts and worker collectivities, Muñoz's future-oriented performance theory helps make farm workers visible as social actors, and union protests as "anticipatory illuminations" of better worlds or performances of the future in the present.[23]

If farm worker futurism projects a particular, often prescriptive new social order, farm worker futurity performs the givenness of future existence, a utopian prospect in contexts where access to a future is unequally distributed. *OED* definitions of the word are suggestive for theorizing "futurity" as a critical speculative practice: "1. The quality, state, or fact of being future"; "2. Future time; the future; a future space of time"; "3. What is future. a. What will exist or happen in the future; future events as a whole. Also those that will live in the future, posterity." These definitions focus on the facticity of the future, the fact of the future's inevitability if unknowability, a given if contentless future. Drawing inspiration from such etymologies I theorize farm worker futurity as the imaginative labor of presupposing a future as such. Farm worker futurity both posits and performs the future as given possibility, based on the expectation of an unknown and uncertain "future space of time." With such expectations farm worker visual culture "enacts the future in the present." The capacity to imagine a future as such within the limits of the here and now ultimately raises creative speculative questions about how material conditions would have to be transformed in order to support widespread expectations of the future. So while I focus on the contradictions of farm worker futurisms I also highlight moments of materialist futurity which ask who can expect a future, who cannot, and why.

Agribusiness Futurism

For much of the twentieth century, powerful corporate interests have promoted forms of agribusiness futurism devoted to technological progress as a means of solving labor problems. Agribusiness futurism projects a corporate utopia in which technology precludes labor conflict and where new machines and biotechnical research eliminate some workers while enabling the expanded exploitation of others. Agribusiness futurism fetishizes new technology in an effort to eliminate resistance and subordinate workers of color to the machinery of production. While optimistically framed in terms of progress and new tomorrows, agribusiness futurism presupposes a barely disavowed sadism directed at workers newly disciplined through technology, a quality critically foregrounded in farm worker union media, and more broadly, in science fiction that reflects on

Agribusiness Streamline Moderne. The barn and silo for the 1933–34 Chicago World's Fair renders agribusiness futurism in architectural form. Photograph by International Harvester Company; courtesy of Wisconsin Historical Society.

California agribusiness. Agribusiness futurism articulates high-tech capitalism to white masculinity and heterosexuality, linking agricultural technology to the future of patriarchal white family life. Throughout this study I suggest that agribusiness futurism and its discontents have powerfully shaped culture and politics in California, the United States, and the world.

Starting in the 1930s the International Harvester Company (IH), maker of mechanical reapers, tractors, and other agricultural machines, became one of the most influential promoters of agribusiness futurism. As sociologist C. Horace Hamilton observed in 1939, along with machinery IH sold farmers "a set of ideas about the social advantages of mechanization" and "the theory of social and technological progress."[24] For the 1933–34 "Century of Progress" World's Fair in Chicago, International Harvester built a giant hall, in the shape of a streamlined barn and silo, to showcase its farm implements.[25] The exhibit included displays of the kinds of com-

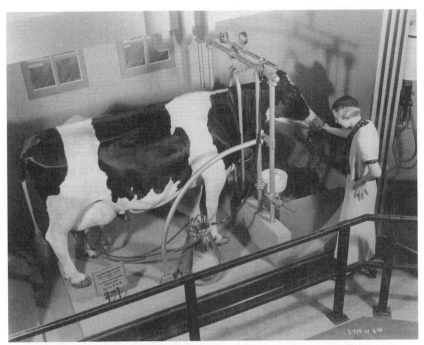

The magic of mechanization. The queen of the "Century of Progress" World's Fair pretends to feed an animatronic cow. The sign placed just below the mechanical vacuum attached to the mechanical udders reads "THIS PURE-BRED HOLSTEIN COW IS BEING MILKED WITH A McCORMICK–DEERING SINGLE-UNIT MILKER." Photograph by International Harvester Company; courtesy of Wisconsin Historical Society.

plicated machinery that were in the process of taking over the vast agricultural fields of California, including harvester–threshers, cultivators, corn pickers, mowers, tractors, and mechanical cotton harvesters. While there were no electric sheep, the dairy exhibit did include the demonstration of a milking machine on an animatronic Holstein that "could moo, switch its tail, turn its head, wink its eyes, chew its cud, breathe and give milk" (actually, imitation milk pumped via a pipeline in the mechanical cow's leg and out its ersatz udders).[26]

The exhibit also included daily outdoor demonstrations of a remote-controlled tractor on a replica of a family farm. As the company brochure described the scene:

A mechanical man in farming clothes, seated comfortably on the front porch of a small farmhouse . . . converses with the spectators by means of an invisible loud speaker, and apparently directs every movement of the tractor. Broadcasting equipment, carefully concealed in the house, speaks for the farmer, and, by means of small electric switches, *starts and stops the tractor and steers it in any direction desired.* When the demonstration is completed, the tractor disappears through mechanically-operated garage doors at the rear of the farmhouse. Will the farmer of the future be able to sit on his front porch while directing all his farm work? Will it be possible to sit in an office in Chicago or New York and direct the operation of fleets of tractors throughout the world? Will it be possible by these methods to operate farm properties in both hemispheres and gather harvests in practically every month of the year? What are the possibilities of radio control in housework, industrial work, transportation, and especially warfare? These are a few of the unanswerable questions with which the weird spectacle of a driverless, yet perfectly controlled tractor, excites the imagination.[27]

Combining the appeal of popular science and midway attractions, both exhibits presented agricultural technology as a magical means for saving labor so that even the cow's production of milk is mechanized, or, in the words of a *Popular Science* article about the radio-controlled tractor, "Robot Plows while Farmer Rests."[28] At the same time the exhibit promotes spectator identification with white male corporate farmers and promises the imaginative pleasures of using technology to "direct" or "control" labor on a massive scale.

Here and elsewhere the company used robots to depict the promise of technology as a means of labor control. IH exhibits at fairs and public demonstrations in the late 1930s, for example, featured Harvey Harvester, a talking robot made out of machine parts and wearing a round, wide-brimmed hat resembling a metallic sombrero.[29] Recalling the tractor, the robot was controlled from a remote location where his master could observe passersby and mobilize its mechanical voice in conversation with spectators.[30] The dream of labor discipline and control presented by such spectacles is a durable one, reappearing in IH exhibits at state fairs in the early 1960s in the form of "Tracto the Talking Robot."[31] In its promotional materials the company photographed white children and women posed next to these mechanical Mexican farm workers. Remarkably,

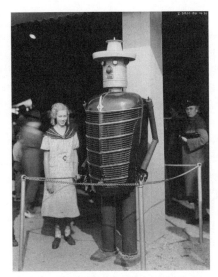 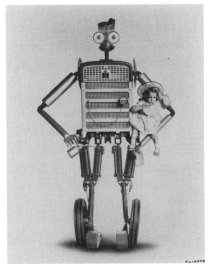

Future farm workers. *(Left)* At a 1938 Iowa fair, a white girl poses with metal-sombrero-wearing robot "Harvey Harvester," safely enclosed by a chain-link fence. *(Right)* In a 1960 promotional photo, a white child is held by "Tracto the Talking Robot." Photographs by International Harvester Company; courtesy Wisconsin Historical Society.

such images appeared at moments of heightened union organizing and in historical contexts where working-class men of color had often been constructed as sexual threats to white women. In contrast with its historical moment, when the exploitation of women of color in agriculture was expanding, agribusiness robots were imagined as "male" workers of the near future that posed no danger to white women and children because they combined both labor and sexual discipline, figured in the photo of Harvey Harvester by the chain that surrounds his waist. The IH farm worker 'bots promised to serve white families and the company framed its exhibits as family fun, as if to connect agribusiness technology to idealized forms of white reproduction and the family farm.

A similar kind of agribusiness futurism is suggested by the way IH redesigned its iconic line of tractors. In the late 1930s the company hired the industrial design firm Raymond Loewy Associates to modernize its tractors. From his Chrysler Building exhibits at the 1939 "World of Tomorrow" New York World's Fair to his 1973 designs for NASA's Skylab, Lowey had a long and influential career as an industrial futurist. During the Great Depression he was famous for his streamlined trains, cars, appliances, product packaging, and commercial architecture. Complementing IH's barn and silo from the World's Fair, Loewy also streamlined the Farmall and Caterpillar tractors, topping or completely encasing their engines with a smooth metal shell.[32] As Jeffrey L. Meikle puts it, based in ideas about aerodynamics, the design style "expressed the public's desire to overcome the economic and social frictions of the depression, to flow through time with as little resistance as a teardrop auto through air."[33] Streamlining promised to smooth over conflict by projecting an alternative future of friction-free accelerated progress. Or, to paraphrase Joshua C. Taylor, IH's redesigned product line promoted "the dream of a fascinating future world" where tractors go faster, "mechanisms are eager to function well for the good of man, and every form slips easily into its purposeful role."[34] Premised on the elimination of resistance, it projected a world beyond material contradictions, including labor conflict. According to Christine Cogdell, streamlining also "served as a material embodiment of eugenic ideology" that idealized a distinctly white-supremacist future. Both eugenicists and designers "considered themselves to be the agents of reform, tackling problems of mass (re)production, eliminating 'defectiveness' and 'parasite drag' that were thought to be slowing forward evolutionary progress. Both were obsessed with increasing efficiency and hygiene and the realization of the 'ideal type' as the means to achieve an imminent 'civilized' utopia."[35] Streamlining, in other words, anticipated the development of white perfection beyond the degeneracies of people of color.

Corporate warfare against labor establishes the conditions of possibility for the emergence in the 1930s of these agribusiness futurisms, making them visual components of what Carey McWilliams called "farm fascism." Just a few years after the new, streamlined tractors began appearing in the San Joaquin Valley, McWilliams published *Factories in the Field,* in which he analyzed the "new type of agriculture" there that was "large scale, intensive, diversified, mechanized."[36] He began with the wheat boom of the 1870s and 1880s, when big California growers were early adopters of the huge new combine harvesters and the state became a giant laboratory for forms of agricultural mechanization that would be exported to other parts of the United States and the world.[37] In the 1882 preface to the Russian translation of the *Communist Manifesto,* for example, Marx and Engels write that the United States was the site of "a gigantic agricultural production" and "step by step the small and middle land ownership of the farmers, the basis of the whole political constitution, is succumbing to the competition of giant farms."[38] By the 1910s and '20s

Agribusiness streamlining. In the 1934 advertisement on the left, the tractor's crankshaft, suspension, steering column, and other component parts are exposed and protruding. Its design is backward looking, recalling a Victorian fetish for complex mechanisms that anticipate what has more recently been called a "steampunk" aesthetic. By contrast, in the 1939 advertisement for the design by corporate futurist Raymond Lowry below, the tractors are streamlined for an "up-to-the-minute appearance" and "modern styling." International Harvester Company; courtesy Wisconsin Historical Society.

agricultural engineers and farm implement manufacturers such as IH produced improved tractors and combines for California with the express goal of eliminating workers.[39] The decade of the 1930s witnessed intensified efforts to organize agricultural workers in the fields and canneries, leading to numerous strikes and violent, sometimes fatal attacks by management and police. At the same time, state- and corporate-sponsored researchers developed new mechanical planters, cultivators, and sorters that further mechanized agriculture. McWilliams concluded that "the eventual mechanization of most types of agriculture is a foregone conclusion," and that the resulting displacement of workers would spur future efforts at unionization.[40]

Immediately after World War II and in the midst of continuing labor organizing and actions, agribusiness interests self-consciously promoted a newly reformulated futurism of Cold War consensus and labor control. Corporations continued to look forward to a time when technological progress would, in Galarza's ominous phrase, "eliminate people from production," or at least eliminate farm workers who resisted, made demands, and organized. "Mass displacement of workers," according to Galarza, "was regarded by the industry as a mark of efficiency," while "psychologically, the use of machines spread a comforting euphoria" in agribusiness circles by promising a future safe from the demands of labor.[41] IH's Cold War retail spaces seemed to make similar promises by ordering or "standardizing" differences and symbolically resolving contradictions and conflicts. In 1946 Loewy redesigned the company's entire retail presentation—including a color-coded graphic system and a new company logo—for organizing the three hundred thousand parts and products sold. The reimagining of product packaging extended to dealerships; using language reminiscent of scientific research and even space exploration, the company commissioned Loewy to design a "prototype" for what it called the dealer's "Base of Operations." Lowey wrote that the Base of Operations was designed "so as to be fully standardized (modular) and easily expanded or contracted."[42]

In the face of ongoing labor conflict in agricultural industries, the national and international standardization of retail spaces helped establish a reassuringly unified and consistent corporate brand. Or as the company's magazine for dealers, *Harvester World,* put it in 1948, "The obvious stability and permanence of the Base of Operations store inspires confidence that efficient service is waiting inside the doors."[43] The storefront combined contrasting horizontal and vertical planes: a long, white rectangular box

EXTERIOR AND INTERIOR VISUALIZATION

BASIC STANDARD NUMBER ONE

The mid-century architecture of agribusiness futurism. International Harvester's "Base of Operations," designed by corporate futurist Raymond Lowey. International Harvester Company; courtesy Wisconsin Historical Society.

with a floor-to-ceiling glass display room topped by a long, thin overhanging roof bisected by a red rectangular tower or "pylon" that prominently displayed the IH logo.[44] The redesigned showroom's combination of color-coded vertical and horizontal planes employed opposing aesthetic elements to produce what *Harvester World* called a "pleasing contrast" that resolved material conflicts visually and thus served as an apt frame for the laborsaving and disciplining devices displayed inside.[45]

IH advertised the new dealerships as "modern," "scientific," "progressive," and "strides into the future" because of their role in promoting mechanization and labor saving.[46] According to a 1947 publication commemorating the company's hundredth anniversary, the new Base of Operations was "an essential part of the mechanization of American agriculture."[47] IH converted its retail and service spaces into robots of a sort, machines for selling agricultural mechanization and the dream of replacing recalcitrant farm workers. This project was implicitly framed in Cold War nationalist terms as part of the technological progress IH promised the world. One story in *Harvester World* includes photos of different realizations of the design and concludes that the red pylon is a "symbol of postwar progress," with a thousand of the new dealerships built or planned in the United States and others built or planned for Canada, Mexico, Australia, Brazil, Chile, Paraguay, Uruguay, Egypt, Syria, and Palestine.[48] In another story, titled "Progress in the Desert," the magazine described a Base of Operations in Syria as "an outpost of Harvester dealer progress."[49] The first prototype built outside the United States, however, was in Hermosillo, Mexico, where, according to a 1946 story, the "IH pylon" was "now an international beacon." As if to visually emphasize the forms of technological progress International Harvester purveyed, the first page of the story included a photo of the dealership's modern exterior as two men on a burro-drawn cart pass by, while the next page reproduced an image of the dealership's interior and three streamlined tractors. This Base of Operations in Mexico gives form to a "progressive spirit" because it promises to displace workers like the two men and their cart. Ironically, this "international" version of the prototype, a design dedicated to eliminating workers from production, opened on International Workers' Day or May Day.[50]

IH also established numerous Bases of Operation in the San Joaquin Valley of California. According to a 1951 *Harvester World* article called "Way Out West in the Land of Cotton," California's "jet-like ascent" among the plantation set was made possible by the development of IH's mechanical cotton picker, the machines that reminded Galarza of something out of science fiction. The magazine approvingly quoted a large Kern County cotton grower about the wave of the future: "You can't plant five or six thousand acres of cotton and expect to pick it by hand. Takes too many people or too much time or both—and it costs too much. One of our biggest jobs is to adapt our ways of farming so as to take best advantage of the picking machine, while at the same time we improve our efficiency with planters, cultivators, and other equipment. We've got to be all-machine."[51] As Miriam J. Wells explains in her history of California agribusiness, growers used such mechanization to "solve their labor problems by eliminating unruly workers." Investments in the research and development of new laborsaving machines were often spurred by periods of farm worker unionization and vice versa, as farm worker unions responded to new forms of mechanization with renewed organizing efforts.[52]

But while mechanization in cotton and other agricultural industries displaced thousands of workers, it also expanded the scale of production in ways that required an increasing supply of low-wage labor, particularly during and immediately after World War II. Agribusiness retooled for the war effort, supplying vehicles and food for the military, and after the war the industry used its new capacities to expand commercial production. Technology enabled more land to be cultivated and encouraged the formation of huge agricultural corporations since only the largest companies could afford to fund research and development and purchase and deploy the results.[53] Thus between 1940 and 1982 the total number of farm workers in California increased 233 percent.[54] Rather than eliminating farm workers, then, technology enabled agribusiness to restructure and discipline an expanded workforce. Automation enabled the deskilling and downgrading of certain tasks, as when, for example, packing operations were "moved from town sheds to movable assemblies on wheels" and the jobs were reclassified as unskilled fieldwork, while women were substituted for men and paid less.[55] Recalling McWilliams's prediction that mechanization would spark renewed labor organizing, a postwar boom period in the technological development of productive forces in agribusiness coincided with a series of farm worker union actions in the San Joaquin Valley between 1947 and 1952.[56] Agribusiness efforts to design a future free from conflict between capital and labor actually reproduced and extended such conflicts.

The history of the bracero program, for example, suggests that rather than eliminating the contradiction between capital and labor, the use of technology widened it. Mechanization further enabled the exploitation of low-wage, noncitizen Mexican guest workers or braceros, who were particularly subject to subordination within the machinery of production. In *Strangers in Our Fields* Galarza analyzed the technological dimensions of the bracero program, arguing that it was molded by corporate interests and reflected "the vertical integration of government with private interests" in California agriculture.[57] The state in effect subsidized agribusiness futurism by providing and administering the supply of cheap, noncitizen labor that made the development and deployment of agricultural technology possible and productive. As part of his research for the book in the early 1950s, Galarza visited and photographed a variety of the massive institutional spaces where braceros were housed, including a huge cattle corral with open privies in Yuba City, a military base surrounded by barbed wire, and a county fair cattle pavilion in Stockton.[58] As I argue in the next chapter, large-scale institutional housing was an important and contested part of the technology of agricultural production since it was self-consciously engineered to discipline workers and preclude union organizing. The front and back covers of *Strangers in Our Fields* form a single eight-by-ten-inch green-tinted photographic image captioned "Recent arrivals from Mexico feeding a battery of bean harvesters."[59] It depicts a crew of workers using pitchforks to load beans onto slanted conveyor belts that rise to the top of massive mechanical threshers. In the bottom left corner of the photo, the large metal gears and chain of one conveyor are captured in relative close-up in the foreground, while rows of similar machines stretch into the horizon, cutting diagonally across the image. The machines dominate the field of vision and dwarf the men who "feed" them in ways that prefigure the analysis of the bracero program and mechanization inside the covers of the report, where Galarza describes how employers define farm workers as "unskilled" even when they are skillfully operating machines. Work crews harvesting beans, for example, are divided into groups of those who feed the threshers, those who ride the moving machines and change boxes, others who work behind the threshers with rakes and shovels, and still others who load full boxes onto trucks or stack empty ones. And yet, despite this complex division of labor and skill, and in violation of bracero program regulations, the crews Galarza interviewed generally received the same low wage as "unskilled" harvesters who did not work with such large and potentially dangerous machines.

Recalling the standardization and flexible modularization of the redesigned IH storerooms, braceros were employed as generic labor, "moved from one type of work to another in a flexible, sometimes informal manner," but paid at the same rate regardless of the different skills or risks involved.[60] Mechanization helped to construct farm workers as inherently unskilled, as if the machines they fed had also symbolically swallowed up their practical knowledge and technical proficiencies. When calculating wages, agribusiness corporations fetishized technology, denying a portion of the workers' contributions to production by imaginatively attributing worker skill to the machines they operated. This technological deskilling, moreover, served to legitimate not only worker exploitation but also capital's speculative externalization of risk, whereby the increased profits of mechanization come at the expense of lost limbs and other career-ending injuries. Confronted with this situation, Galarza reframed agribusiness futurism in dystopian terms that recall *Sleep Dealer*. As Galarza asks in *Merchants of Labor: The Mexican Bracero Story*, "Is this indentured alien—an almost perfect model of the economic man, an 'input factor' stripped of the political and social attributes that liberal democracy likes to ascribe to all human beings ideally—is this *bracero* the prototype of the production man of the future?"[61]

At the same time as postwar agribusiness futurism attempted to re-engineer labor, it also altered the California landscape in ways that further subordinated farm workers. In addition to revolutionizing agricultural production, science and technology radically transformed the environment in visible ways. Scientists and engineers rationalized irrigation by channeling rivers into reservoirs, sinking deep industrial-sized wells, and covering the state with a "system of ditches, control gates, settling ponds, pipes, siphons, pumps, and sluices that constrained water to do anything, even to flow uphill."[62] San Joaquin Valley visual fields have been significantly remapped by the proliferation of agricultural sites of production dominated by spectacular forms of technology on a scale that imaginatively diminishes farm workers. Galarza, for example, describes mechanization in terms of its visual effects, as when he writes about how technology "became awesome, like the motorized cotton picker; graceful, like the spidery walnut pruner; delicate, like the electronic lemon sorter; or spectral, like the eighty-foot land leveler moving through clouds of its own dust."[63] And as in the last example of the spectral leveler, Galarza often focuses on forms of technology that loom large and imposingly in the visual field: "Mounted on large wheels, pipe assemblies anchored to portable towers could creep and wheel by electronic control, watering a thousand acres at a time, their thin jets tracing arches of sunlit spray against the sky."[64] He further uses metaphors from military battles and parades to compare the sight of machines in the agricultural fields to army units on the battlefield, including the mechanical cotton harvesters moving "in formation." In such passages agribusiness technology resembles an occupying army, and this impression is reproduced in the numerous examples of agribusiness advertising and promotion focused on massive machinery dwarfing surrounding workers.

Similarly, agribusiness interests have made extensive use of media technologies such as film and television to promote corporate interests and undermine unions, in part by celebrating the industry's use of technology and connecting it to ideologies of scientific rationality, masculine power, and nationalist white ingenuity.[65] In agribusiness ads, fetishistic images of gleaming, massive agricultural machinery become what Stuart Hall calls points of ideological condensation that articulate agribusinesses to key ideological terms of white-supremacist capital formations based in the exploitation of low-wage workers of color. I juxtapose such images to something like their photo negatives, the forms of farm fascism that such imposing visions of agribusiness machinery both represent and displace.

In addition to the development of farm machinery, according to Galarza, postwar California agribusiness also benefited from "laboratories in the state universities where the skills of agricultural engineers, plant scientists, entomologists, and soil physicists were enlisted" in a biotechnical offensive. Publicly funded but supplemented by private donations from banks and corporations invested in producing and marketing California produce, university researchers developed "varieties of fruits and vegetables adapted to handling in bins, defoliants, precision drill seeding, electronic selection, flotation, heating, hedge pruning, shaking, cradling, and packaging." Agribusiness thus reengineered nature to better integrate it into the laborsaving machinery of production.[66] Researchers simultaneously developed powerful chemical fertilizers, herbicides, and pesticides, the last with particularly significant health consequences for workers. In the 1990s, for instance, it was estimated that a thousand farm workers died every year from pesticide poisoning while over three hundred thousand got sick, suggesting the extent to which farm workers are rendered vulnerable to illness and shortened life spans.[67]

The use of pesticides in agriculture emerged in dialectical relation to modern warfare, and technologies used in war were partly transferred not only to agricultural pests but also to farm workers. After World War I the first experiments in crop dusting were performed by the U.S. War Department, and the military origins of such research continued to shape the industrial uses of pesticides and responses to it for decades. According to historian Edmund Russell, "In the first half of the twentieth century, the science and technology of pest control sometimes became the science and technology of war, and vice versa. Chemists, entomologists, and military researchers knew that chemicals toxic to one species often killed others, so they developed similar chemicals to fight human and insect enemies. They also developed similar methods of dispersing chemicals to poison both."[68] Russell concludes that the institutional links between agriculture and the military were complemented by a shared set of metaphors based in "annihilating" or "exterminating" pests. The military origins of pesticides have also shaped their use in California agriculture, where corporate growers have often treated labor like the enemy—which is not to suggest that the literal aim of pesticide use has been to exterminate workers, but rather that their widespread deployment is part of a larger militarized industrial formation that treats technology as weaponry and imagines worker well-being as the potential enemy of future profits.

After World War II, framed by its military origins, "chemical farming" was increasingly integrated into agribusiness futurism, where it joined the idolization of machines to form a high-tech agribusiness perspective of domination over labor.[69] The combined fetishization of machinery and chemistry is suggested by the extensive use of planes and helicopters. Just five years after the publication of Rachel Carson's *Silent Spring* had focused popular attention on the dangers of pesticides, and in the middle of historic UFW strikes, the J. G. Boswell Corporation in the San Joaquin Valley, the largest privately owned farm in the world, commissioned a TV documentary called *The Big Land* (1967) that celebrated pesticides and, more broadly, an agribusiness gaze linking technology and scientific rationality to white male capitalism.[70] The film uses aerial shots to elicit wonder at the corporation's technological mastery of the landscape, including images of huge tractors and gigantic cotton harvesters. It also includes scenes of a manager's helicopter flight to survey the vast fields with their orderly "patterns of green and gold" that symbolically link the manager's power to his panoptic domination of the visual field. By crosscutting between personalizing close-ups of him in the helicopter and shots of the rows of cotton from his vantage point, the documentary invites the spectator to imaginatively identify with the perspective of the white male corporate head looking down on his factory in the fields.

At the same time, *The Big Land* showcases white male company scientists who supervise experiments executed by farm workers of color. Indeed, the film features numerous male workers of color, mostly anonymous, who are seen irrigating fields with shovels in hand, on vehicles spraying pesticides, sorting seeds, and grading and packing cotton. These workers carry out the instructions of corporate researchers but are never presented as researchers themselves. One scene, for instance, focuses on a white scientist's efforts to produce a more pest-resistant strain of cotton, and he is shown supervising a number of Mexican workers, whom he directs to check the experimental plants for insects. Unions often argued that agribusiness treated workers like farm machines, and *The Big Land* supports such claims by depicting Mexicans as instruments of scientific rationality but not its agents. Such scenes recall the earliest scientific experiments in which, according to Donna Haraway, the workers who helped perform them were excluded from the privileged category of scientific observer. White, male, and upper class in its historical origins, the objectivity and transparency of the scientific observer depends on his performative or "experimental" difference from "colored, sexed, and laboring persons" marked as particular, biased, and self-interested, and hence more properly the objects of observation rather than its "self-invisible source."[71] By effectively elevating and ennobling a white agribusiness gaze in opposition to farm workers fixed in the visual field, *The Big Land* invites viewers to identify with the top-down perspective of agribusiness and take visual pleasure in the high-tech domination of land and labor.

Technologies from Below

Part of the machinery of farm fascism, planes and helicopters are prominently featured in UFW activism and art, where artists often link pesticide use to war and the militarization of civilian life. The most widely seen example is probably the opening of the UFW documentary about pesticides titled *The Wrath of Grapes* (1986), where a helicopter fills up the frame and the sound of whirring blades and dissonant music combine on the soundtrack, recalling period images of U.S. military helicopters in Central America. Such representations further recall earlier juxtapositions of crop dusters and U.S. warplanes in Vietnam as in "Vietnam Campesino" (1970) by El Teatro Campesino, the farm worker theater group organized by Luis Valdez as part of the UFW.

At about the same time, in the early 1970s, the Central Valley artists' collective the Royal Chicano Air Force (RCAF) was formed and began to produce art and graphics in support of the UFW. Many members of the RCAF had been farm workers or were the children of farm workers, and the group's use of airplane imagery is partly a response to crop duster attacks on workers. As RCAF member Juanita P. Ontiveros recalled in the TV documentary *Pilots of Aztlán: The Flights of the Royal Chicano Air Force,* "It was the local growers' sons that flew the crop dusters . . . They would dust and they dared each other on who would fly down the lowest until they ended up getting people to throw themselves on the cotton sacks. And of course you would feel all, it was like dew falling on your skin, you would feel all the pesticides."[72] In this context the RCAF deployed images of biplanes and their pilots but decorated them with UFW colors and icons, especially the union's stylized black thunderbird.[73] The world of the RCAF was built on earlier efforts by the UFW to produce spec-

Agribusiness helicopter as weapon. *The Wrath of Grapes* (1986).

tacles such as the mass march on Sacramento that were visible to aerial news media. Similarly, the RCAF elaborated an alternative reality where they formed an imaginary aerial counterforce to agribusiness domination of the visual field in California. In dialectical answer to agribusiness futurism, the RCAF produced futuristic images of Chicano technologies of flight, as in Esteban Villa's painting of a woman astronaut, *Third World Astro Pilot of Aztlán,* and Ricardo Favela's drawing *UFW Cooperative Space Station #Uno* (Plates 1 and 2). Similarly, like the UFW, which formed its own clinic and cooperative gas station, the RCAF converted a space-age gas station in Sacramento into the "Aeronaves de Aztlán Automotive Collective." The collective contexts of such farm worker futurisms mark them as utopian alternatives to agribusiness futurism and its idealization of technology in the service of labor exploitation and private property.

As this brief account of flight in California agriculture suggests, technology has been a double-edged sword, serving to help reproduce and dismantle the forms of material inequality presupposed by the regional agribusiness economy and related spaces of large-scale, low-wage agricultural production. In significant parts of the world and especially in the

Farm Worker Flight. This poster for a Royal Chicano Air Force Cinco de Mayo celebration appropriates agribusiness technology for farm worker purposes. Esteban Villa (1973); courtesy of CEMA and Esteban Villa.

global South, technology has supported not only increased labor exploitation but also an expansion of labor hierarchies and divisions of labor organized in terms of race, gender, and nation. Ideologically, technology has anchored discourses about the superiority of white Western patriarchal capitalism, and inequality has often been explained or justified by appealing to the scientific rationality and technological ingenuity of white men in the capitalist West and the scientific irrationality and technological disingenuity of women and people of color the world over. Such ideas have rationalized settler colonialism, slavery, racialized and gendered oppression, imperial warfare, and neocolonial development policies.[74]

Over the course of the nineteenth and early twentieth centuries, the combination of transportation and communication—trains and telegraphs—helped make modern forms of European imperialism seem not only possible but also natural and desirable. Along with steamships, according to Michael Adas, trains and telegraphs served as technologies of European colonial expansion in Africa, India, Southeast Asia, and Australia. Trains and telegraphs have also served as vehicles of U.S. settler colonialism and westward expansion, as well as U.S. financial imperialism in Latin America. At the same time, colonial powers have employed transportation and communications technologies as means of counterinsurgency, using trains to quickly transport troops and telegraphs to transmit military intelligence in response to uprisings. Finally, trains and telegraphs became not only powerful physical but also "symbolic manifestations of the European colonial presence," racialized and gendered idealizations of "complexity, scale, and power" proclaiming "the European's mastery of time and space."[75]

On the other hand, such mastery has never been guaranteed and forces of rebellion and anti-imperial resistance have often appropriated technologies of time–space compression for their own ends. During the Mexican Revolution, Pancho Villa's forces used the combination of trains and telegraphy to outmaneuver the armies of a Mexican state that had invited U.S. capital investments in local transportation and communication infrastructures. Such technologies also supported labor organizing, as Mexican railroad workers in both Mexico and the United States formed radical unions.[76] Mexican workers have further used trains and telegraphs as technologies of transnational labor migration and communication. Migrants in the early twentieth century traveled by train from the interior of Mexico to the U.S.–Mexican border and, once in the United States, they used telegraphy to communicate with family and friends and to wire money back to Mexico. The ample records of such telegraph messages and money transfers enabled Mexican researcher Manuel Gamio to track migrant networks for his famous study, *Mexican Immigration to the United States*.[77] Hence, while modern colonial state powers used technology to dominate populations and territories, Mexican migrants used it to traverse national borders. And whereas dominant communications and transportation regimes in Mexico were aimed at producing surpluses for U.S. investors, Mexican migrant workers used the same technologies to move money from the United States back to Mexico. While not directly antagonistic to capitalism and state imperialism, early twentieth-century Mexican migrant appropriations of technology were nonetheless irreducible to their demands and in practice often exceeded, inverted, and opposed them.

While Adas and others argue that many U.S. Americans linked modern technologies to ideologies of white supremacy and nonwhite inferiority, working-class Mexicans developed popular forms of futurism that showcased their own technological facility and ingenuity. Bruce Sinclair reminds us that the postwar fetishization of "great men and technological progress drove research into rather limited and exclusive channels that centered on big capital, complex technologies, and the small fragment of the population acting on that narrow stage" in ways that effectively barred people of color. For these reasons, it has been at work that many people of color have experienced their "most crucial encounter with machines and technological systems."[78] Foundational research in materialist Chicana feminism, such as Vicki L. Ruiz's *Cannery Women, Cannery Lives: Mexican Women, Unionization, and the California Food Procession Industry, 1930–1950* and Patricia Zavella's *Women's Work and Chicano Families: Cannery Workers of the Santa Clara Valley,* which analyzes historical and contemporary intersections of race, gender, and labor in an important industrialized segment of agricultural production, further suggests that the dominant white patriarchal gendering of technology makes work a unique point of technological engagement for women of color.[79] More recently, low-wage labor has been a means of access to computer technology for women of color.[80]

Drawing on labor-related contexts, working-class Mexican migrants have long fashioned vernacular techno-cultures. A famous *corrido* of the Mexican Revolution, for instance, describes Villa magically commandeering and flying an enemy plane and hanging enemy soldiers from telegraph poles, whereas the early twentieth-century "Corrido de Pensilvania" represents Mexican migrant workers who use the train to escape the cotton fields of Texas. Formally, many *corridos* constitute aesthetic mediations of the new experiences of time–space compression produced by train travel, as in José Limón's analysis of the Celaya *corrido* about the movement of Villa's forces by train. The song is organized contrapuntally, alternating between the formal innovations and changing images of succeeding stanzas, and the repetition of a larger rhythmic structure that, Limón argues, mimics the train travel it narrates. As he writes, "the imagistic and scenic novelty of each stanza is artistically counterpointed to the recurrent rhyme and rhythm" in ways that recall the experience of "Villa's peasant soldiers riding in their troop trains" as they "watched the changing scenes of the landscape from northern Coahuila to south–central Guanajuato even as they heard the repetitive rhythm of the train carrying them down the tracks to their destiny at Celaya."[81] In this way we might understand the *corrido* as a vernacular attempt to take advantage of the possibilities of new technologies, experimenting with them in ways that counter dominant U.S. American ideologies of Mexican technological inferiority.

Américo Paredes suggested that early twentieth-century *corridos* served as alternative working-class communications technologies that competed with print media and the telegraph. The narrator of "El Corrido de Gregorio Cortez" notes that news of the hero's capture is transmitted by telegraph, but the song's extensive circulation makes it, too, a means of quickly transmitting information across wide distances, or, in other words, a popular technology of time–space compression. Connecting the present to the past and maintaining ties to Mexico while in the United States, migrant appropriations of technology produced forms of virtual co-presence, whereby they could imaginatively inhabit different times and spaces at once. Migrant technologies thus collapsed spatial distances and displaced linear time, such that different historical moments (the revolutionary past and the postrevolutionary present) and places (in Mexico and the United States) could imaginatively coexist.

The dissemination of radio had similarly contradictory consequences for dominant and subaltern groups. On the one hand, as Brian Larkin argues, in Africa radio has been part of the infrastructure of colonial rule and an example of the "'colonial sublime,' the use of technology to produce an overwhelming sense of grandeur and awe in the service of colonial power," while in the United States radio has been harnessed for state power, official nationalisms, and white supremacy.[82] On the other hand, as Barbara Savage demonstrates in her study *Broadcasting Freedom: Radio,*

War, and the Politics of Race, 1938–1948, radio also became a means of opposing racism, and, as I have argued elsewhere, a technology for transgressing national borders and the racial segregation of social space.[83] In 1930s Los Angeles, activist broadcasters Josefina Fierro and Pedro J. Gonzalez used radio to organize Mexican agricultural and other low-wage workers. Fierro was the daughter of a Mexican anarchist mother and grew up in and around the agricultural fields of the San Joaquin Valley before moving to Los Angeles and eventually launching a popular radio program devoted to local and international politics. She also successfully used her show to mobilize listeners for mass marches on employers and the state capital in Sacramento. Gonzalez had been Villa's telegraph operator during the revolution, but by the late 1920s he had moved to Los Angeles where he became a popular live musical performer and radio host who organized benefits and support for Mexican workers threatened with deportation. Both shows were precursors to the radio broadcasts of San Joaquin Valley farm worker unions in the 1940s and 1960s, most notably the UFW's Radio Campesino, itself a formative precedent for the role of radio in mobilizing the 2006 immigrants' rights protests.

Farm Worker Futurism builds on such histories but focuses specifically on farm worker appropriations of film and video technologies as examples of what Sinclair calls "people using their politics to rethink technologies." Sinclair draws on bell hooks to argue that, for black people, cameras became "crucial to how they could picture themselves" in historical contexts "where someone else usually controlled the ways in which African-Americans were represented." Historically used to counter distortions and circulate alternative images, photography constitutes, according to hooks, "a powerful location for the construction of an oppositional black aesthetic." As Sinclair concludes, "This power to define reality provides a starting point from which to shape politics and culture differently. And it works two ways: cameras in black hands—just like the technology of music in black hands—allows for the creation of an alternative image, but that image also enables African-Americans to represent themselves as skillful in the management of those technologies."[84] Similarly, I argue that for farm workers, cameras became important means for constructing an oppositional brown aesthetic dedicated to visually redefining reality. Cameras in brown hands not only enable the creation of images critical of corporate agriculture but also serve to counter the raced and gendered ideologies of farm worker technological inferiority and disingenuity informing agribusiness labor exploitation. In the late 1940s, California farm workers sought out cameras in order to counter agribusiness imagery. By creating and promoting both dynamic photo montages and a documentary film, Galarza's union attempted to make visible for a national audience a seemingly alien world where, in violation of Cold War democratic values, human beings were being treated like animals and things. In the 1960s and 1970s the UFW made and distributed films documenting their struggles to force agribusiness companies to bargain with the union, and in the 1980s it employed cutting-edge communications technologies, including video and computer graphics, in the battle against pesticides. So while farm workers of color have been imagined as technologically naïve and primitive, they have in fact often been early and innovative users of new technologies, drawing on long and dense material histories to construct complex, often oppositional technological cultures.

Farm Worker Futurism, Farm Worker Futurity

In contexts where life chances are unequally distributed and farm worker life expectancy disproportionately low, unions and their supporters have tried to mobilize media technologies to open spaces for farm worker futures. But as the previous discussion of agribusiness futurism suggests, *Farm Worker Futurism* departs from narratives of technological determinism and focuses instead on how, as material means of production, technologies also anchor and organize critical speculation in the form of political ideas and affects. My analysis of the imaginative life of technology in California's agricultural political economy builds on recent studies of low-wage migrant workers, including David Naguib Pellow's and Lisa Sun-Hee Park's *The Silicon Valley of Dreams: Environmental Injustice, Immigrant Workers, and the High-Tech Economy*; Stephen J. Pitti's *The Devil in Silicon Valley: Northern California, Race, and Mexican Americans*; and Alicia Schmidt Camacho's *Migrant Imaginaries: Latino Cultural Politics in the U.S.–Mexico Borderlands*. Pellow and Park historicize the health and environmental costs of high-tech industries in Silicon Valley in relationship to the region's prior domination by agribusiness, and as their title suggests, *The Silicon Valley of Dreams* focuses on both dominant corporate representations and the creative and imaginative work—what we might call the speculative labor—of workers literally organizing to save their own lives.[85] Similarly, the title of Pitti's study foregrounds the imaginative aspects of political economic history, with the Devil serving as a metaphor for racial formations in the Santa Clara Valley. In the epilogue, "Devil's Future," he concludes that "the history of Latinos in Silicon Valley," including as farm workers, "explodes local myths about the area's universal prosperity and social peace."[86] Finally, drawing on Camacho's book, I analyze the significance of technology in both agribusiness and farm worker social imaginaries. Camacho uses the term "migrant imaginaries" to "encompass the world-making aspirations of Mexican border crossers," and she derives it from the work of Cornelius Castoriadis, who proposed the concept of "social imaginaries" as a corrective to economic determinism. From this perspective, the material social relations of agricultural production are inseparable from the symbolic fields of affect and meaning through which people imagine themselves as social subjects— which is to say that the work of imagination, notably in cultural representations and practices, is integral both to dominant real-world building and to projects of social transformation from below, for as Camacho reminds us, "social relations must first be imagined by subjects in order to be comprehended and acted on."[87]

In what follows I juxtapose the history of two social imaginaries, "agribusiness futurism" and "farm worker futurism," which are usually at odds but sometimes in sync. In response to corporate dreams of a time when farm workers are reduced to the machinery of production, farm worker unions like Galarza's National Farm Labor Union and the more famous UFW responded with alternate visions of social reality that contradicted the techno-utopias of agribusiness. Unions used visual technologies to project alternatives to existing social conditions, other worlds that transcend inequality and injustice *here* and *now*, in *this* life, not the next. Cesar Chavez's famous slogan—*sí se puede* / it can be done— encapsulates the "speculative," alternative world-building qualities of the farm worker movement, qualities that resonated with postwar decolonization and Third Worldist movements.

Like the (inter)planetary perspective of many science fictions, the worlds that farm workers built were shaped by global concerns. While often imagined as part of a regional or at most national movement, farm worker unions used visual technologies in ways that reveal their participation in Cold War international politics. In chapter 1 I analyze how the racialized anticommunism of the blacklist period framed the photos and films made by agribusiness and farm worker unions, while in chapter 2 I discuss UFW filmmaking in relationship to Latin American Third Cinema and anti–Vietnam War films, and UFW video in relationship to popular accounts of video- and audiocassettes during the Iranian Revolution. Finally, in chapter 3, I suggest that the technological visions of California agribusiness in the films of George Lucas and the activist art of Ester Hernandez and Barbara Carrasco critically engage the Cold War militarism of the 1970s and 1980s. However, while agribusiness and farm worker futurisms are generally antagonistic, they are also partly shared social imaginaries, and *Farm Worker Futurism* thus analyzes instances where unions replicate agribusiness ideas about whiteness, private property, Cold War geopolitics, and the transformative power of technological progress.

These two futurisms are illuminated by the speculative fictions they have inspired, literature and films that extrapolate future worlds from histories of California corporate agriculture. Mexican migrant workers are the protagonists of three recent works: the films *Sleep Dealer* (2008) and John Carlos Frey's *Gatekeeper* (2002) and the novella *Lunar Braceros* (2009) by Beatrice Pita and Rosaura Sánchez. Displacing farm workers and agribusiness in time and space, these science fictions generate forms of "cognitive estrangement," or a dialectic between historical social realities and another imaginary world, that suggests a critical interpretation of the limits of the actual world.[88] I return to each of these texts in subsequent chapters, but here I emphasize their common conceptual elements: all three depict future scenarios where capitalists control new high-tech production facilities that reproduce older forms of migrant labor exploitation familiar from the history of California agriculture even as they suggest comparisons to contemporary prisons and immigration detention centers. They foreground migrant workers who are subject to extreme forms of violence and control at the hands of state and corporate forces, thereby offering visions of the future that estrange commonsense understandings of farming as pastoral and the source of democratic freedoms. Instead they bear an uncanny resemblance to the farm fascism that McWilliams diagnosed in the late 1930s. Taken together, *Sleep Dealer, Gatekeeper,* and *Lunar Braceros* retrospectively sound the death knell for prior moments of agribusiness futurism by narrating near and distant futures where technology has not replaced workers but expanded their exploitation. These three works additionally provide views of future worlds where even the most limited reforms and legal rights won by the farm workers' movement have seemingly disappeared, undermining the ritualized nostalgia for progress reproduced by many institutional memorials to Chavez and the UFW.

Contemporary speculative fiction about migrant workers, in other words, provides a critical vantage point on past ideological representations of California's future. Works by Frey, Pita and Sánchez, and Rivera also suggest new ways of reading older, canonical science fictions as preoccupied with agriculture. As a genre partly defined by curiosity about technology, authoritarian social orders, and immigration to new worlds, science fiction has often found inspiration in high-tech agribusiness, with its massive machinery of social control and vast body of migrant workers, strangers in a strange land. Indeed, the subgenre of farm worker science fiction has a long history, beginning in 1868, with the publication of Edward S. Ellis's dime novel *The Steam Man of the Prairies*. Frequently cited as one of the first U.S. science fiction novels, it tells of an ingenious young white boy who invents a giant steam-powered iron man that he uses to travel west, terrorize and kill Indians, and search for gold. *The Steam Man of the Prairies* was published at the dawn of the late nineteenth-century wheat boom and the mass mechanization of agriculture, and it recalls the easy movements of giant harvesting combines across the flat plains of Kansas and California when the narrator emphasizes how readily the eponymous steam man strides across the prairies. *The Steam Man* seems to anticipate the subsequent invention of a steam-powered harvester in the San Joaquin Valley, as well as the fantasy of replacing intractable workers with mechanical ones mobilized by "Harvey the Harvester" and "Tracto the Talking Tractor." The novel was immensely popular, spawned a number of successful sequels and imitations, and influenced the interests and tastes of numerous twentieth-century writers and readers, including Robert Heinlein (see chapter 1). Similarly, Hugo Gernsback's influential novel *Ralph 124C 41+: A Romance of the Year 2660* (1911/1925) features a chapter called "Give Us Food" that depicts in great detail the many miraculous technical innovations of the giant, automated "Accelerated Plant Growing Farms" of the future. Images of futuristic or alien forms of high-tech agriculture—on land, underground, under the sea, in space, or on distant planets—are a common feature of science fiction and popular science and technology magazines in the twentieth century, whereas science fiction stories and novels have often depicted forms of space colonization in relationship to histories of settler colonialism and yeoman farming.[89]

Each of the following chapters builds on such histories in order to claim farm worker futurism as an influential intertext for past visions of the future in works by Robert Heinlein, Philip K. Dick, George Lucas, and other canonical science fiction artists. Science fiction writers and cultural producers turn to agriculture because it has been freighted with so much ideological and affective weight about the future of so many important things—democracy, family, gender, race, capitalism, and international relations, to name a few. Science fiction centers agriculture in part because California's agricultural economy has been so important to visions of the future in the nation and the world. Science fictions about agribusiness interests suggest the extent to which they have colonized the future and successfully made political claims to it. But historically, both mainstream and oppositional speculative fictions have also been drawn to agribusiness contexts because of the gravitational pull of farm worker futurisms, and *Farm Worker Futurism* thus makes visible otherwise obscured social movement contributions to critical thinking about competing political mobilizations of the future.

The importance of California agriculture for the nation and the world is central to chapter 1, "'To the Disinherited Belongs the Future': Farm Worker Futurism in the 1940s." Its thesis is based on Galarza's archive of the strike he helped lead in the late 1940s, including photographs, photo essays, and a documentary film called *Poverty in the Valley of Plenty.* As part of the strike against the DiGiorgio Fruit Company over wages and living conditions, Galarza built on a migrant labor techno-culture of time–space compression in order to organize workers in collective research on and documentation of the strike and the working and living conditions that motivated it. The results were used to construct press releases, including collages of photos organized on a rectangular grid that formally mimicked agribusiness mechanization while imaginatively displacing it by projecting a different world of union organizing. These utopian images were shattered when the company took legal action that effectively banned *Poverty* and destroyed the union. This outcome had lasting implications, encouraging agribusiness corporations to expand their use of technology to control workers and prompting union leaders to increasingly adopt a defensive anticommunism. Galarza's visual projection of materialist futurity was in these ways undermined by Cold War corporate futurism.

The next chapter, "From Third Cinema to National Video: Visual Technologies and UFW World Building," examines the relationships between the worlds envisioned in UFW film and video, on the one hand, and visions of Cold War geopolitics, on the other. In 1971 Chavez discussed plans for constructing elaborate media-making facilities and a wide range of projects partly modeled on films about different regions of the decolonizing world. While these ambitious plans never fully materialized, the UFW did make *Fighting for Our Lives* (1974), a documentary that turned the cameras on high-tech agribusiness, baton-swinging police, and strike-breaking thugs in ways that visually linked the California fields to scenes of imperial military violence in Southeast Asia. By the 1980s, however, the UFW had stopped organizing strikes and focused exclusively on promoting the grape boycott, using the new technologies of home video to generate forms of virtual intimacy or "co-presence" between consumers and the victims of pesticide use, particularly as embodied by Chavez, who engaged in a spectacular public fast in order to advertise the boycott. In this way the union attempted to build a national audience by framing pesticide harms in nationalist terms and by turning Chavez into a nationalist icon. Whereas *FFOL* connected the union to anti-imperial struggles in the global South, the UFW's video projects in the 1980s implicitly appealed to nationalism at a moment of resurgent U.S. imperialism in Central America and the Middle East under the Reagan administration. The UFW, in other words, ultimately emphasized nationalist "futurism" over more radical forms of "futurity."

In chapter 3, "Farm Worker Futurisms in Speculative Culture: George Lucas and Ester Hernandez," I suggest that the technological visions of California agribusiness in the films of George Lucas and the art of Ester Hernandez connect agribusiness to influential forms of white male agrarian populism that supported the Cold War militarism of the 1980s. Made by a native of the California agricultural community of Modesto, *Star Wars* provides a revealing speculative rendering of a dominant ideological perspective in the recent history of California and national politics: a kind of pastoral, free market, white individualism defined in dialectical relation to farm workers. By contrast, with her print in support of the UFW titled *Sun Mad* and other works, Hernandez, who is also from a Valley agricultural community, linked Mexican workers and white consumers similarly affected by pesticides in ways that undermined nativist and corporate articulations of whiteness. Her images of skeletons are part of a larger body of farm worker visual culture in the 1980s and 1990s that helped make visible the forms of violence and destruction obscured by the articulation of white masculinity to high-tech agribusiness.

In the afterword, "Farm Worker Futurism Now," I examine the influence of the farm worker movement beyond California's agricultural fields in the context of new labor systems and new labor movements. I conclude by analyzing the rearticulation of farm worker futurism in recent speculative fictions in film and literature; in the contemporary immigrants' rights movement; in conflicts between management and labor in the production of computer hardware; and in the anti-prison movement.

Farm Worker Futurism suggests an extensive reordering of things in the Foucauldian sense of a dramatic transformation in how we think about the modern organization of power/knowledge across a range of intellectual fields and disciplines. Each case study foregrounds subaltern epistemologies, or ways of seeing and knowing the world from below, that challenge or significantly revise more conventional academic ways of producing knowledge about power.[90] For example, *Farm Worker Futurism* significantly shifts the center of gravity of U.S. film and media studies toward the analysis of the visual politics of agribusiness economies. Elsewhere I have argued that the emergence in Los Angeles of film production in general and sound film in particular was partly a response to the local presence of Mexican migrant workers, including their collective and interactive cinematic practices that contradicted the passive, individualist subjectivity presupposed by dominant modes of Hollywood spectatorship.[91] Here I make a related set of claims about the farm worker presence in California's various agricultural valleys—the Imperial Valley, Coachella Valley, the Santa Clara/Silicon Valley, the Sacramento Valley, and especially the San Joaquin Valley. Shifting critical attention from urban centers (like Benjamin's Paris, or California cities such as Los Angeles and San Francisco) to regions of agricultural production suggest that farm worker futurisms have served as vital conditions of possibility for contemporary media politics—which is to say that farm worker futurisms have significantly inspired and shaped dominant media histories, often providing their political and historical horizons of intelligibility.

Centering farm worker futurism also departs from and transforms nation- and identity-based epistemologies for understanding visual culture and politics, including ethnic studies approaches to film and media organized around group identities. Overlapping with modes of literary analysis that intervene in dominant constructions of literary value by recovering and analyzing underappreciated works by writers of color, ethnic studies research has made valuable contributions to film studies by taking as its unit of analysis films by directors of color. While building on such work, my own approach to film and visual culture is an effort to approximate the epistemological perspectives of farm worker futurism, which often presupposes complexly collective and collaborative modes of production, dissemination, and spectatorship, as well as non-identitarian, transnational modes of social organization. In contrast with work organized around individual authors/auteurs and racial identities ("Chicano film," "Asian American cinema," etc.), my focus on farm worker film and visual culture foregrounds conflicted and contradictory interracial, transnational social formations. While sometimes imagined as synonymous with particular racial/national groups, "farm worker" is a historically changing, internally differentiated category that, as used here, has included Italians, poor southern whites, African Americans, Chinese, Japanese, Filipinos, Yemeni, and Mexicans. Rather than marking a racial or national identity, then, the term "farm worker" defines a matrix of domination, resistance, incorporation, and rearticulation. It is linked to other terms like race, class, gender, sex, and nation but irreducible to them, a relatively autonomous social category around which an entire machinery of power/knowledge has been built. Indeed, adopting the perspective of farm worker futurism suggests that, to the extent they are centered on individual films, auteurs, and racial identities, such ethnic studies epistemologies may formally converge with those of agribusiness, with its possessive individualism and the atomized, "divide and conquer" racializations of its work camps and strikebreaking practices.

The trajectory of *Farm Worker Futurism* from a post–World War II farm worker strike in the San Joaquin Valley to a UFW-supported strike against Apple in the Silicon Valley presages a similar shift in thinking about the history of social media. In the 1950s, at the conclusion of the DiGiorgio strike and as part of both his organizing and research into labor conditions and the bracero program, Galarza turned from the San Joaquin Valley to other agricultural regions of California, notably the Santa Clara Valley, a prominent site both of agribusiness domination and an emergent IT industry. Rebranded in the 1980s as "Silicon Valley," the region's IT companies have largely superseded agribusiness both economically and in public memory; and yet the companies that produce the hardware and shape the culture of new digital media were built on the historical substrate of agribusiness and incorporated many of its political ideologies and labor practices. At the same time, low-wage workers of color in the Silicon Valley, building on the organizing activities and tactics of the UFW and the NFLU, launched some of the first successful organizing drives in the high-tech industry.

Since the 2006 immigrants' rights protests, when large numbers of young protestors in Los Angeles and elsewhere organized demonstrations via social media, researchers have recognized Latino immigrants as forming part of the vanguard of digital political activism. While often greeted with surprise in mainstream media accounts, the Latino students who used social media sites and text messaging to organize school walkouts did not come out of nowhere but instead built on longer histories of technological innovation among working-class people of color in California. Farm workers, in particular, have always been early and creative adopters of new media technologies of time/space compression, from telegraphy and film and video cameras to mobile phones. Whereas conventional accounts of the history and dissemination of digital technology adopt a top-down perspective, foregrounding farm worker futurism requires a re-historicization of social media from below.

Focusing on farm workers also changes how we think about the history of political ideology and practice. While there is widespread consensus over the contemporary influence of neoliberalism, as an explanatory framework the concept overemphasizes the power of elites. In contrast with theories of neoliberalism as a set of dominant discourses and practices imposed on the mass of people from on high, *Farm Worker Futurism* adopts a model of power based in the clash of contesting forces and the dynamics of contestation, incorporation, and dissent. Partly in response to theories of neoliberalism that in effect threaten to erase or deconceptualize the struggles of black people, Clyde Woods, in his work on post-Katrina Louisiana, rearticulated the term by linking it to the history of struggles over southern plantation economies. In Woods's account, plantations become paradigms or experimental laboratories for the formation of what has come to be called neoliberalism.[92] I would make a similar claim about the historical origins of neoliberalism in the agricultural fields of California, where individual white market freedoms have been defined in relationship to farm workers. To see neoliberalism in this way is to understand it as a reactionary political economic formation built on the backs of farm workers and other low-wage workers of color.

This farm worker optic further reveals the powerful articulation of neoliberalism to ideologies and fantasies of gender and sexuality. Historically, an agribusiness-dominated political economy has supported and been supported by subjectivities formed out of a constellation of ideological signifiers—white, male, heterosexual, individual, high-tech—defined in opposition to farm workers figured as colored, feminized, queer, collective, and technologically primitive. Such clashing race–gender–sex–tech constellations are central to the forms of neoliberalism that have emerged in the agricultural valleys of California, structuring the formation of conflicting gazes and contested visual fields.

Finally, centering farm worker futurism generates new ways of thinking about time, temporality, and the politics of "the future." Speculative, futuristic genres have come to dominate media culture across a range of platforms, and this book invites readers to think about how such genres draw on histories of farm worker futurism. Additionally, however, *Farm Worker Futurism* provides new resources for thinking critically about images of the future and their social and political implications. In his analysis of "catastrophic, 'near-future' visions" of disaster, Fredric Jameson famously argued that such representations suggest a widespread waning of the ability to imagine a future, in the West at least, in other than dystopian and reactionary terms. "These imaginary near futures . . . no longer strike us with the horror of otherness and radical difference," Jameson argues, because they figure not the future but the intensified dangers of the present. Such near-future dystopias suggest that "there is only the present and that it is always 'ours.'"[93] In contrast with hegemonic near futures that disappear or demonize the poor and the working class, *Farm Worker Futurism* displaces dominant visions of the future with farm worker futurisms, and, in particular, with subaltern claims on what José Muñoz called "futurity," or the critical expectation of the future as open-ended possibility.[94]

1 "To the Disinherited Belongs the Future"

Farm Worker Futurism in the 1940s

The corporate power historically faced by farm worker unions has been partly defined by a constellation of ideas about agriculture, technology, and white heterosexual masculinity. That constellation is revealingly represented and influentially elaborated in the work of science fiction writer Robert Heinlein, whose popularity and influence would be hard to overestimate.[1] As H. Bruce Franklin writes in his critical biography *Robert A. Heinlein: America as Science Fiction,* Heinlein was born in 1907 in a small Missouri farming community at a time when family farms were being replaced by "mechanized agribusiness, sweeping people off the countryside into the booming new cities."[2] In the early twentieth century his father worked as a traveling salesmen for a farm implement company called Midland Manufacturing, and then for a family company called Heinlein Brothers Agricultural Implements, before finally taking a job with International Harvester, the agribusiness giant for which Heinlein's grandfather worked as a salesman, clerk, and bookkeeper in Kansas City, Missouri. In this new agricultural–industrial–urban center he became an avid reader of the "first science-fiction dime novel," Edward Ellis's *The Steam Man of the Prairies* (1868), as well as its popular copycat series *Frank Reade and His Steam Man of the Plains,* works that I suggest were historical mediations of period agribusiness technologies.[3] Combined with his subsequent military service, Heinlein's early exposure to the world of agribusiness technology shaped his subsequent interest in high-tech narratives of space travel.

After receiving a medical discharge from the navy for tuberculosis in 1934, Heinlein moved to Los Angeles, where he became involved in local Democratic Party politics. He was eventually elected to the West Hollywood Democratic Club's board of directors and helped organize Upton

Sinclair's "End Poverty in California" (EPIC) campaign for the California governorship. The socialist Sinclair ran on a platform of using government credit to buy failed factories and farms and redistribute them to the unemployed. While Heinlein may have considered such large-scale state redistribution of wealth beyond the pale, he found Sinclair's critique of monopoly capitalism appealing. Heinlein, "whose family's farm-equipment business had been superseded by an emerging monopoly (International Harvester) and whose own small-business ventures had been unable to compete in this era of life-and-death struggle between corporate monopoly and small enterprise," tended to idolize individual entrepreneurs (like the boy inventors in his early reading) and small farmers.[4] In 1935 Sinclair assigned Heinlein the task of investigating strikes and vigilante violence in the Imperial Valley, where agribusiness monopolies reigned with a heavy hand.

In his history of California vigilantism Mike Davis argues that in the early 1930s farm workers confronted a "semi-fascist, closed society whose employing classes, especially in the Central Valley and Southern California, were habituated to vigilante violence as a normal mode of industrial relations." Davis concludes that "farm fascism assumed its definitive form" in the Imperial Valley, in response to strikes by Mexican and Filipino farm workers who were supported and partly organized by the Communist Cannery and Agricultural Workers Industrial Union (CAWIU).[5] Agribusiness interests not only mobilized the local police to break the strike but also organized vigilante posses of between 40 and 150 men, including growers, ranch foremen, small businessmen, and American Legion members. After 1933 and in the face of new efforts by the CAWIU to organize lettuce workers, "the big grower–shippers in El Centro sought complete militarization of the Valley's middle and skilled working classes" by organizing the "Imperial Valley Anti-Communist Association" with somewhere between seven and ten thousand members.[6] Imperial Valley vigilantes broke up union meetings, beat union members and their supporters in the street, and kidnapped them and ran them out of the area. According to biographer William H. Patterson Jr., Heinlein was "appalled and outraged" by the vigilante violence he witnessed during his fact-finding trip.[7] Upon his return to Los Angeles he made a presentation before the West Hollywood Democratic Club in which he screened a newsreel about the strike and concluded that the "constitutional rights of workers in Imperial Valley have been abrogated by some of the citizens and elected officials in [an] amazing display of vigilante activities."[8]

More than a decade later, in roughly the same years as the highly publicized farm worker strike that is the focus of this chapter, Heinlein imaginatively returned to the Imperial Valley in a haunting suspense story,
"Water Is for Washing" (1947), about an earthquake in its "open desert
and irrigated fields." The story follows an unlikely group of survivors—a
traveling businessman, a "vagrant," a white girl child, and a "Nisei" boy
child—who race to higher ground in an effort to avoid a post-quake tidal
wave.[9] As the water rises the two men take turns, with one lashed to a concrete post marking "sea level" and supporting the children on his shoulders while the other treads water. Ultimately the businessman and the
children survive until morning when the water recedes, but the "vagrant"
(also called "the tramp" and "the bum") is swept away to his death and
subsequently buried by the businessman in a shallow grave.

The story's meaning is elusive, but it suggests a pair of competing interpretations that partly correspond to the contradictions in "commonsense" white populist perspectives on agriculture, which often oscillate
between critiques of corporate agriculture (and corporate capitalism
more broadly) and attacks on union organizing among people of color
(and the political power of the latter in general). Is the vagrant a figure
of the impoverished and the disinherited from the EPIC campaign, including the Mexican and Filipino workers Heinlein saw beaten by agribusiness vigilantes? Given how Imperial Valley agribusiness interests, in
collaboration with the state, engineered massive infrastructures for the
control and mobilization of vast amounts of water, perhaps the tidal wave
in the story symbolizes the combined forces of agribusiness technology
and vigilante violence. But the vagrant's description of the ensuing disaster also suggests a contrary reading: "The Pacific Ocean has broken
through . . . That's the Gulf. I was in a cantina in Centro when it came
over the radio from Calexico. Warned us that the ground had dropped
away to the south. Tidal wave coming. Then the station went dead."[10] The
earthquake, in other words, has destroyed protective geological formations to the south of the Imperial Valley, leaving it vulnerable to a tidal
wave from the Gulf of California in northern Mexico. Does the disaster
then refer to waves of communist Filipino and Mexican farm workers?
Heinlein's increasing anticommunism, combined with his frankly racist novels about the invasion of the West by Asian armies (*Sixth Column*,
1941) and the enslavement of whites by African warlords from a parallel
universe (*Farnham's Freehold*, 1964) support such a reading of "Water Is
for Washing."

The contradictory combination of anti-agribusiness and anti–farm worker speculative fiction is revealingly represented in Heinlein's novel *Farmer in the Sky* (1950). In the late 1940s and early 1950s he wrote a group of popular books glorifying space travel, including a series of works for adolescent boys from which *Farmer in the Sky* is drawn.[11] These later works, according to Franklin, depicted the conquest of space in optimistic and romantic language "pulsing with missionary zeal for a colossal human endeavor" that turned boys into men on a harsh alien world.[12] *Farmer in the Sky* is set sometime after 1998, when food shortages resulting from overpopulation compel the novel's protagonist, a California teenager named Bill Lermer, to contract with the "Colonial Commission" and immigrate with his family to a farming colony on Ganymede, one of Jupiter's moons. They had been promised "free land" for farming, but upon their arrival it is revealed that the housing facilities for the interplanetary immigrants are inadequate and that "there wasn't enough processing machinery to go around"—the massive tractors and rock crushers required to terraform the planet. As a result, they are told that "it might be two or three years before any particular immigrant got a chance to process his first acre of ground."[13] If they are to eat in the meantime, the immigrants must indenture themselves to earlier immigrants with already established lunar farms.

In a chapter called "Share Croppers," a recent immigrant to Ganymede named Saunders protests against the implied dishonor: "I'm a farmer. Always have been. But I said 'farmer,' not sharecropper. I didn't come here to hire out to no boss. You can take your job and do what you see fit with it. I stand my rights!"[14] But Bill quickly realizes that if he wants to "homestead" in space someday he has no choice but to rent himself out as "stoop labor" to a benevolent family farmer referred to as "Papa Schulz."[15] Bill and his father ultimately borrow the necessary machinery and terraform a five-acre parcel, build a rock farmhouse, and begin growing food on their own plot of land. Bill subsequently joins a "pioneer party" of other young men to scout new possible farmland. Along with another boy he discovers a mysterious crystal cave containing "a sort of tractor thing," an elaborate mechanical vehicle resembling a giant metal centipede that the boys surmise was left behind by aliens.[16] They ride the strange tractor out of the crystal cave and back to the safety of camp and finally to their new "homesteads," where Bill expresses his identification with the machine's alien makers: "They controlled their environment. They weren't animals, pushed around and forced to accept what nature handed them; they took nature and bent it to their will. I guess they were men."[17] This encounter with alien yet familiar masculine farm technology finally seems to prompt his decision to remain on Ganymede, where it was "new, hard, and clean," and become a "farmer in the sky."

The novel projects a critical alternative-future rejoinder to its actually existing present, where agriculture was dominated by corporate interests that had largely squeezed out family farms.[18] At the same time, however, *Farmer in the Sky* poses the speculative question: What if an exemplary white U.S. American boy was forced to become a lowly farm worker? Anticipating a number of similar science fiction narratives, the novel constitutes a sort of race and gender thought experiment that subjects its white male protagonist to conditions experienced by racialized migrant farm workers. Even the bare bones of Bill's narrative recall the story of many working-class Mexican migrants to the United States: limited access to work and food prompts dangerous, long-distance travel; upon arrival the migrant discovers that housing and employment conditions have been dramatically misrepresented; the migrant is forced by circumstances to accept difficult and debilitating "stoop labor," a form of agricultural work that growers argued Mexicans were naturally well suited for, and that reproduced farm worker abjection.[19] The novel's striking cover by Clifford Geary, who illustrated Heinlein's juvenile space fictions, foregrounds stoop labor. Recalling period photos of farm labor in the San Joaquin Valley, the cover depicts a Ganymede farm with a pitchfork-holding farmhand standing up and resting in the foreground while in the receding distance a tiny, stooped-over figure works amid the rows of crops.[20] Rather than becoming bent and broken by stoop labor, or beaten down like the Mexican and Filipino farm workers Heinlein encountered in the Imperial Valley, Bill ultimately rises, and becomes a successful settler. The white space immigrant is not limited to materially and symbolically diminishing forms of racialized work such as "sharecropping" and stoop labor— he is a heroic "homesteader," "pioneer," or "settler" colonial who stands up on his own two feet and bends the world to his will. From this perspective the futuristic white farm worker serves to denigrate actually existing farm workers who do not similarly make the passage to white male yeomanry, who by implication are more "like animals, pushed around and forced to accept what nature handed them." Finally, technology serves as a key marker of the difference: whereas farm workers of color are supposedly dwarfed and dominated by industrial farm machinery, the white farm boy is able to master the alien tractor.[21]

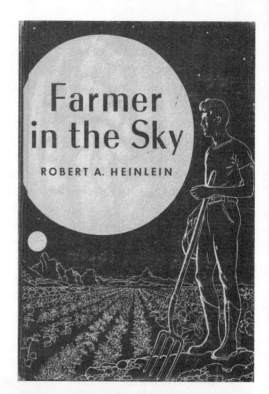

Sharecropping in space. The cover and a detail for the first edition of Robert Heinlein's *Farmer in the Sky* (1950) depicting agricultural "stoop labor" on Ganymede.

In what will prove to be an influential move in the history of California and U.S. political discourse, Heinlein attempts to imaginatively wrest technology from agribusiness in order to serve a futuristic vision of the white family farm implicitly defined in opposition to farm workers of color. But as we shall see, he did not anticipate the extent to which the conjoined futures of whiteness and agricultural technology had already been colonized by agribusiness. California's San Joaquin Valley agribusiness and labor have a long history of struggling over technology, including visual technology, and its privileged relationship to corporate whiteness. Agribusiness companies have used their superior access to mass media to control representations of production and set the terms and conditions of employment, successfully marginalizing media that focus on racialized labor exploitation in order to circulate their own more celebratory and heroic images of the industry in news stories, advertising, photos, and films. In the decade or so after World War II, California agribusiness corporations invented influential media identities that combined residual idealizations of a white patriarchal family farm, on the one hand, with the fetishization of emergent forms of "white" science and technology for mass production, on the other. At the same time farm worker unions used photography, film, and other media technologies to document and publicize work and living conditions and to mobilize support from workers, unions, civic organizations, and consumers. Appropriations of cameras and other media by farm worker unions have thus constituted both a material and symbolic force, making exploitation visible while simultaneously seizing the means of visual reproduction in ways that directly challenge the agribusiness deployment of "white" technology in the visual field.

This chapter centers on an important precursor to the United Farm Workers, Local 218 of the National Farm Labor Union, and its 1948–50 strike against the DiGiorgio Fruit Company headquartered in the southern San Joaquin Valley. The strike helped to establish a variety of successful organizing tactics, including media campaigns, which were subsequently used by the UFW. While the strike is discussed in numerous labor histories, the conflicts over technology that accompanied it have received little attention. An important exception is *Spiders in the House, Workers in the Field* by Ernesto Galarza, one of the strike organizers.[22] The book is a history of the strike and the legal battles over a documentary film the union made in collaboration with a Hollywood union called *Poverty in the Valley of Plenty* (1948). In a precedent-setting case, DiGiorgio won a libel suit against the unions involved in making the film and suppressed it. The film's significance, however, depends on situating it amid the larger networks of agribusiness and union media, most notably the numerous photo essays that made up the union's publicity campaign and on which the film was partly based. Galarza, a Mexican immigrant and onetime farm worker, organized the union's publicity. While his book *Farm Workers and Agri-business in California, 1947–1960* is a classic in labor history, and his memoir *Barrio Boy* is part of the Chicano/a literary canon, his photographic work remains largely unknown to scholars. In addition to drawing on numerous examples of agribusiness media and histories of industry and labor in the San Joaquin Valley, particularly works by Galarza, this chapter is thus substantially based on an examination of Galarza's archive of personal papers, including numerous photographs, photo essays, and other kinds of union publicity.

As part of the strike, Galarza built on what I described in the introduction as a migrant labor techno-culture of time–space compression in order to organize workers in collective research on and documentation of the strike and the working and living conditions that motivated it. Agribusiness companies such as DiGiorgio attempted to annex the living arrangements of farm workers to the machinery of reproduction by renting out single-family shacks or tents organized into a complex system of segregated work camps. Galarza's photo essays show how corporate housing posited farm workers as machines, but they also indirectly suggest the ways agribusiness used housing to reproduce racial inequality and heterosexual families as economic units and components of production. One aim of the union's media campaigns was to build support among different union members and unions across racial and gender lines, and Galarza's photo collages represent a multiracial strike involving men and women in ways that suggest, by negation, the intricate combination of racial segregations and gendered divisions of labor that constituted the conditions of agribusiness (re)production on a mass scale.

Widely circulated in newspapers and union publications, Galarza's photo collages projected an alternative world of union organizing that displaced the limits of actually existing conditions, and in this sense exemplify a kind of campesino modernity as social movement speculative fiction. In the present context, the notion of social movement speculative fictions refers to collective projects devoted to using technology to imagine alternative future worlds, based in the immediacy of present material conditions while projecting their near-future suspension or reversal. This is well represented by the flag of the race- and gender-integrated NFLU, which represents the union's planetary perspective with the image of an eagle hovering over the earth. Seemingly orbiting around the eagle like a satellite is the union's circular insignia representing a cotton boll, a plow, and a hoe, emblems of the product and technologies of agricultural production. These elements of the flag suggest the union's appropriation of technology, in contradistinction to agribusiness visions, where farm workers serve the mechanical means of production. The union eagle is further encircled by the union slogan, "To the Disinherited Belong the Future." The NFLU thus staked its strike on claims to a future currently owned by agribusiness and, like a ruthless corporation from a farm worker remake of *The Matrix* films, corporate powers would fight tooth and nail to protect their investments. The banner is an emblem of what in the previous chapter I called "futurity," or the presupposition of a future as such. In contexts where farm workers face limited options, shortened life spans, and ideologies of their impending obsolescence, to claim a future at all was a radical act. In a related way Galarza's photo collages oppose agribusiness futurism with farm worker futurity, or the utopian projection of a future as collective possibility.

The Postwar Agribusiness Mediascape

According to Cesar Chavez, in 1944 he joined the U.S. Navy and while on shore leave was arrested for refusing to move from the "whites only" section of a Delano, California, movie theater to the section reserved for blacks, Filipinos, and Mexicans.[23] In the navy, he encountered forms of labor segregation among black, Filipino, and Mexican sailors that recalled similar arrangements in the cotton and beet fields around Delano where he grew up. His arrest for resisting segregation was the first of many subsequent arrests over his long career as a labor leader.

If Chavez departed for Delano from San Diego—traveling by car, bus, or hitchhiking—he would have traveled north through the Los Angeles Basin, then up over the steep Tejon Pass and down into the oil fields and factory farms of Kern County in the San Joaquin Valley. If it was a clear day he might have seen from the top of the Pass vast tracts of DiGiorgio Fruit Company farmland laid out like a jumbled sheet of green and brown graph paper on the Valley floor. Traveling north on Highway 99, Chavez would have passed by many of the work camps and small towns of the regional agribusiness belt, including Arvin, Wasco, McFarland, and, of course, Delano. In the 1940s Arvin and Delano were effectively satellites of the DiGiorgio Fruit Company, and segregated movie theaters had been the norm in the area since the advent of cinema there. The Mexican immigrant socialist activist Josefina Fierro recalled an incident in the mid-1920s when her mother similarly refused to relinquish her seat in a segregated movie theater in the cotton town of Madera.[24] And in his 1947 study of San Joaquin Valley agribusiness communities, anthropologist Walter Goldschmidt noted that farm workers made up a significant portion of the film audience in the region's segregated theaters.[25]

The Delano police ultimately released Chavez without charges since he hadn't broken a law; instead, he had contravened a dominant norm in an area ruled by agricultural interests. One sign of agribusiness dominance in the Valley was the fact that communities such as Wasco and Arvin remained unincorporated in the 1930s and 1940s, a situation favored by large growers since they didn't have to pay taxes for city services and infrastructure and because they could effectively run the towns where many of their workers lived without interference from local elected officials.[26] Even when communities like Delano were incorporated, they were still largely controlled by big agriculture, as suggested by the fact that the segregation of movie theaters mirrored the segregation of farm workers of color in local agribusiness housing.

Starting roughly in the 1920s and 1930s, agribusiness in the San Joaquin Valley developed a system for controlling production and reproduction that significantly relied on media technologies. As the anecdote about Chavez suggests, agribusiness exercised significant influence over movie theaters—the region's most popular commercial entertainment and one of the few public spheres that incorporated farm workers, in however subordinated a fashion. At the heart of corporate agriculture's efforts to control the media was the Associated Farmers of California (AFC), a statewide interest group aggressively devoted to low wages and strikebreaking. With important members in the southern part of the Valley, including DiGiorgio, the group had publicly denounced John Steinbeck's *The Grapes of Wrath* as communist propaganda and in Kern County its members helped ban the novel in public libraries. AFC further attempted to stop the making of the film version of the book and, failing that, it organized a boycott against Fox, the studio that made it, and tried to prevent the film from screening in the Valley.[27] Ultimately more influential, however, was what Carey McWilliams called AFC's "carefully organized propaganda department" with its regular bulletins for members, widely distributed publications, and steady stream of statements and releases for the press. Such campaigns, according to McWilliams, led to the passage in rural communities of anti-picketing laws and special emergency ordinances that effectively equated strikes with natural disasters requiring state action.[28]

AFC used media technology to influence public opinion but also to police labor. As *Fortune* magazine put it, the agribusiness interest group was "run by big growers but supported and manned by the little ones who pay dues and wield pick handles and rifles" when a strike breaks out.[29] Members of the AFC pledged themselves to report to the local sheriff "in case of trouble," and in the 1930s they were deputized by the thousands to confront striking farm workers. AFC tactics further included running union members out of town, disrupting their meetings, attacking work camps, and collaborating with the police to spy on union members. As part of its anti-union espionage the group engaged in an extensive system of surveillance and information collection and organization. McWilliams, for instance, reports that by 1935 the AFC had produced a set of files on about one thousand "dangerous radicals" with front- and side-view photographs that they circulated to over a hundred police officers in the state. To revise Althusser's famous formulations about state power, we could say that media technologies were important parts of both the ideological and the coercive apparatus of agribusiness.

The DiGiorgio Fruit Company was one of the most influential members of AFC. In the late 1930s DiGiorgio held forty thousand acres of fruit land in the United States as well as vast tracts in Central and South America, making it the largest producer of fresh fruit in the world.[30] The company was worth $24 million by the time of the strike, which included eleven thousand acres of vegetables, fruit orchards, and grapes divided between its Delano and Arvin properties.[31] Despite or perhaps because of such massive scales, many agribusiness companies projected media images of themselves as family farms. As Galarza explains, agribusiness ideology included the fantasy that "agri-businessmen are farmers, men of earthy minds and bodies dressed in overalls, the direct descendants of the Jeffersonian yeomen, the elite of the republic."[32] DiGiorgio, for instance, drew on traditions of white agrarian reproductive masculinity with its trademark image of the DiGiorgio "Jolly Farmer," a smiling icon in a checked shirt, overalls, and a straw hat.[33] By the 1930s the industrial nature of agribusiness was hard to deny, and so agribusiness corporations developed new ways to link themselves to ideologies of whiteness via the industry's connections to high technology.[34] But in the case of the DiGiorgio Fruit Company, its white media image was complicated by the fact that its founder and public face, Joseph DiGiorgio, was an Italian immigrant, an identity not readily assimilated to whiteness.

Agribusiness Technology and Whiteness

The title of a recent scholarly anthology asks *Are Italians White?* In California and elsewhere, the answer is complicated. On the one hand, Thomas A. Guglielmo and David Roediger argue that historically, Italian immigrants to the United States were treated as white in many important ways. According to Roediger, Italians were viewed as "legally fit for naturalized citizenship and political participation even before naturalization," setting them apart from African Americans and Asian and Mexican immigrants.[35] And as Guglielmo argues, Italians were often afforded the status and benefits of whiteness in terms of greater residential mobility, eligibility for state relief funds, and more access to movie theaters, restaurants, and other racially exclusive or segregated public places than were African Americans.[36] On the other hand, however, the Italian immigrant's claim on whiteness has sometimes been tenuous and uncertain. As Stuart Hall notes, modern Italy has been divided between "the industrializing and modernizing 'North' of Italy" and "the peasant, underdeveloped and dependent 'South,'" making Antonio Gramsci's analysis of the "Southern Question" relevant to the study of colonial race relations in other contexts.[37] Another historian, Jennifer Guglielmo, further explains that most late nineteenth- and early twentieth-century Italian immigrants to the United States were peasants and workers from the south who "were considered racially 'other' by the northern Italian ruling class," particularly given the south's relative proximity to Africa. These ideologies crossed the Atlantic, she concludes, "and informed the thinking of native-born white Americans who also denigrated southern Italians as prone to violence, whether of a revolutionary or a criminal nature."[38] In parts of the United States, particularly in late nineteenth- and early twentieth-century Louisiana, Italians were compared to black people, not only because of southern Italy's African connections but also because Italian immigrants often lived near black people, worked "black" jobs such as farm labor, and were sometimes lynched.[39]

In addition, Italian immigrants had a reputation for radical politics in the late nineteenth and early twentieth centuries, culminating in the 1927 execution of the anarchists Nicola Sacco and Bartolomeo Vanzetti, that often put them at odds with notions of white Americanism. The decade of the 1920s also saw the red scare and deportation raids directed at im-

migrant anarchists and socialists, notably Italians, and the passage of the
Johnson–Reed Act (1924) establishing immigration quotas partly directed at limiting immigration from southern Italy. Italians were at times,
in the words of Roediger, "outside the sure protections of white supremacy," and many late nineteenth- and early twentieth-century Italian immigrants may not have completely known the U.S. racial order, "bought
into whiteness," or "mobilized as whites." As several of the contributors to
Are Italians White? argue, whereas some Italian socialists and anarchists
espoused forms of antiblack racism, others critically disidentified with
whiteness, denounced lynching, and supported the Mexican Revolution.[40]

During the same years a number of Italian immigrants migrated to
California to work in agriculture and some built great fortunes, foremost
among them Joseph DiGiorgio, whose formative dates and milestones
span from the 1890s through the 1920s, the period during which the
whiteness of Italians was most in flux. His father was a small farmer and
the head of a cooperative lemon-packing house in Cefalù, Sicily, in southern Italy that packed his lemons and those of other farmers in the area. In
1888 or 1889 he sent fourteen-year-old Joseph first to New York and then
ultimately to Baltimore to help with the distribution of lemons. In 1904
DiGiorgio founded a lucrative auction house called the Baltimore Fruit
Exchange, and soon after he incorporated the Mexican American Fruit
and Steamship Company with banana plantations in Cuba and operations
in Jamaica, Mexico, and Nicaragua that rivaled the powerful United Fruit
Company. During the first two decades of the twentieth century DiGiorgio
purchased vast tracts of citrus land in Florida as well as a large fruit packing and shipping company and farmland in California. Finally, in 1920, he
established the DiGiorgio Fruit Company in the San Joaquin Valley.

In the decades preceding DiGiorgio's arrival in the Valley, there had
been an influx of Italian immigrants, partly spurred by the passage of
the Chinese Exclusion Act of 1882, and many of them worked harvesting crops.[41] California was divided over the desirability of Italian immigration to the state, with some anti-Chinese organizations and big growers (including some Italians) promoting Italians as white alternatives to
"oriental" farm labor while nativist writers and officials denigrated Italians for their supposed criminality and resemblance to the Japanese.[42]
Similarly, in Hollywood during the 1920s the southern Italian immigrant
Rudolph Valentino was celebrated but also vilified in part because, as
film scholar Miriam Hansen argues, his Italian identity orientalized and
blackened him.[43] In *White on Arrival: Italians, Race, Color, and Power in*

Chicago, 1890–1945, Thomas A. Guglielmo suggests that by the 1940s Italian Americans were increasingly seen—and saw themselves—as white.[44] Ironically, this state of affairs was perhaps encouraged by a final historical challenge to the white Americanism of Italians at the start of World War II. When the United States entered the war the state classified all non-naturalized immigrants from Japan, Germany, and Italy as "enemy aliens." As a result, 260 Italians were interned at Fort Missoula in Montana, while those not interned were subject to a series of regulations including a curfew and travel restrictions. They were also required to register with the government as "enemy aliens" and to carry photo IDs. Moreover, thousands were displaced from their homes to newly defined "restricted zones" on the West Coast. However, whereas earlier in California history Italian immigrants were compared to the Japanese, during the war the two were ultimately distinguished from each other. Whereas Italians were imprisoned in the hundreds, approximately 110,000 Japanese were interned. Moreover, in contrast with the Japanese, the Italians' suspect status was short-lived—the attorney general officially rescinded their classification as "enemy aliens" on Columbus Day, 1942.[45] The history of Italian immigrants in California thus suggests that they became white partly in opposition to Japanese.

A significant number of DiGiorgio's Japanese workers were interned, clearly marking the difference between Italians and Japanese in terms of class and the distinction between management and labor. In the 1930s a few Issei-operated Japanese work camps housed workers for DiGiorgio's Sierra Vista Ranch, but during internment they were either closed or used by Mexican and Filipino workers.[46] Wealthy, powerful, and a proudly naturalized U.S. citizen, DiGiorgio was not subjected to the threat of detainment faced by some Italian Americans, yet even after the war newspaper and magazine profiles continued to emphasize his difference from other white Americans. A generally celebratory story about DiGiorgio featured in the August 1946 issue of *Fortune,* for example, calls him "colorful" and "full of *pastafazoi* [sic]." It further describes his speech as "picturesque" and renders it as dialect ("This suppose to create employment . . . so what they do? . . . They through outa work the box-factory help"; "If an insec' try to eat his way through this root, he take a hundred years"). On the first page of the article is a photo of DiGiorgio at nineteen and, even though the editors note that it was taken in Baltimore, they have superimposed him over a background view of "his birthplace in the Sicilian town of Cefalù." Finally, a photo of DiGiorgio with several of his non-Italian executives is captioned "Much of DiGiorgio's success can be attributed to his flair for checking his Latin inspirations against the shrewdness and farming skill of all the native Americans whom he has brought up in the business over the years."[47] Two years later, the *San Francisco Chronicle* published a story about the ongoing Arvin strike in its Sunday news magazine that made fun of DiGiorgio's "Italian" way of speaking English. The news magazine's cover featured a sketch of the mustachioed corporate head gesturing with large, hairy hands.[48] Even given the newly more secure whiteness of Italians, not to mention his immense wealth and power, DiGiorgio was still depicted in ways that recalled earlier moments when Italian whiteness was more in question.

At the same time, however, the media also represented DiGiorgio as a master of technology and industrial engineering on a massive scale in ways that partly countered his ethnic othering. The *Fortune* feature, for example, depicts him as a larger-than-life giant of industry, the scope of his technological reach and vision rivaling the size of his vast agricultural holdings. The article represents the wide-angle gaze of the big grower as he surveys his expansive factory in the fields.[49] It includes, for example, a high-angle, panoramic color photo of one of DiGiorgio's Kern County ranches that covers the top of two pages. If the photo represents the white male gaze of high-tech agribusiness, as it were, then others, like the photos of the corporation's railway depots and its massive winery, represent dramatic feats of white male engineering. The story begins with a description of DiGiorgio traveling by chauffeured car over the Tehachapi Mountains, when he asks the driver to stop so he can survey the San Joaquin Valley below:

> Looking down on DiGiorgio Farms, the heart of his nationwide ownership of 26,000 acres, he saw a rectangle of green six miles long and three miles wide . . . The whole perimeter of his land was marked by a row of tamarisk, slightly darker green than the leaves of his vines and plum trees. A pale green strip to the north was his asparagus . . . Nearer, at DiGiorgio's left, lay the small town of Arvin. Not far beyond Arvin, and within his ranch's limits, DiGiorgio spied the monolithic concrete of his new winery. At this point in the road DiGiorgio has expressed the same sentiment to many friends: "All this I create myself. Before I drill the wells, all was desert."[50]

Like a high-tech Moses, DiGiorgio makes water flow in the desert and appropriates to himself the power of creation in ways that obscure the

Wide-angle agribusiness gaze. The DiGiorgio ranch, *Fortune* (1946).
Ernesto Galarza Papers, Special Collections M0224; courtesy of
Department of Special Collections and University Archives, Stanford
University Libraries.

agency of farm workers, who imaginatively become, like wells and concrete, mere means of production.

The portrait of DiGiorgio accompanying the *Fortune* story further depicts his command of workers as an extension of his technological dominance. In the artist's sketch introducing the story, DiGiorgio stands in
the center of the image, between his railroad depot and winery on the
right and rows of grapes on the left. The tracks that stretch back and
disappear into the horizon are matched by a row of workers with identical straw hats who pack the fruit into boxes and place them on a conveyor
belt, suggesting that they have been incorporated into the machinery of
production. The figure of DiGiorgio is at the controlling intersection of
two technological grids dominating the landscape. As if to emphasize the
commanding power of his vision, he holds a pair of sunglasses in his right
hand, uncovering a gaze that looks directly at the viewer; by contrast, the
workers' eyes are hidden behind the brims of their hats and their heads
are bowed, ostensibly to concentrate on their work but symbolically as if
they had submissively averted their gazes in recognition of their boss's superiority. The farm workers' gender is rendered obscure and ambiguous
by hat and pose, and within the economy of the agribusiness visual field
the workers are visually feminized and queered in relationship to the gaze

of the corporate head. In related fashion a 1946 *Time* story called "The Fruit King" begins with a description of the domineering gaze DiGiorgio fixed on his workers: "Amid the sunshine and fruit trees on his 10,000-acre ranch near Arvin, Calif., Joseph DiGiorgio, 71, imperiously watched workmen pour concrete for what will be the world's largest winery."[51] Such articles suggest that he controls not only the environment but also the technologies of agriculture, including labor. And while Mexicans had not yet become the majority labor force in the fields, the incorporation of so many straw hats could be read as their synecdoche, thus encouraging viewers to take vicarious pleasure in DiGiorgio's employment of Mexican farm workers as implements of production—which is to say that *Fortune* symbolically whitens corporate capital by defining DiGiorgio's business prowess in terms of his technological power over a racialized, feminized, and queer labor force.

Representations of DiGiorgio's power over technology thus whiten the company and assimilate it to patriarchal reproductive futurism. The *Fortune* profile foregrounds images of phallic power such as the corporate head's penetrating gaze, the massive size of his holdings, his "monolithic" concrete winery and well drilling. As Laura Pulido reminds us, big growers in the southern San Joaquin Valley are almost exclusively male.[52] Media representations of DiGiorgio effectively normalize and even celebrate this male orientation. He is often described as an appealingly "cocky" risk taker, for example.[53] And while he has no children of his own, DiGiorgio is

The master's gaze. Portrait of Joseph DiGiorgio with farm workers,
Fortune (1946). Ernesto Galarza Papers, Special Collections M0224;
courtesy of Department of Special Collections and University Archives,
Stanford University Libraries.

nonetheless depicted as the patriarch of his extended family, employing
his brothers (but not sisters) and grooming his several nephews (but not
nieces) to ultimately take over the corporation. And the bronze bust the
town's middle-class leaders erected in his honor at the Arvin community
center, a photo of which is included in the *Fortune* story, suggests that the

company's paternalism extends to local social relations. By representing his power over the machinery of production the media thus constructs DiGiorgio as a white man, with an emphasis on both words.

Michael Rogin's *Blackface, White Noise: Jewish Immigrants in the Hollywood Melting Pot* is, among other things, an account of race, ethnicity, technology, and corporate power in Hollywood that illuminates the situation of agribusiness companies such as DiGiorgio. Rogin focuses on the generation of Jewish immigrants who developed the Hollywood studio system in the 1920s, at about the same time that DiGiorgio was building his San Joaquin Valley empire: "The men creating mass production studios were rising from their working-class and petty entrepreneur roots to positions as captains of industry. They were transforming local scenes of maker/distributor/audience interaction into centralized hierarchies that revolved around producer power, mass markets, and star fame. As was not the case with the artisanal mode of film production, and with the exception of certain directors and stars, a clear line now separated owners and executives from workers." While there isn't an exact analogue to the star system in agribusiness, the other kinds of centralized Hollywood hierarchies Rogin describes were also operative in the history of agribusiness, where small family farms were quickly displaced by large factory farms that produced for mass markets and that were starkly divided between management and labor. In order to naturalize such hierarchies, according to Rogin, the Jewish studio heads had to become Americanized heterosexual white men by "interpreting gentile dreams," particularly dreams about race and gender, and converting them into films. His prime example is Hollywood's first feature-length talking picture, *The Jazz Singer,* a fantasy version of the studio heads' own biographies that depicts a Jewish immigrant who becomes a star by performing in blackface and by marrying a white American woman. By focusing on Jewish blackface performers, the moguls "appropriated an imaginary blackness to Americanize the immigrant son."[54] Key to Rogin's argument is the way that new sound technology enabled Jewish performers, and by extension corporate leaders, to find their voices as heterosexual white men by appropriating black voices. Hence, one important and underappreciated implication of Rogin's argument is that media technology has been symbolically coded as white and normatively male and that struggles over technology are also struggles over race, class, gender, and sexuality.

A similar argument could be made about the use of technology just a few hours north of Hollywood, in the southern San Joaquin Valley, where technology and mechanization helped link agribusiness corporations—even when founded by Italian immigrants—to the ideological values of heterosexual white masculinity. Whereas farm workers are represented as ignorant, unskilled, and technologically primitive in management accounts, agribusiness corporations represent themselves as modern and high-tech. In such contexts technology becomes an entrepreneurial tool or weapon for struggling with other men of capital, and it is implicitly articulated to ideologies of market competition and white male risk taking over and against feminized, racialized, and queer technological inferiors.[55] Thus the media spotlight on agribusiness technology, farm machinery, and the engineering of mass production helps to connect capitalism to influential ideas and fantasies about white masculinity. In a sort of capitalist hagiography, *Fortune* and other mainstream sources complement depictions of DiGiorgio as a master of machines with narratives about his successful speculative ventures in fruit auction houses and financing, as well as his remarkable foresight in anticipating national and international markets. These narratives romanticize capitalism and the figure of the factory farmer while conferring on the field of agricultural production some of the extreme, quasi-religious reverence for the market that has characterized U.S. (neo)liberalism. DiGiorgio's biography is represented as a uniquely "American" success story, in which a poor immigrant works hard, competes against others, takes risks, masters machinery and markets, and rises to the top of his industry. The media image of the company centered on DiGiorgio was, in Stuart Hall's phrase, a "point of condensation" that combined diverse associations to technology, whiteness, masculinity, capitalism, and nationalism.[56] The figure of the capitalist himself became a multifaceted fetish that partly displaced and obscured workers.

The Agribusiness Gaze

Early in the NFLU strike against DiGiorgio, a group called the National Sharecroppers Fund published a pamphlet with a picture of John and Stella Gorman and their four children in their living quarters at the Arvin Farm Labor Camp that came to the attention of Republican New Dealer Harold L. Ickes.[57] On Thanksgiving 1947, one day after DiGiorgio had evicted sixteen striking families from company housing,[58] Ickes published a nationally syndicated newspaper editorial titled "Plight of the Migrant Farm Laborers" that supported the nearly two-month-old strike and used the photo of the Gormans as its centerpiece, describing their bare, "one-room shack" as fit for "serfs" and "farm slaves." In response, a group of agribusiness elites produced a widely disseminated photo pamphlet called *A Community Aroused*.[59] It reproduced the Ickes editorial in order to refute it with photos of farm worker wage checks along with images of company housing and other structures—minus the workers who supposedly inhabited and used them. The largest portion of the pamphlet, the "Seeing Is Believing" section, featured fourteen photographs of housing and other facilities on and around the DiGiorgio ranch, including a tree-lined "Street View" of the camp showing solid, neat family homes, a recreation hall, tennis courts, a swimming pool, a nearby church and school, and, finally, the famous "Bronze Bust of Mr. Joseph DiGiorgio in Courtyard at Arvin Community Center. The bust was presented by residents of Arvin area in recognition of Accomplishments as Pioneer of Area and for Efforts in Community Betterment." Similarly, the pamphlet's authors speak as "Citizens" of a settler community in ways that recalls white nativism: "We are the pioneers who built Kern County . . . among the people who made America great." Here the authors of the pamphlet attempt to align agribusiness with coded forms of settler colonial whiteness by representing DiGiorgio and other big growers as "pioneers" who "built" the county. And part of what they have built, it suggests, is an attractive neighborhood of homes fit for good Americans. In a Cold War–inflected twist, the pamphlet contrasts the kind of people who "made America great" with union organizers, whom it vilifies as outside agitators, "crack-pots and left-wingers and associates of known Communists."

As Galarza and the union repeatedly pointed out, however, the homes and facilities represented in *A Community Aroused* were used by managers and foremen, not farm workers.[60] Even so, the photos provide an eerie window into the agribusiness visual imaginary, where structures of production take the place of people. The only human faces in the pamphlet appear in the first photo, a group shot of the "community aroused," the local agribusiness elite whose image attests to the impartial witnessing represented by the pamphlet's documentary style. And yet recalling fetishistic representations of DiGiorgio as the sole agent of massive agricultural transformations, this opening photo betrays its debt to an agribusiness mediascape where elite figures fill the frame and farm workers vanish into the machinery of production, in this case company housing. As Marx argued with regard to factory owners, agribusinessmen have attempted to reduce workers to the status of machines by annexing life beyond the fields to the production process. In order to justify paying the lowest wages possible, corporate growers had an interest in generating and perpetuating conditions in which workers could reproduce their labor power at the lowest cost possible, and this has often meant providing housing for workers as a part of their wage. While framed in benevolent paternalist terms, the provision of company housing was thus in fact a hidden means of exploiting workers.

One challenge the union faced was how to make exploitation visible in contexts where agribusiness corporations worked so hard to hide it. The difficulty of seeing exploitation is, of course, a general feature of life under capitalism, where ideologies of free labor help to mask it, but agribusiness corporations have been particularly adept at the arts of invisibility. As Galarza details in *Farm Workers and Agri-business,* agricultural corporations developed numerous deceptive means of measuring productivity and accounting for wages that helped to obscure increased appropriations of surplus value. In the same book, he argues that the agribusiness practice of segregating workers in terms of race had the effect of limiting worker perspectives on the larger political and economic relations that dominated the field of their struggles. Whereas corporate executives had access to a broader view of networks of capital and state power, farm workers had an immediate, local, and fragmentary vision more conducive to conflict than cooperation among different groups of workers, a situation that favored management.

Agribusiness executives thus presumed to control the field of the visible in the Valley in ways that limited the ability of unions to effectively organize. During the almost two years of its duration, the company denied that there was a legitimate union, that the workers had any real grievances, or that a strike was even occurring. Complementing such denials, DiGiorgio and the other members of the agribusiness association to which it belonged published glowing photo essays about working conditions and full-page ads denouncing the union in local newspapers. How could the union possibly compete with a management media machine that was seemingly able to make strikes disappear?

The Farm Worker Mediascape

The NFLU produced media not only for the general public but also for union audiences, aimed at organizing union activities. Despite its limitations, which I will detail below, I begin with a discussion of the union-made film about the DiGiorgio strike, *Poverty in the Valley of Plenty,* as a way to theorize a broader farm worker mediascape.[61] Whereas starting in the early decades of the twentieth century dominant modes of theatrical film exhibition presupposed the "classical spectator," a normative viewer who sat quietly absorbed in a feature-length narrative film, union film screenings employed what film scholars call pre-classical forms of exhibition and spectatorship but which, in the present context, would be better described as anti-classical or anti-normative. The anti-normative spectators presupposed by farm worker unions were positioned as active participants in public events that combined films with live performances and critical commentary. One handbill for a free community center screening of *Poverty in the Valley of Plenty* sponsored by labor and civic organizations in Buffalo, New York, advertises a heterogeneous program for the evening: "ENTERTAINMENT" ("Talented dance, comedy, and song numbers"); a "SOUND MOVIE" ("Documentary scenes of the strike made on the spot by film unionists"); a lecture about "THE STRIKE and what it means to you by Buffalo Trade Unionists"; and finally, "COMMUNITY SINGING." Billed as a "Citizens Rally to Support the DiGiorgio Strikers," the event took place in the summer of 1948, in the middle of the strike, and so was partly aimed at generating interunion solidarity and material aid. Films for farm workers, such as *Poverty,* were exhibited in union halls, community centers, and churches, and they presupposed the audiences for such venues, incorporating representations of union meetings as the double of, and proffered point of identification for, union audiences. *Poverty* includes scenes of a strike meeting, for instance, and more famously, in *Salt of the Earth* (1954), the blacklisted leftist film about a mining strike involving white and Mexican men and women, a union meeting is the setting for some of the most dramatic action. Locally, in a San Joaquin Valley context defined by the absence of democratic institutions, a civil society limited to middle-class clubs and the chamber of commerce, and a mediascape dominated by agribusiness interests, the union meeting as movie theater was a politically important space. In their handbill for one of the first public screenings of *Poverty* in 1948, the local of the NFLU "invites you and your family . . . Everyone, yes, everyone, regardless of race, creed, or color."[62] Here union film exhibition is part of a utopian counter-public sphere that represents an alternative to segregated local social spaces, including movie theaters.

As the DiGiorgio strike indicates, the farm worker mediascape also included music, radio, magazines, newspapers, and especially documentary photo essays. Though better remembered as a labor organizer and historian, Ernesto Galarza was a key figure in this history of farm worker media. He was born a few years before Heinlein, in 1905 in Jalcocotan

The union hall as theater: a union meeting in *Salt of the Earth* (1954).

in the state of Nayarit, Mexico, and also like the science fiction writer, Galarza migrated with his family at an early age to an urban agricultural center, Sacramento, California. There he learned English, did well in school, and during the summers worked as a drug store clerk, a messenger, a court interpreter, and in the agricultural fields and canneries. Galarza completed a bachelor's at Occidental College in Los Angeles (1927), a master's at Stanford (1929, with a thesis titled "Mexico and the World War"), and a doctorate in Latin American history at Columbia (1944). His dissertation, based on fieldwork in Mexico, was titled "La industria electrica en México." Hence, his graduate work suggests the kind of world perspective and interest in technology that would define much of his subsequent career. While finishing his dissertation, Galarza combined both of these interests as one of the editors of the CIO publication *Photo-History*. According to Michael Denning, it was "one of several attempts to create a Popular Front picture magazine, . . . a short-lived but exceptionally powerful photo magazine which documented contemporary history, selling popular accounts of the war in Spain and the rise of the CIO for a quarter."[63] *Photo-History* combined the visual styles of large-format photo magazines (such as *Life*), newsreels, and mass-circulation newspapers. Each large, almost fourteen-by-ten-inch page of the magazine was a collage of text and image, with superimposed or floating headlines, photographs, reproductions of artwork and magazine engravings, newspaper stories, images of historic documents, protest posters, political cartoons, and multiple kinds of figures and graphs. The magazine's visual pedagogy used photographic and textual collage to generate active viewing practices in ways that anticipated and modeled the critical activities of union organizing itself.[64] Working on *Photo-History* shaped Galarza's visual aesthetic and sense of formal experimentation as a means of union organizing.

In 1947 Galarza joined the Southern Tenant Farmers Union. The STFU, which began in Arkansas, and then spread to Missouri and Texas, was a response to the collapse of tenancy and the displacement of black and white sharecroppers, tenants, and small farmers.[65] As Neil Foley has shown, it was divided by contradictions. While the union was unique among labor organizations in that it organized black, Mexican, and white farm workers, it often did so in segregated locales. Furthermore, while the union's initial success was among sharecroppers, it was also open to tenants and small farmers, embraced both wage workers and wage payers, and maintained an ideological commitment to the yeoman farmer that was often at odds with the conditions of farm workers in industrial agriculture. Part of

Galarza's job with the union apparently involved collecting photographs of sharecropper housing, and given his subsequent efforts to organize white and Mexican workers, he must have appreciated the union's commitment to organizing across the color line, in however limited a fashion.[66] By 1947 the union was renamed the National Farm Labor Union and moved west, where it refocused on farm workers.

In the San Joaquin Valley, Galarza continued to serve as the union's director of research and education, which partly meant organizing meetings; in this capacity, according to Stephen Pitti, he promoted a dialectical relationship between meeting segregation and desegregation. Recalling the STFU, he led separate meetings for whites and for Mexicans, literally and figuratively speaking different languages to each, in the first case emphasizing class solidarity and antiracism, in the second employing rhetoric from Mexican cultural nationalism. His job also involved using visual culture in interrelated forms of pedagogy, intelligence gathering, and publicity. In an effort to combat white racism against Mexican unionists and strikebreakers, for example, Galarza presented slide shows about living and working conditions in Mexico to white farm workers from Oklahoma and Texas. Finally, Galarza organized collective discussions and field research in order to generate photo press releases for a "nationwide propaganda" campaign to provide a "protective shield" for the striking workers, and for a variety of different union publications in order to rally support.[67] Building on the work of rank-and-file researchers, Galarza entered an intense publicity contest with agribusiness, among multiple audiences, over how to see local labor relations.

Galarza also helped to make exploitation visible by repeatedly publishing documentary photographs of the living conditions of DiGiorgio workers. In small labor newspapers, more mainstream regional papers, and, in one case, a national magazine *(Businessweek)*, he circulated images of the shoddy tents and impoverished shacks provided by the company. His reports often appeared in the *Kern County Union Leader Journal*, like the story titled "Not Tobacco Road," illustrated with the photo of a farm worker shack.[68] Such poor family housing was part of contemporary efforts to replace families with single men on the farms. In order to discourage families and other collective living arrangements, over the course of the 1940s and early 1950s growers like DiGiorgio increasingly promoted barracks-like housing made for single males rather than single-family dwellings. Without dependents, it was argued, single men were cheaper to employ, and so corporations let family housing units decay, or tore them down and replaced them with barracks.[69] Galarza's photographs of decaying single-family tents and shacks thus capture a critical moment in management's efforts to use housing to regender the workforce to the detriment of single women workers and relatives of workers.

The photos further captured the shift toward a corporate disciplinary model of worker housing. Starting in the 1930s, agribusiness had argued against the federally sponsored work camps like those made famous in *The Grapes of Wrath*, claiming that "farmers can take care of their own labor." But according to Galarza, statements of grower paternalism masked their interests in destroying the camps because they had served as home bases for union members and organizers. "In the flux of perpetual migration," these labor camps had emerged as "stations of repose from which harvesters could take a broader and more tranquil look at their condition. But the broader view is reserved for those who hold power, and sharing it with those who came and went with the seasons was totally contrary to the lessons of business experience."[70] Corporate interventions in housing, then, were partly meant to discipline workers by placing them under company surveillance and control. The low wages and the malign neglect of family housing represented in Galarza's photo press releases, combined with the increasing corporate promotion of work camps as total institutions, contradicted DiGiorgio's beneficent image of "corporate paternalism."[71]

Galarza's publicity campaigns thus alternated between representations of exploitation and utopian images of union world building. A good example of the latter is a story titled "A 'Twenty-Mile' Picket Line: Ranch Workers Organize to End 'Grapes of Wrath' Era" that Galarza published in the *Trade Union Courier* in 1948.[72] Contradicting management denials, the story was illustrated with a photograph of a huge crowd, captioned "Mass demonstration by more than 15,000 union members support the strike of the AFL National Farm Labor Union workers at the DiGiorgio farm." In the main text Galarza commends the AFL "relief caravans" that brought food and clothing to the striking workers, but concludes that "the main show is the picket line, where little groups of men and women from Arkansas, Oklahoma, Texas, Kentucky and Mexico keep watch." In opposition to agribusiness media spectacles and the domineering gaze of management, here the picket line becomes the "main show," as if the union movie theater had been made mobile, while a heterogeneous group of farm workers and their supporters "keep watch." The photo for this story was ultimately reproduced by *Businessweek* in its coverage of the strike.[73]

The farm worker mediascape: advertisement for *Poverty in the Valley of Plenty.* Ernesto Galarza Papers, Special Collections M0224; courtesy of Department of Special Collections and University Archives, Stanford University Libraries.

As this example suggests, Galarza's press releases often focused on the contributions of both men and women. His photo for the mass demonstration included large numbers of women, whereas another press release included one depicting two women with signs in front of a line of strikers, captioned "It's a good fight against DiG, and the whole family joins in. The

MASS PICKETING, reinforced by California A.F.L. unionists, didn't prevent . . .

"The main show is the picket line." NFLU strike against the DiGiorgio Fruit Company in *Businessweek.* Ernesto Galarza Papers, Special Collections M0224; courtesy of Department of Special Collections and University Archives, Stanford University Libraries.

line above is made up principally of women."[74] Another story, published in the *Union Reporter,* included an intricate photo collage. Recalling the kinetic, proto-cinematic colleges in *Photo-History,* here Galarza combines visible evidence of a grievance in terms of a meager pay stub; close-up photos of strikers, including a Mexican worker; a corporate truck transporting scabs; and, finally, images of a countermovement of union solidarity in the form of the relief caravans.[75] As in *Photo-History,* Galarza's collage invites the viewer to scan images in multiple ways, searching for larger connections or patterns, among, for example, low wages, the company's use of scabs, and the integrated nature of the union.

That particular collage and others also suggest connections between the local and other union organizations. Galarza constructed similar photo collages to represent two "Friendship Caravans" made up of union representatives from Southern and Northern California in solidarity with the farm workers union, reportedly including a young Cesar Chavez. Given the agribusiness domination of regional social space, the caravans constituted a dramatic disruption in the visual field. In the first, Southern

At the top of this picture you see a former employe of the $20,000,000 Di Giorgio Corp. display-ing a pay check for eleven cents. Next to him are scabs riding to work on a Di Giorgio truck. Mid-dle left is a strike relief parade in front of the main gate to the ranch. Middle right is Fred Chavez, a Mexican member of Local 218 NFLU—on strike. At the bottom of the picture, the button on J. R. Mitchell's battered hat shows he is a member of the striking local. To his right is a car in the second relief caravan to the strikers. In the very center of the picture, President Jack Shelley of the California State Federation of Labor gives instructions to the drivers of the relief caravan.

Galarza's photo collage anticipates union futures. Ernesto Galarza Papers, Special Collections M0224; courtesy of Department of Special Collections and University Archives, Stanford University Libraries.

California caravan, hundreds of cars and trucks loaded with donations of food and clothing drove through the center of Arvin—under local police, sheriff, and highway patrol escort—to the DiGiorgio ranch, where they greeted the line of striking farm workers before delivering their donations to the local labor temple and riding to Bakersfield's "Melody Bowl" theater for an evening of union music and dancing. Galarza surrounded his news story about the caravan with a series of photos which, when scanned clockwise starting in the upper-right corner of the page, mimic the movement of the caravan and emphasize the size and diversity of the union movement. Formally, then, the collage encourages the sort of visual scrutiny and active thinking encouraged by the union movement it promotes. Galarza organized this and other collages of photos on a rectangular grid that formally resembled agribusiness mechanization (as represented, for instance, in *Fortune*'s DiGiorgio portrait) while imaginatively displacing it by projecting an alternative world of union organizing. Taken together, these utopian constructions of union collectivity are exercises in farm worker futurity, positing the ongoing, future existence of a union not yet recognized by management or the state.

The documentary film *Poverty in the Valley of Plenty* was made amid all the volleys and countervolleys of visual publicity exchanged between the DiGiorgio Fruit Company and the NFLU.[76] The film was produced by the American Federation of Labor's newly formed Film Council, which was cochaired by Roy Brewer and Ronald Reagan, the presidents of the conservative Hollywood unions, the International Alliance of Theatrical and Stage Employees (IATSE) and the Screen Actors Guild (SAG), respectively. The filmmakers attempted to give the viewer a broad, systemic view of corporate agriculture by using DiGiorgio as an influential example of trends in the industry at large. *Poverty* depicts worker grievances, especially in terms of housing; re-creates the early history of union organizing and the start of the strike; describes management efforts to break it, including the employment of scabs; and represents union solidarity in the form of a relief caravan and a mass meeting of farm workers resolved to continue the strike.

Poverty in the Valley of Plenty is clearly indebted to Galarza's press releases. Some of the narration is taken directly from them, and like Galarza's reports, *Poverty* also foregrounds the struggles of women and makes critical use of documentary images of housing. Commenting on the recent wave of mechanization and its consequences for workers, the film juxtaposes scenes of decrepit housing with shots of several tractors in front of a sturdy storage shed as the voice-over continues, "Now if they were tools or farm equipment they would be housed in a nice clean waterproof shed . . . [cut to shacks] . . . but they're just human, so consideration isn't necessary." Similarly undercutting heroic, agribusiness images of scientific and technological progress, subsequent scenes represent a violent, material instance of the interface between man and machine on the farm: shots of a one-handed worker securing a grapevine to its support using a prosthetic metal hook. According to the voice-over narration, "This man is not a veteran of the war—he is a veteran of the farm and there is no compensation for the loss of the limb. There is no law requiring a farm corporation to carry compensation for their employees." As the film shifts to scenes of male and female farm workers applying pesticides and carrying shovels through the fields, the narrator concludes that they are "working under conditions that were prevalent at the close of the Civil War." Here the tools and technology of modern farming, including pesticides and, of course, the mechanical prosthetic limbs worn by the wounded, represent not the triumph of progress but a regression to nineteenth-century conditions.

In addition to union meetings *Poverty* was screened in a variety of venues, including "college campuses, churches, luncheon clubs, conventions and farm labor gatherings throughout the country."[77] Through a special agreement with Paramount Television Productions, KTLA in Los Angeles broadcast the film in May 1948.[78] As Brewer wrote in July 1948, shortly after its completion the film had already been seen by tens of thousands of people.[79] The central goal of the broadcast and the screenings in nonunion venues was to publicize a boycott of DiGiorgio products among urban audiences. Finally, NFLU president H. L. Mitchell showed it to members of a subcommittee of the House Committee on Education and Labor in 1949 as part of an effort to prompt state regulation of agribusiness.[80]

Such screenings did not continue, as DiGiorgio successfully pursued libel suits against Paramount Television Productions, the Hollywood Film Council, the Los Angeles Central Labor Council, and the NFLU that effectively suppressed the film. *Poverty* was vulnerable to agribusiness power in part because of the ways it departed from its source material. In contrast with Galarza's press releases and photo essays, which produced a vision of union power and solidarity out of a multiracial, gender-integrated collage of photos, the film juxtaposes white union crowds and noble white faces with images of Mexican strikebreakers or "wet backs" recruited by the company. The filmmakers' whitening of their source materials expresses the ideology of the conservative unions that made the movie. The national leaders of the NFLU shared with "corporate" Hollywood unions such as SAG and IATSE a commitment to anticommunism and a related resistance to discussions of racism for fear of undermining the United States relative to the Soviets. Hence, in the context of Cold War nationalism and the limits it set to racial representation, the union filmmakers attempted to claim for farm workers the ideological power of images of white populism—which partly explains why so many shots of white farm workers in the film recall iconic photos by Dorothea Lange of dust bowl refugees or images from John Ford's film version *The Grapes of Wrath* (1940). Ironically, then, by filtering Galarza's press reports through the lens of whiteness, the makers of *Poverty in the Valley of Plenty* visually reproduced forms of segregation like those that had historically benefited management.

Partly vindicating Galarza's alternative visual strategies, the attempt by other union leaders to claim whiteness for labor failed in the face of agribusiness counterclaims. In the libel suit that successfully suppressed the film, lawyers for DiGiorgio emphasized scenes that juxtaposed worker housing to the bust of Joseph DiGiorgio. By 1947 the corporation was largely managed by others, but DiGiorgio continued to represent it in advertisements and public relations ventures. The film undermined this valuable public image, this "possessive investment in whiteness," not only by connecting the DiGiorgio bust to scenes of exploitation but also by suggesting that striking workers, and not high-tech agribusiness, represented white nobility and virtue.[81] The company's triumph in the libel suits thus reasserted a relative corporate monopoly over the visual technologies of whiteness, and by extension over the articulation of whiteness to technology more widely. Whereas Galarza and the Mexican and white members of the local NFLU he helped organize were devoted to an anti-racist future, like Heinlein, the makers of *Poverty in the Valley of Plenty* wagered the future on white populism plus technology and lost to agribusiness.

Coda: The Future That Came to Pass

The conclusion of the NFLU strike against the DiGiorgio Company had lasting consequences for the subsequent history of speculative technologies in the fields of California agriculture. In the first place, it represented an important victory in the ongoing agribusiness efforts to rationalize and mechanize the industry in ways that limited its vulnerability to worker

demands. Published over twenty years after the strike, Galarza's study
Farm Workers and Agri-business in California, 1947–1960 tells of how
corporate agriculture effectively used mechanization to discipline farm
workers and destroy their unions, including the local of the NFLU. During
the late 1940s and early 1950s, according to Galarza, the fields began to
be seeded and fertilized by aircraft, and irrigation was further rationalized as engineers "laced" together a complex system of water controls
and conveyances.[82] At the same time, he continues, corporations dedicated to eliminating workers increasingly turned to the awesome and
futuristic forms of mechanization enumerated in the previous chapter.
But mechanization further led to the expansion of production and thus
also an expanded exploitation of newly deskilled and gender-stratified
forms of low-wage farm labor. The deployment of machines increasingly
led agricultural jobs to be recategorized as lower in skill and so male
workers were paid less, or the jobs were redefined as women's work
with a lower pay rate. Mechanization in the fields was also meshed with
the bracero program, which imported roughly two hundred thousand
guest workers a year from 1948 until the program's conclusion in 1964.
Braceros were processed by U.S. officials en masse, as if on a giant bu-
reaucratic assembly line that Mae Ngai has analyzed as a kind of "imported colonialism." INS officials in Texas handled groups of hundreds
of workers at a time, interviewing, fingerprinting, and photographing
each one. They were also fumigated, briefly examined by a doctor, and
x-rayed to detect tuberculosis. Braceros were in fact imported at a pace
set by the state's rationalization of the visual field, which determined
that each machine could on average photograph 175 men every hour.[83]
Galarza's study of the program, *Strangers in Our Fields* (1956), which
was researched and written in the wake of the DiGiorgio strike, features on its cover a photo of braceros feeding produce to giant mechanical threshers that seem ready to swallow them up like malevolent alien
robots from period science fictions films.

The DiGiorgio Fruit Company's lawsuit ending the strike effectively
reinforced agribusiness domination of the regional mediascape by limiting the ability of farm worker unions to mobilize visual technologies.
The settlement made token judgments of one dollar against the plaintiffs
but required the destruction of all known prints of *Poverty*, with the one
exception being a print in the possession of DiGiorgio. "It was a curi-
ous turn," Galarza concluded, whereby "only those who had condemned
it could view it openly; those who had sponsored it and agreed with it

could show it only at grave peril."[84] Moreover, the legal battle over the documentary helped establish the preconditions for the subsequent Cold War attacks on *Salt of the Earth*, the groundbreaking collaboration between Hollywood leftists and members of a new Mexican mining community. One of the Hollywood union leaders who helped make *Poverty*, Roy Brewer, reacted to its suppression by leading efforts to suppress *Salt*. It is as if, in response to the prior defeat, Brewer attempted to prove labor's nationalist, anticommunist credentials by red-baiting *Salt* and workers of color. As president of IATSE, Brewer became the lasting friend and mentor of the similarly anticommunist Ronald Reagan. Later, as governor of California, Reagan effectively red-baited another union of workers of color, the United Farm Workers.[85]

Corporate control of visual technologies meant it would be over twenty years before a farm worker union would make another film, as I suggest in chapter 3. In the meantime, however, one of the NFLU's successors in the region and a precursor to the UFW, the Agricultural Workers Organizing Committee (AWOC), was sued for exhibiting *Poverty* in 1960. In the intervening decade Galarza had become a board member of the union in California and so was also named in the suit. While at a labor convention AWOC's director of publicity and training, Louis Krainock, heard about a film he thought was called *Poultry in the Valley of Plenty*. When he ordered it from the United Auto Workers it turned out to be a copy of the banned film. The print thereby became part of the union's small library of "labor films" that were screened at farm worker meetings. During the spring and summer months of 1960, *Poverty* was booked almost every night in places such as Stockton, Woodlake, Strathmore, Marysville, Olivehurst, Empire, Riverbank, and Westley, Northern California towns dotted with farm labor camps. The audiences were of modest size; thirty-five to forty people reportedly attended the screening in Woodlake. "At some of the exhibitions," according to Galarza, AWOC head Norman Smith "added his personal commentary to the narration on the sound track . . . Smith's organizing fervor, always warm and frequently hot, went up a degree or two whenever he viewed the film."[86] During and after the screening, Smith and Krainock detailed for audiences the differences between the two contexts yet concluded that the contemporary conditions of farm workers mirrored those of the strikers in *Poverty*. Testifying to the tenuous, embattled nature of the historical memory reconstructed here, the AWOC exhibitors of *Poverty* knew nothing of the film's prior legal history. As part of the second suit, the union's print was subpoenaed as evidence, and, in contrast to the DiGiorgio legal team, the AWOC lawyers were unable to see the main evidence against their clients until it was screened in court. Despite the NFLU's efforts to claim the future for the disinherited, agribusiness was ultimately able to assert its superior claims.

Finally, as the fate of *Salt of the Earth* suggests, the struggle over visual technology in the fields was embedded in Cold War geopolitics, with destructive consequences for farm workers. The violent response to communist organizers in the fields of the 1930s made anticommunism seem like a precondition for labor organizing in the region, and the national leadership of Galarza's local chapter of the NFLU had long been anticommunist. The DiGiorgio victory was thus the culmination of a long chain of anticommunist labor orthodoxy that would shape and ultimately limit the United Farm Workers' more famous efforts to mobilize visual technologies, as we shall see in the chapter that follows.

2 From Third Cinema to National Video
Visual Technologies and UFW World Building

Philip K. Dick's novel *A Scanner Darkly* (1977) was written in the wake of the highly visible UFW strikes and boycotts, while the author was living in Southern California's racially segregated Orange County. As Dick described his suburban Fullerton condominium complex in "Strange Memories of Death," his late 1970s autobiographical story, "This is Orange County. Money rules. The very poor live to the east of me: the Mexicans in their barrio. Sometimes when our security gates open to admit cars the Chicano [*sic*] women run in with baskets of dirty laundry; they want to use our machines, having none of their own. The people who lived here in the building resented this. When you have even a little money—money enough to live in a modern, full-security, all-electric building—you resent a great deal."[1] The barrio that his building tries to keep out was no doubt home to the many Mexican immigrants working in the region's agricultural fields, farm workers whose presence there shadows the conclusion to *A Scanner Darkly*. Set in the "future" year of 1994, the novel focuses on an Orange County drug agent named Fred who goes undercover as "Bob Arctor" and lives with a group of other poor white men who are addicted to the mysterious "Substance D" (also called "slow death" or simply "death"). This character is increasingly torn between his identities as policeman and drug addict until the drug wins out. With much of his memory wiped by Substance D and with newly diminished mental capacities, Fred–Bob becomes a pawn in a government plot to infiltrate the massive hidden plantation where the drug is grown. At the end of the novel, a government agent commits Fred–Bob to a residential drug treatment facility called "The New-Path Foundation" that is actually a front for the mass production of Substance D. At the "New-Path" facility, a fictionalized version of the infamous drug rehabilitation cult called Synanon,

Fred–Bob's identity is further destroyed by group "therapy" meetings involving extreme forms of sexist and homophobic verbal abuse.[2]

As part of his destructive remaking, Fred–Bob's head is shaved, he is renamed "Bruce," and at the end of this transformative ritual Mike, his supervisor at the facility, tells him that he is now ready to be a farm worker: "'You can't make yourself think again. You can only keep working, such as sowing crops or tilling on our vegetable plantations . . . or killing insects. We do a lot of that, driving insects out of existence with the right kind of sprays. We're very careful, though, with sprays. They can do more harm than good. They can poison not only the crops and the ground but the person using them. Eat his head.' He added, 'Like yours has been eaten.'" His brain eaten by Substance D, "Bruce" has been reduced in the eyes of his supervisor to the state of a farm worker debilitated by pesticides, a kind of mechanical living death:

> You have been sprayed, Mike thought, as he *glanced* at the man, so that now you've become a bug. Spray a bug with a toxin and it dies; spray a man, spray his brain, and he becomes an insect that clacks and vibrates about in a closed circle forever. A reflex machine, like an ant. Repeating its last instruction. Nothing new will ever enter his brain, Mike thought, because that brain is gone. And with it, that person who once *gazed* out . . . This creature beside me has died . . . There is little future, Mike thought, for someone who is dead. There is, usually, only the past. And for Arctor–Fred–Bruce there is not even the past; there is only this . . . The living, he thought, should never be used to serve the purposes of the dead. But the dead—he *glanced* at Bruce, the empty shade beside him—should, if possible, serve the purposes of the living. That, he reasoned, is the law of life. (emphasis added)[3]

And so "Bruce" is transferred to a New-Path farm in the Northern California wine country, assigned to a prefabricated cabin he will share with another Substance-D-diminished farm worker, and given a tour by the New-Path executive director and the farm-facility manager. During the tour the new farm worker sees a field of "lovely little blue flowers" behind rows of corn and, in a gesture familiar from agricultural "stoop labor," bends down to examine them. "You're seeing the flower of the future," the director tells him. "But not for you . . . Back to work, Bruce." Still stooped over, "Bruce" thinks, "That was it: I saw Substance D growing.

I saw death rising from the earth, from the ground itself, in one blue field, in stubbled color." The farm-facility manager and the director *"glanced* at each other and then *down at the kneeling figure,* the kneeling man and the *Mors ontologica* planted everywhere, within the concealing corn. 'Back to work, Bruce,' the kneeling man said then, and rose to his feet" (emphasis added).[4]

A *Scanner Darkly* recalls Robert Heinlein's *Farmer in the Sky* in that both novels focus on white men who are reduced to the level of racialized farm workers. Bob's new status as a farm worker is visually emphasized in the cinematic version of *A Scanner Darkly* (2006), which was produced through a process called "rotoscoping," in which animators trace over live-action film footage. The concluding scenes of the animated *A Scanner Darkly* were traced over live film shot in the agricultural fields near Dick's Orange County condo. Wearing a pesticide spray pack and walking through a corn field, Bob–Fred–Bruce, played by the mixed-race actor Keanu Reeves, stops when he sees a carpet of blue flowers amid the rows of green. He stoops to examine them when he is interrupted by the farm director. In contexts where life chances are unequally distributed, and, in particular, where farm workers are disproportionately vulnerable to premature death, Heinlein and Dick both zero in on the prospect of white masculinity brought low. But whereas Heinlein narrates his hero's downward arc only to stage white transcendence in ways that denigrate actually existing, nonwhite farm workers who do not similarly rise, the future represented in *A Scanner Darkly* leaves no room for fantasies of white progress. The manager and director look at each other and then *"down at the kneeling figure,* the kneeling man and the *Mors ontologica* planted everywhere,"* as if their mutual recognition of each other required looking down on the farm worker amid the visual field of death. These hierarchical relations of looking are well represented in the film version, where the image of Bob kneeling is presented in a high-angle shot, as if from the standing perspective of the condescending farm director. *A Scanner Darkly* thus presents a devastatingly lucid representation of processes of abjection in which farm workers freeze into the "living dead" under an agribusiness gaze.

The farm worker as the living dead recalls Galarza's question: "Is this indentured alien—an almost perfect model of the economic man, an 'input factor' stripped of the political and social attributes that liberal democracy likes to ascribe to all human beings ideally—is this *bracero* the prototype of the production man of the future?" The conclusion of *A Scanner Darkly*

Slow death: envisioning farm worker abjection in *A Scanner Darkly,*
directed by Richard Linklater (2006).

The agribusiness gaze in *A Scanner Darkly.*

engages that question with an elegant and incisive anatomy of what it
means to be stripped of the liberal democratic political and social attributes of "the human" and, conversely, what it means to be proudly—even
aggressively—clothed in them. Here the farm worker is viewed as the living dead because he supposedly works without thinking, like a machine
or an insect. From this perspective the farm worker approximates the

dream of agribusiness futurism for obedient workers, subordinated without dissent to the machinery of production. In the view of management figures in the novel, the farm worker is exiled from human time, with no past or future. For such creatures "there is only this," meaning the perpetual present of farm labor, punctuated by the repeated injunction, "Back to work, Bruce . . . Back to work, Bruce." Simple and "brainless," Bruce has become a mere tool, lacking the kind of technological rationality that white men have often attributed to themselves and to European and Anglo-American culture more broadly. In a revealing formulation his supervisor thinks the new farm worker has no subjective interiority and that "the person who once *gazed* out" was gone. In this passage one of the implicit attributes of liberal democratic personhood is the possession of a sort of interior thinking eye or gaze, something that is supposedly wanting in Bruce—which is to say that "the dead" serve the living not only materially, with their labor, but also symbolically, as the other over and against which the superiority of agribusiness subjectivities and values are defined. In contrast with farm workers who only work, managers think, have memorable pasts and promising futures, and possess powerful and perceptive gazes that justify their dominance over the visual field.

This chapter analyzes the contradictory consequences of the UFW's efforts to critically analyze and intervene in just such an agribusiness-dominated visual field. In 1971 UFW president Cesar Chavez and a group of close advisers discussed plans for constructing elaborate media-making facilities and a wide range of projects partly modeled on films about different parts of the decolonizing world. While these ambitious plans never fully materialized, the UFW did make *Fighting for Our Lives* (*FFOL*, 1975), a widely screened documentary that remains largely unanalyzed in histories of the union. *FFOL* turned the cameras on high-tech agribusiness, baton-swinging police, and strikebreaking Teamsters in ways that visually linked the California fields to scenes of southern police violence during the African American civil rights movement as well as to imperial military violence in Southeast Asia and Latin America. For these and related formal and political reasons, I situate *FFOL* as part of a radical "Third Cinema" tradition. At the same time, however, *FFOL* can also be read in a contrary way that connects the union to conservative patriarchal Catholicism, trade union anticommunism, and techno-fetishism. Departing from recent revisionary histories of the UFW organized in terms of its decline, I argue, on the other hand, that the UFW was constitutively contradictory, combining in its foundations revolutionary and reactionary futurisms.

The contradictions of UFW futurism shaped the union's innovative adoption of the new media technologies of the late 1970s and 1980s—video cameras, videotapes, and videocassette recorders (VCRs). Historically video was associated with revolutionary movements and the threat of terrorism, and the UFW's use of video built on its reputation as a medium of radical transformation. But the union's use of video was at the same time part of a broader effort to claim video technologies for U.S. Cold War nationalism. UFW home video aimed to generate forms of virtual intimacy or "co-presence" between consumers and the victims of pesticide use, particularly as represented by a fasting Chavez. Through the imaginary intimacy of video, the union attempted to build a national audience by framing pesticide harms in nationalist terms and by turning Chavez into a nationalist icon. At a moment of renewed U.S. imperial interventions in Central America and elsewhere, such appeals to nationalism contradicted and contained the more radical, global-revolutionary tendencies of UFW futurisms.

Farm Workers and the Agribusiness Visual Field

Given the extent and structure of agribusiness domination in California, the emergence of the UFW is nothing short of amazing. Agribusiness corporations have historically treated farm workers as disposable, mere means of production like tractors, short-handled hoes, or even pesticides. To paraphrase Marx, in their efforts to accumulate capital, big growers have "unblushingly asserted" the "proprietary rights of capital over labor power" and treated farm workers like "beast(s) of burden," "instruments of production," or "machines."[5] Large California growers not only promoted but also often celebrated the use of pesticides that poisoned and killed farm workers. The worker was thus no more protected from destruction than any other means of production worn out or used up in the process of accumulating capital. In the years leading up to the founding of the union that would become the UFW, moreover, agribusiness drew on and reproduced racist views of Filipino, Yemeni, Mexican, and other farm workers of color as uniquely abject and naturally well suited to their status as mere means of production. These views were reinforced by the assumption among the growers and their allies that farm workers were beings without a meaningful past or a future beyond the fields. Without power or the entitlements and protections of citizenship, and employed in jobs framed as demeaning "stoop labor," farm workers have often been viewed as a particularly degraded class of workers—which in part explains how

Plate 1. Esteban Villa, *Third World Astro Pilot of Aztlán* (1984). Sketch for tile design, California Ethnic and Multicultural Archive (CEMA), University of California, Santa Barbara. Courtesy of Esteban Villa and CEMA.

Plate 2. Ricardo Favela, *UFW Cooperative Space Station #Uno* (1983). Color pencil drawing, California Ethnic and Multicultural Archive (CEMA), University of California, Santa Barbara. Courtesy of Ricardo Favela and CEMA.

Plate 3. Ester Hernandez, *Heroes and Saints* (1992). Courtesy of Ester Hernandez and Department of Special Collections, Cecil H. Green Library, Stanford University Libraries.

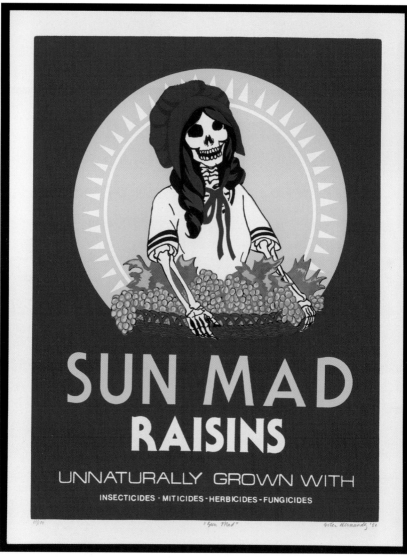

Plate 4. Ester Hernandez, *Sun Mad* (1982). Silkscreen print. Courtesy of Ester Hernandez and Department of Special Collections, Cecil H. Green Library, Stanford University Libraries.

California agribusiness interests could successfully prevent farm workers from gaining the right to unionize and collectively bargain until the mid 1970s, some forty years after other workers were guaranteed such rights by federal law. In a sort of "secular excommunication," farm workers have been "alienated" from certain "rights or claims of birth" and often exiled from human history and community.[6] Recalling *A Scanner Darkly,* employers and others have often defined their own privileged relationship to their past and future prospects in opposition to farm workers imagined as without a meaningful history or future. Finally, the farm worker as a mere means of production was ultimately enforced by the threat of violence at the hands of private security forces, the local police (who often effectively worked for agribusiness), and pro-agribusiness vigilantes.

One sign of farm worker reduction to the machinery of production is the fact that such workers have often been the objects but rarely the subjects of works of art in the age of mechanical reproduction. There is a vast archive of iconic photos and films *of* farm workers, for example, but many fewer well-known examples of visual media produced *by* farm workers.[7] As I argued in the introduction, the exploitation of farm workers depends on technologically mediated forms of visual culture, including the agribusiness-dominated relations of looking that have symbolically reproduced farm worker subordination and abjection. Meanwhile, in agribusiness film and other visual media, corporate leaders are depicted as powerful masters of the gaze who dominate the visual field from on high, as in the TV documentary *The Big Land* (1967).[8] The film opens with aerial shots of a wide and flat valley landscape diagonally bisected by a levee: on the left is Tulare Lake, held at bay by the levee, and on the right are rows and rows of cotton. A deep, authoritative male voice states that "man, machines, water, and land" are "the elements of an empire" that requires "big men" with a big vision. The farmer has become a "giant" who "no longer serves the land, the land serves him." Thanks to such giants, the waters have been dammed and "man has begun the conquest of the earth." These scenes are accompanied by triumphal-sounding music that recalls the theme songs of period TV shows about California ranching empires such as *Bonanza* (1959–73) and *The Big Valley* (1965–69). At such moments the film appeals to representations of the nineteenth-century frontier and to contemporary images of outer space as the "final frontier" in order to endow an agribusiness perspective on the Valley landscape with the heroism and power of settler colonialism and white science and technology.

By contrast with its heroic depiction of management, *The Big Land* represents farm workers as the anonymous objects rather than the subjects of the gaze. Made by the corporate "giant" it celebrates, the film encourages audiences to identity with agribusiness via the objectification of farm workers. Agribusiness relations of looking are further dramatized in several scenes of white corporate managers observing and directing Mexican farm workers. The film's visual appeal to presumably non–farm worker spectators represents a mode of agribusiness futurism that combines *scopophilia,* or a pleasure in looking, with a kind of technological *epistemophilia,* or a pleasure in knowing that, together, promise to "satisfy curiosity through looking and hence produce mastery by 'seeing how things work.'"[9] The generation of mastery by "seeing how things work" applies both to the machinery of production and to farm workers, who become working "things" under a sadistic agribusiness gaze that dominates by imaginatively taking workers apart, discovering what makes them "tick," and learning how to best control them.

The short-handled hoe represents a revealing instance of scopophilia plus epistemophilia, or the production of mastery by seeing how (workers as) things work. Before they were banned in 1975, short-handled hoes were employed throughout California, where growers insisted on them for working sugar beets, strawberries, lettuce, and other row crops. Cumulatively, the repeated use of the short-handled hoe, which required workers to bend over at the waist or kneel as they moved down the rows, produced debilitating back injuries that often led to the early end of working careers. Agribusiness companies, however, subordinated the health and well-being of workers to the machinery of production, arguing that the profitability of the industry depended on the tool's use and that, in any case, Filipinos and Mexicans were naturally suited to it. In a chapter titled "Sentience and Slavery: The Struggle over the Short-Handled Hoe," Sarah S. Lochlann Jain analyzes testimony from the hearings that ultimately led to the short-handled hoe being banned, and concludes that the farm workers needed to demonstrate their "humanness" and capacity for injury in the face of the growers' assumptions that the worker's body "is part of his own prosthetic assemblage—the technology of agricultural production of which the worker was one part and the hoe was another and the boundaries between the two were insignificant."[10]

Farm workers using short-handled hoes have been common subjects for photographers, who often employed the conventions of landscape photography to frame workers in a visual field made up of geometric rows of crops. In 1956 commercial photographer Leonard Nadel was commissioned by the Ford Foundation's Fund for the Republic to produce a visual counterpart to *Strangers in Our Fields,* Ernesto Galarza's study of the bracero program. The result was a collection of thousands of photographs, many of them widely circulated in public and among lawmakers, including long- and wide-angle shots of braceros performing stoop labor in the lettuce and pepper fields of the Salinas Valley. Nadel makes visible the role of the short-handled hoe in management's observation and control of farm workers. Since workers had to bend over while using the tool, overseers could see they were resting when they stood up. The tool was thus a means of surveillance that enabled management to adopt a sort of panoramic perspective on the field of production, viewing at a glance who was kneeling and working and who was standing and not working. The tool helped make the worker's labor visible to the bosses, reproducing an unequal set of visual relationships whereby big growers were the subjects, or we might say "owners," of the gaze, while farm workers were its objects. The inequality of these relations of looking were furthered by the way the short-handled hoe required workers to repeatedly reproduce a posture—bent over, with bowed head and often on bended knee—symbolically linked to gendered and raced qualities of abjection such as subservience, weakness, or primitiveness, and implicitly contrasted with the superior-class qualities of independence, power, and advanced civilization conventionally coded as white and male. While most of Nadel's images of braceros working with short-handled hoes picture them in such postures, in a number of photos they awkwardly look up at the camera, suggesting exceptions to the general rule that farm workers perform their subordination by lowering their heads and averting their gazes. In this way the compulsory use of the short-handled hoe and the visual field it presupposed was a means for reproducing, both materially and symbolically, unequal relationships between raced and gendered capital and labor.

Despite farm worker efforts to ban the short-handled hoe, over fifteen years after Nadel captured his images UFW volunteer Rick Tejada-Flores's photo series "Stoop Labor Salinas Valley" (1972–75) foregrounded how the tool helped discipline bent working bodies by making their labor visible against the grid of industrial agricultural production.[11] "Stoop Labor Salinas Valley" is an extensive series that includes thirty photographs, and viewing the series as a whole has a repetitive, cumulative effect that

Farm workers fixed in the visual field. Braceros using short-handled hoes in a Salinas, California, pepper field. Photograph by Leonard Nadel (1956); courtesy of Smithsonian National Museum of American History, http://americanhistory.si.edu/collections/search/object/ nmah_1354613.

symbolically recalls the worker's repeated bending and injuries. Some images partly reproduce the bosses' perspective of panoramic surveillance in long, wide-angle shots of workers amid extensive rows of crops, their bent outlines brought into relief against the horizon. Tejada-Flores also intersperses medium-range or close-up shots of individuals or pairs of workers that make details of clothing, hair, eyes, and hands visible in particularizing and animating ways. In one striking image a farm worker's large transistor radio is visible, strapped on at the waist, highlighting his use of technology rather than total reduction to it. In "Stoop Labor / Short Handle Hoe" the union artist casts a de-reifying gaze on farm workers that visually marks their difference from the tools of production. (Tejada-Flores would go on to help shoot the UFW documentary *Fighting for Our Lives*.) Thus, whereas California agribusiness assumed a naturalized set of looking relations and a corporate gaze that saw farm workers as part of the machinery of production, UFW visual culture focused a critical gaze on the growers and made visible the visual construction of farm workers as machines.

Refusing to avert the gaze: a bracero using a short-handled hoe in a Salinas, California, pepper field looks up and into the camera. Photograph by Leonard Nadel (1956); courtesy of Smithsonian National Museum of American History, http://americanhistory .si.edu/collections/search/object/nmah_1354602.

The farm worker movement was the subject of a number of sympathetic documentary films in the second half of the 1960s that represented union efforts to intervene in an agribusiness-dominated visual field. The films were made in the middle of the Delano grape strike and boycott that began with protests by the Agricultural Workers Organizing Committee (AWOC), a largely Filipino union, against a system of wage disparities in the Coachella Valley organized in terms of race and citizenship such that for the same work harvesting grapes Mexican braceros were paid $1.40 an hour, Filipinos $1.25, and Mexican Americans $1.10. Led by Larry Itlong, AWOC members launched a strike demanding wage parity, and the union appealed to the National Farm Workers Association (NFWA), the precursor to the UFW founded by Chavez and Dolores Huerta, to join the strike, which they ultimately did. The Delano grape strike was thus launched against the technologies of racial segregation long employed by agribusiness. As noted in the previous chapter, the segregation of the DiGiorgio work camps was replicated throughout the Valley so that in the 1960s Mexicans, Filipinos, Puerto Ricans, blacks, Yemenis, and Anglos were segregated into different bunkhouses and cafeterias. Journalist John Gregory Dunne visited DiGiorgio's Mexican camp during the Delano grape strike and found impersonal, barracks-like living quarters and a mess hall that reminded him of the army, with a machine that "stamps out over three thousand tortillas a day."[12] Agribusiness made significant investments in such technologies as a means of labor control since the engineering of segregated living quarters, mess halls, and pay scales made worker cooperation across lines of race more difficult.

In response, farm workers began picketing a four-hundred-square-mile area around Delano, while also organizing a consumer boycott of grapes, both of which were calculated to attract media attention. Confrontations between strikers and the police were broadcast on the national news, and a visit and announcement of support from United Auto Workers president Walter Reuther brought national visibility to Delano.[13] At the same time newspapers and national magazines published interviews with Chavez and articles and photo essays about the strike, and in this context Mark Harris began what would become his two documentaries about the movement, titled *Huelga* (1966, 1968).[14] The young filmmaker had started out to make a documentary about the history of the Industrial Workers of the World before turning to his cinema verité works about the Delano grape strike, suggesting the internationalist context within which the farm workers' movement was situated. Harris recalls that when they filmed Chavez at union headquarters he "was just becoming aware of what it meant to be a media star and was beginning to edit himself as he talked to the press. So this may have been the beginning of his self-consciousness about his image. He was listening to himself as he was talking to us."[15]

If Chavez appeared careful and self-conscious at the prospect of being filmed, it was not only because he had been newly thrust in the media limelight, but also because technologies of sight and sound had emerged as major practical strategic problems for the union. As Dunne discovered, a strike against agribusiness posed unique challenges. The more familiar setting for a U.S. labor strike was an industrial factory, which, however large, was self-contained and with a discrete number of entrances and exits where strikers could attempt to disrupt production by persuading scabs not to cross a picket line. By contrast, the factories in the fields of the San Joaquin Valley occupied miles and miles of land, and management could respond to a picket at one tract by moving scab workers to another tract where they could not easily be seen and confronted by strikers or captured by the media. Union volunteers in "scout cars" spent long hours in surveillance and detection activities in an effort to tackle this new terrain, driving past vast agribusiness lands with binoculars and alerting union headquarters by two-way radio when work sites were discovered so that "a caravan of roving pickets" could be dispatched. The growers attempted to evade detection by shuffling workers among multiple sites, moving them to the center of a vineyard where they were more difficult to see from the roadside, or by parking a line of cars along the edge of a field to obscure the view of picketers. Management also broadcast music over car radios and loud speakers to drown out the bullhorn appeals from picketers to scabs to leave the fields. In another example of the privileged aerial perspective presumed by agribusiness, one grower used his private plane to search for union caravans so he could radio his foreman to move operations elsewhere. The agribusiness elite responded to the strike's perceived challenge to their domination of the region in general and of the visual field in particular by using farm technology to attack a union gaze. Some growers buzzed picket lines with tractors to raise blinding dust clouds, while others "drove down the edge of their property line with mechanical sprayers shooting insecticide and fertilizer at the strikers" in ways that recall the history of treating pesticides and other technologies as weapons aimed at labor control. Farm fascism often involved violent physical assaults on the sight lines of strikers such that growers, according to Dunne, "walked up and down the picket line, stamping on the toes of the strikers, tripping them up, or elbowing them in the ribs," even kicking them. And local police ultimately reinforced the agribusiness presumption of entitlement over the visual field. In one telling incident, when Chavez and a Catholic priest flew over a field and tried to use a bullhorn to communicate with workers too far from the road to be reached by pickets, police arrested them for violating the grower's air space.[16]

In this struggle over the visual field, cameras were key. The title of Richard Steven Street's history of photography and California farm workers, *Everyone Had Cameras,* is taken from an interview with UFW volunteer Leroy Chatfield, who recalls that cameras were ubiquitous on all sides of the strike. Agribusiness companies paid private photographers to capture images of strikers, while their local police allies "engaged in massive photographic surveillance." Delano police took thousands of still and moving pictures on the picket line, detained union caravans to question and photograph strikers, photographed the license plates of union supporters, and sent the information to state and federal authorities. At the same time, the Kern County Sherriff Department compiled a photographic database of five thousand suspected strike supporters. As Dunne sardonically concludes, "Cameras, in fact, seemed to be indispensable artifacts of keeping the peace in Delano."[17] On the other hand, strikers strove to disrupt the police database project, by taking an inordinate time answering questions or by making faces while being photographed and forcing the police to shoot multiple takes. Many strikers carried their own cameras, including Chavez, who walked the picket lines with a donated Nikon camera. Not only did volunteers produce photos for the union's newspaper, *El Malcriado,* as well as the leftist, labor, and religious press, but the presence of cameras also sometimes shielded workers from the worst extremes of police and other forms of violence.[18]

Hence, while cameras and other "speculative" technologies were weapons of labor control, they also provided opportunities for creative, alternative uses by the union. Chavez and others anticipated cameras and carefully designed and planned the look of pickets and pilgrimages to appeal to audiences, including photographers, and to make for more compelling images. As movement photographer John Kouns recalled, "Chavez really knew the value of photography and what it could do for the union. He was very visually aware. I don't think he did anything during the first year of the strike without considering how it would look on film. To an extent that few realized, much of what the NFWA did was conceived with the idea of shaping the visual record to their advantage . . . Photography strongly influenced their tactics and thinking."[19] Given their limited access to visual technologies and the means of reproducing and distributing them, the union designed visual spectacles in an effort to attract cameras and direct them by a kind of virtual remote control.

A good example of the NFWA's efforts to redirect media technology was the famous three-hundred-mile march, or *peregrinación,* north through the middle of agribusiness country on California Highway 99 from Delano to Sacramento. The march was inspired by another incident of the use of farm technology as weapon of labor control: after picketers were sprayed with pesticides and fertilizers by a big grower's ranch crews, a group of workers proposed a protest pilgrimage to the company's headquarters in New York. Chavez thought the great distance involved made the plan impractical, but with images of the recent Selma civil rights marches in mind he fixed on a shorter but still ambitious pilgrimage to the state capital. Sacramento was selected as the destination in order to pressure a reluctant Governor Pat Brown to intervene on the side of farm workers and to bring state and national attention to demands that the growers recognize and bargain with union leaders. With the slogan "Penance, Pilgrimage, and Revolution," the march started in Delano on March 17, 1966, and ended in the capital on Easter Sunday. As the high-angle and areal shots of the march in *Huelga* and other works suggest, the farm worker *peregrinación* was designed to be visible to aerial news media in visually compelling ways and thereby aimed to commandeer a futurist vantage point from above that was often monopolized by agribusiness.

Both rhetorically and visually, the march constituted a millenarian, revolutionary disruption of agribusiness time and space that resonated with other contemporary anti-imperial, Third Worldist movements. As Chavez, Huerta, and Luis Valdez wrote in "The Plan of Delano," which was modeled on the Mexican revolutionary manifesto the Plan de Ayala, "The Pilgrimage we make symbolizes the historical road we have traveled in this valley alone, and the long road we have yet to travel, with much penance, in order to bring about the Revolution we need . . . We will strike. We shall pursue the REVOLUTION we have proposed . . . Our revolution will not be armed, but we want the existing social order to dissolve; we want a new social order."[20] As a strike modeled on Lent pilgrimages, the time of the *peregrinación* literally interrupted the industrial time of agricultural production. The march also countered the agribusiness domination of Valley social space by symbolically claiming it for farm workers.

While the terminus of the pilgrimage and the spectacle of thousands of marchers arriving in the capital were important elements of union strategy, the process of the march itself was perhaps of greater consequence for farm worker world building. The march up Highway 99, through agribusiness country and the small barrios of the San Joaquin Valley, drew out poor black, Filipino, Mexican, and white spectators, many of whom joined the growing movement of people on the freeway. The protest thereby produced a public horizon of visibility for working class people of color as it moved through the plantation towns like those described in previous chapters, where public institutions were dominated by agribusiness interests and the local police.

The march as a dynamic material and visual claiming of public space is effectively captured in films that attempt to reconstruct it by alternating between freeway pilgrims and spectators, editing together shot–reverse shot sequences connecting the two in a kind of visual call and response. The part of *Huelga* (1968) about the *peregrinación* comprises a sequence of shots that simulate a movement that cuts through agribusiness-dominated spaces and grows along the way by converting spectators into participants: medium shots of marchers and flags visible through rows of bare grapevines and fruit tree branches; a shot from closer up of a marcher carrying an NFWA banner at the head of the line of other marchers; a long, wide, high-angle shot of walkers moving along the 99 as the march cuts between expansive tracts of grapevines; a medium shot of the line of marchers as they advance toward the camera; close-ups of individual marchers on the freeway, including Chavez squinting in the Valley sun as the cameraperson joins the march; a shot of the line moving away from the camera; a shot of marchers from the perspective of spectators on the side of the freeway, some of whom seem to fold themselves into the line as it passes; shots of the growing line of marchers, many of whom seem to look directly into the camera; and, finally, the mass of marchers arrive in the capital.

Meanwhile, the voice of Luis Valdez on the sound track underlines the coherence of this sequence of different shots with a set of reflections on the ways the march disrupted an agribusiness construction of reality:

It seemed *fantastic,* you know, how could we march three hundred miles? We organized here at the office and there were a couple of hundred people in line to march to Sacramento. And then we got out of Delano and we got to Ducor, which was a seventeen-mile walk,

Progress of the march on Sacramento. Scenes from *Huelga*
(1968), directed by Mark Harris.

and that started it I guess. We were received by a separate family of farm workers and then from there it was the next town and then the next town and the line kept growing and little bands of farm workers would join us along the way, and there was an immense feeling of solidarity you know. Like we're not alone, what do you know we're not alone, there are a lot of people that know what's going on in Delano. Farm workers, they would pick up little flags and wave them and march with us, and just *seeing* that line grow was *fantastic*. Or walking along the freeway, if you had suggested that to a farm worker you know a year ago, a year and a half ago, he would have thought you were a little unbalanced. I think anyone would have thought you were a little unbalanced, walk along the 99 with a flag? [laughs] It did something really tremendous to keep the people walking along. There was this feeling of solidarity you know, we have a right to be here. (emphasis added)

Here "fantastic" marks the march's critical departure from what is reasonable, rational, and normal from the perspective of agribusiness visions of reality, where workers are extensions of the machinery of production. Such scenes from *Huelga* and similar ones from the union film *Nosotros Venceremos / We Shall Overcome* represent the emergence of a mobile farm worker counter-public.[21] The march thus constituted a rupture in the agribusiness domination of the visual field and the emergence of farm workers into a new kind of visibility, anticipating the end of agribusiness and the projection of another world.

Farm Worker Third Cinema

Chavez and other union organizers envisioned the farm worker movement as part of a larger struggle of poor people against wealth and power and viewed the Southwest as part of the global South. Chavez famously translated Gandhi's strategies of nonviolent resistance in British India and Martin Luther King's strategies in Selma to the southwestern agricultural fields. Less well-known is the UFW's alliance with the Black Panther Party (BPP). According to Lauren Araiza, the two groups articulated commonalities of class across race lines, starting with the BPP's decisive support of the boycott of the Safeway supermarket chain in Oakland, California. Oakland's Panthers joined the boycott in part because Safeway had refused to donate food to the party's Free Breakfast for Children Program. In 1972 Chavez joined BPP founding member Bobby

Seale in a joint press conference at Oakland's Merritt College, after which they met with students from Berkeley's Malcolm X Elementary School. Similarly, when the Alcohol, Tobacco, and Firearms Division of the U.S. Treasury Department raided the Panthers in Seattle, the UFW joined protests there in support of the breakfast program and other BPP institutions such as a medical clinic and food bank.[22] The UFW had built its own free medical clinic and collectively owned a gas station in Delano. The fact that the alliance between the BPP and the UFW was partly based in the defense of alternative institutions of collective welfare suggest the kind of "revolution" aimed at by the farm worker movement, in which present forms of state-sponsored capitalism are "dissolved," thereby making room for new collective experiments in social organization. Volunteers from the 1960s and early 1970s further recall union offices decorated with posters of Zapata and copies of Mao's *Little Red Book,* two symbols of peasant revolutions from the south that served as UFW models. Indeed, according to Miriam Pawel, Chavez modeled union marches on Mao's Long March.[23] Similarly, the history of the UFW's famous flag depicting a stylized black thunderbird in a white circle against a red background connects the union to anti-imperial struggles. In the early 1960s Chavez wrote that he "wanted desperately to get some color into the movement, to give people something to identify with, like a flag," so he asked his cousin, Manuel Chavez, to design a flag modeled on the postrevolutionary Mexican flag and the flag of the 1952 Egyptian Revolution against the monarchy and British occupation: "I was reading some books about how various leaders discovered what colors contrasted and stood out best. The Egyptians had found that a red field with a white circle and a black emblem in the center crashed into your eyes like nothing else."[24] The new UFW flag had a similar impact when it was first unveiled "and all of a sudden it hit the people." While Chavez was materially and spiritually committed to nonviolence, the more militant, revolutionary shades of his visual language here subtly mark his radical Third Worldist affiliations.

The UFW also opposed the war in Vietnam because of connections between the farm worker and anti-imperial struggles. The Pentagon helped agribusiness circumvent the UFW boycotts of grapes and lettuce by buying them to feed U.S. troops in Southeast Asia. Similarly, in his 1971 speech at a Vietnam veterans memorial in Exposition Park in Los Angeles, Chavez suggested that a history of militarized agribusiness violence provided a model for the war, and that potentially resistant U.S. farm workers were being encouraged to instead kill Southeast Asian farm workers:

Thousands and thousands of poor, brown, and black farm workers go off to war to kill other poor farm workers in Southeast Asia. Why does it happen? Perhaps they are afraid or perhaps they have come to believe that in order to be full men, to gain respect from other men and to have their way in the world they must take up the gun and use brute force against other men. They have had plenty of examples: In Delano and Salinas and Coachella all the growers carry gun racks and guns in their trucks. The police all carry guns and use them to get their way. The security guards (rent-a-cops) carry guns and nightsticks. The stores sell guns of all shapes and sizes.[25]

Here Chavez analyzes the U.S. war in Vietnam as part of a global war on poor people of color partly made possible by the masculine fetishization of technologies of death and the machinery of war. The speech also makes explicit what is presupposed by many early UFW media projects, which were partly modeled on antiwar media.

In 1970 the UFW initiated plans to produce and distribute its own films, something that was almost unprecedented among twentieth-century social movements of poor people of color. About a month after his antiwar speech Chavez joined a meeting about moviemaking with thirteen other key organizers. The minutes of this meeting suggest various aims for UFW film productions—to help organize farm workers; to elicit support from other unions, church groups, students, and consumers; and to document strike activities in the event of legal proceedings. Members of the union also discussed the most effective combination of visual content and form, paying particular attention to the relationship between film narrative and editing, as they debated and analyzed how to best incorporate film and video screenings into union events. The UFW carefully studied its intended audiences by staging test screenings for farm workers and organizing focus group discussions with consumers.[26] All this strategic thinking suggests that the goal of union media projects was not simply to enable the farm workers to make movies, but more broadly to intervene in a dominant visual field that legitimated farm worker exploitation. Finally, the films chosen as models suggest the union's radical internationalist imaginary, including *Salt of the Earth,* the blacklisted film about a strike of white and Mexican miners, as well as "Films made in Viet-Nam, China and USSR," and in particular films by Felix Greene, the British journalist and filmmaker known for works critical of U.S. imperialism and sympathetic to socialist Cuba, Vietnam, and China.

To accomplish its goals, the union began building its own film and video production facilities. Its first major project was *Fighting for Our Lives,* an Academy Award–nominated documentary about UFW efforts between 1971 to 1973 to force growers in the Coachella and San Joaquin Valleys of California to sign union contracts. The film incorporates funerals for two slain strikers, Nagia Daifallah, a Yemeni immigrant who was killed by a Kern County sheriff on the streets of downtown Delano, and Juan de la Cruz, a Mexican immigrant who was apparently shot by a vigilante. *FFOL* also includes dramatic footage of the police attacking and beating strikers. It was widely screened as a fund-raiser among unions, on college campuses, by church and civic groups, during marches, and even in Europe.[27] As a part of the UFW's organizing efforts, the film helped transform the political landscape in California by pressuring growers to sign contracts and the state to legally recognize the rights of farm workers to collectively bargain in the mid-1970s.

The documentary dramatically reverses dominant relations of looking by turning the camera on the plantation masters of agribusiness. The transgressive force of this reversal is indicated by the ways in which the agribusiness elite, practiced at staring down subordinates but unaccustomed to critical scrutiny themselves, appear uneasy before the camera and unsure of how to best respond to this novel situation. Tenneco vice president Harry Weatherhold tries to cover the lens with his hand, while grower David Valdora attempts to dance away from the camera and turn his back to it. Ray Stafford seems to aggressively confront the camera by almost knocking his oversized eyeglass frames against the lens, as if to reassert the supremacy of an agribusiness perspective that the union had challenged. Finally, John Giumarra acts out by mugging for the camera, belittling the strikers by mimicking them, and manically smiling and waving while seated at his dollar-sign-decorated golf cart. The police captured in the film seem just as uncomfortable and self-conscious, but often with more immediately violent consequences. In one sequence, a line of five policemen march stiffly past the camera, trying to avoid looking at it through the visors of their riot helmets. A second sequence shows a cop focused on spraying Mace at a striker while attempting to avoid the camera, but he can't help nervously looking up and into it. In a third scene a policeman stands guard, billy club at the ready, while other police handcuff strikers. The officer appears tense, perhaps even afraid—not of the strikers, who pose no threat, but of the camera he tries hard not to look at. Finally, there is the remarkable footage of Sheriff Charles Dodge who, in

Reversing the gaze: agribusiness leaders respond to UFW cameras in *Fighting for Our Lives* (1974).

white tie and cowboy hat, at first stands with his back to the camera but as he turns his body, apparently to rearrange his suspenders, seems to meet the camera's gaze. Clenching a cigar between his teeth, the sheriff grimaces as if in pain before turning away and continuing to tug at his suspenders by awkwardly reaching under the back of his jacket. Here the film suggests that the camera's presence physically disturbs what Fanon might call Sheriff Dodge's racialized "body schema" because it reverses the dominant looking relations of agribusiness, subjecting its representatives to the gaze of the UFW.[28]

The growers and the police confronted the UFW camera as a problem because it violated the norms of looking that helped enforce farm worker subordination. Both groups presupposed a world in which their own views of farm workers mattered but where farm worker views of growers and the police did not. One privilege of agribusiness power was the claim to a singular visual consciousness that established the dominant image of farm workers but was not itself subject to the critical gazes of others. This is depicted in *FFOL* by scenes where cameras are used both to directly

Reversing the gaze: the police react to UFW cameras in *Fighting for Our Lives*.

police strikers and to ritually reproduce their abject status. Photographing and fingerprinting strikers while arresting them, or filming them from on top of a police van, the Kern County police used visual technology both to incorporate striking union members into the criminal justice bureaucracy and to symbolically perform farm worker subordination within the visual field. In addition to camera-wielding cops, the growers often carried their own cameras, as in the scenes in the film of grower

Reversing the gaze: Sheriff Charles Dodge responds to UFW cameras in *Fighting for Our Lives.*

Ray Stafford with his 35mm camera. Similarly, after harassing the strikers and preparing to drive away in his dollar-sign-decorated cart, grower John Giumarra gestures for someone off camera to follow him, and this person turns out to be his personal photographer, wearing sunglasses and carrying a camera bag and camera. In contexts where capitalists were accustomed to commanding visual technology as symbols of privilege and as tools for reproducing it, UFW filmmaking posed a formidable threat. Hence, in addition to foregrounding the extent to which farm worker subordination was enforced through violence, *FFOL* further suggests that such violence was partnered with agribusiness efforts to dominate the visual field.

In these ways the film can be read in relationship to the contemporary project of Latin American Third Cinema to decolonize film. Opposed to capitalist, imperialist Hollywood (First Cinema) and European auteurism (Second Cinema), Third Cinema was initially theorized and produced by Latin American filmmakers as a revolutionary film movement devoted

Cameras and labor policing: Kern County police photograph and film striking farm workers.

to anti-imperial content but also to artisanal modes of production, underground means of distribution, alternative screening venues, a collective audience address, and practices of participatory spectatorship aimed at turning audiences into actors—qualities that also defined UFW film culture.[29]

Cold War Farm Workers

In recent years a number of historians and commentators have produced revisionary accounts looking back at the farm worker movement, and while there are a few exceptions, most present a narrative of decline in which, starting in the mid-1970s and at Chavez's insistence, the union largely withdrew from direct organizing, focused narrowly on the consumer boycott and fund-raising, and descended into recrimination, petty tyrannies, and political purges.[30] While such works include important insights that challenge hagiographical accounts of Chavez, they also seem a bit like "déjà vu all over again," repeating charges long made by the union's critics and enemies. Such repetition should make us question the narrative of decline, and indeed I would argue instead that the UFW was contradictory from the very start, combining at one and the same time a Third Worldist, revolutionary opposition to agribusiness futurism with a Cold War–inflected doubling of it.

As I argued in the introduction, big growers militarized production during World War II and extended such practices during the Cold War, when agricultural and military research overlapped, making agribusiness a leader in anticommunist industrial patriotism. While the union was critical of militarization in the fields of California and the world, there was another UFW that was enabled by a patriotic U.S. national frame. Chavez often used tropes of American exceptionalism, claiming in 1967, for instance, "There are things happening in America, such as anti-war rallies and civil-rights demonstrations, that no one has ever seen before. There are very few countries in which such things could happen, but they can happen here, and that's what gives our system its strength. In most countries, all change goes in the other direction, and eventually you end up with an armed revolution."[31] Or conversely, the union leader rhetorically asked how the degraded condition of farm workers was possible in advanced and democratic America. Claiming the ideals of U.S. democracy for farm workers was a potentially powerful political intervention, particularly at a moment when unions were attacked as un-American and their members beaten in the fields. But formulations like "how can that happen in America" risk naturalizing oppression in other countries, where one might expect such conditions to prevail, while reinforcing belief in the uniqueness of American democratic ideals, whose very existence is counted on and invoked to make the farm worker plight visible as an outrage in the first place. These tropes of American exceptionalism thus suggest a second reading of the scenes of violence in *FFOL* in which they presuppose an implied contrast between some other place of state terror and the United States, where such things aren't supposed to happen. If the first reading connects the fight in the fields to the war in Vietnam, the second subtly asserts a difference that was animated by and that implicitly supported U.S. nationalism.

This sort of Cold War Americanism is consistent with the UFW's foundational anticommunism. Historically, with the crushing of the communist Cannery and Agricultural Workers Industrial Union in the 1930s, the remaining unions seeking to organize California farm workers—such as the AFL-CIO and, especially, the UAW—were fiercely anticommunist. After World War II the UAW and AFL-CIO effectively promoted anticommunist unions in the global South as barriers to decolonization.[32] In the United States during the 1960s and 1970s, radical black and white auto workers, including Detroit's League of Revolutionary Black Workers, emerged in opposition to UAW racism and collaboration with management demands for more work for less pay. The league also protested dangerous conditions of work speedup in which, according to Peter Linebaugh and Bruno Ramirez, "the violence of technology" resulted in roughly sixty-five deaths a day in the U.S. auto industry. Linebaugh and Ramirez further argue that during the series of wildcat strikes organized in the U.S. auto industry in 1973, which coincided with the UFW organizing depicted in *FFOL*, the UAW attempted to reassert control over workers through forms of direct violence in which UAW thugs played the part of West Coast Teamsters and attacked striking auto workers.[33] UAW president Walter Reuther was perhaps the most visible spokesman for an anticommunist unionism.[34] Reuther provided sustaining material and symbolic support to the Delano strike and is prominently featured in films and photos depicting it. Chavez and the UFW were highly active in Michigan, in part because of the large number of farm workers there but also because of the support they received from and gave to Detroit's UAW. One sign of the close relationship between the two unions is the fact that the Walter P. Reuther Library at Wayne State University in Detroit is the official repository of the UFW papers.

As suggested by his adherence to Catholic dogma, Chavez shared Reuther's anticommunism. "The Plan of Delano," which capped the pilgrimage to Sacramento, calls for "revolution" while quoting from Pope Leo XIII's encyclical titled *Rerum Novarum* ("New Things"), or "The Rights and Duties of Capital and Labor": "We seek, and have, the support of the Church in what we do . . . In the words of Pope Leo XIII, 'Everyone's first duty is to protect the workers from the greed of speculators who use human beings as instruments to provide themselves with money.'"[35] Biographies of Chavez describe him regularly reading and quoting from this encyclical, and he often returned to it in his speeches. While sometimes remembered as a progressive, pro-labor statement affirming the right of workers to unionize, *Rerum Novarum* seeks to substitute for forms of class conflict a set of reciprocal relations between capital and labor that anticipated the collaborative corporate unionism developed by the UAW and other mainstream unions. The encyclical ultimately argues for an antisocialist alliance between capital and labor in order to safeguard the interrelated rights of private property and the patriarchal family:

> Every man has by nature the right to possess property as his own. This is one of the chief points of distinction between man and the animal creation . . . That right to property . . . must in like wise belong to a man in his capacity of head of a family; nay, that right is all the stronger in proportion as the human person receives a wider extension in the family group. It is a most sacred law of nature that a father should provide food and all necessaries for those whom he has begotten . . . Now, in no other way can a father effect this except by the ownership of productive property, which he can transmit to his

children by inheritance . . . Paternal authority can be neither abolished nor absorbed by the State; for it has the same source as human life itself. "The child belongs to the father," and is, as it were, the continuation of the father's personality; and speaking strictly, the child takes its place in civil society, not of its own right, but in its quality as member of the family in which it is born . . . The socialists, therefore, in setting aside the parent and setting up a State supervision, act against natural justice, and destroy the structure of the home.[36]

Here the right to private property is strongest when concentrated in fathers, whose possessive investment in their children makes private property a "sacred law of nature." For the pope, property and patriarchy persist in a mutually reinforcing embrace: private property is naturalized/sacralized by its articulation to fatherhood, and likewise, fatherhood is made natural and sacred by its association with private property. The problem with socialism—and by extension, communism—is its violation of the possessive patriarchal investments in the heteronormative family.

Given Chavez's devotion to Catholicism in general and endorsement of Pope Leo's encyclical in particular, it is not surprising (though rarely remarked on) that from the very beginning he chose to march under the image of the Virgen de Guadalupe, a figure widely viewed by Chicana feminists as enforcing women's subordination as wives and mothers within the patriarchal family. In her essay "'Indiscriminate and Shameless Sex': The Strategic Use of Sexuality by the United Farm Workers," Ana Raquel Minian argues that with their public criticism of birth control, promiscuity, and queer sexuality and gender presentation, Chavez and the UFW replicated the logics used by the liberal state to subordinate and exclude people of color. The union's "heteronormative discourse," Minian writes, served to assimilate farm workers to a "citizen–ideal," based in forms of sexual respectability, which has also governed the state policing of Mexican and Filipino farm workers.[37] What is thus sometimes underappreciated in retrospective accounts of the UFW is the extent to which its mobilization of Catholicism could also reinforce conservative ideas about private property and the patriarchal family that were historically articulated to Cold War anticommunism, not to mention agribusiness appeals to private property and residual images of the family farm.

Even though the farm workers were themselves red-baited by agribusiness and conservative politicians, in what is often cited as evidence of the UFW's decline the union began a series of purges starting in the mid-1970s, as volunteers were accused of being communists and forced out. As in the case of UFW discourse about gender and sexuality, the union thus reinforced forms of anticommunism that had been used to attack farm workers. Moreover, when read in light of the longer history of Chavez's Catholicism, as well as the larger historical tendency for Cold Warriors to equate communism and queerness,[38] the UFW purges seem to articulate anticommunism and heteronormativity, making red-baiting a sort of queer-baiting as well. This at any rate is one way to interpret the fact that the most popular synonym for "communist" among UFW leaders was "asshole,"[39] thereby making a site of nonreproductive sexual pleasure a symbol of the threat radicals supposedly posed to a union organized under the banner of the Virgin—which is also to say that while the red purges are generally narrated as part of Chavez's tragic fall into a cult of personality, the complex of associations linking the patriarchal family and Cold War anticommunism that they presuppose were constitutive of union ideology from the start.

At the same time as the red purges, the UFW made divisive public declarations in support of Israel that also dovetailed with U.S. nationalism and foreign policy. Chavez circulated to union staff a statement that was subsequently made public supporting Israel during the 1973 Arab–Israeli War, writing that "as individuals committed to the cause of freedom, concerned with the fate of victims of racial, ethnic and religious prejudice and discrimination, we feel a particular sense of solidarity with Israel's struggle to survive as a democracy in peace."[40] According to UFW volunteer Bruce Neuburger, the letter "caused an uproar among some progressives, who wondered how the union could support a state that oppressed and discriminated against an entire people, the Palestinians." Support for Israel, Neuburger concludes, was a "key element of U.S. strategy in the oil-rich Middle east," and Chavez's statement "was an open and clear accommodation to empire."[41] When the UN passed a resolution equating Zionism and racism in 1975, Chavez published a second statement implicitly comparing Mexicans and Israelis: "The recent UN resolution condemning Zionism as racist is an affront to the Jewish people who have been history's primary victims of racism. As an embattled minority who have suffered the humiliation and degradation of racial and economic discrimination in this country, we know first hand the ravages brought about by intolerance and prejudice."[42]

Chavez's seeming identification with Israel partly emerges from a sense of the "families of resemblance" linking Mexicans and Jews who had faced racism, prejudice, and discrimination. In addition to the Catholic mass, Passover was celebrated at union headquarters in Delano, and a number of union members identified agribusiness with the pharaoh and the farm worker struggle with "Israel's liberation from Egypt."[43] Chavez in particular was drawn to the kibbutz as a model for a more just and equitable future. In the late 1980s during UFW video campaigns in support of the grape boycott, Chavez told a Michigan public television audience, "We have to find a way in which the workers can become the owners of the property and do something like they did in Israel."[44] Before that, in 1977, he initiated plans, which were later aborted, for a new combined Catholic and Protestant religious order, "Los Menos," and a communal farm in Oxnard partly modeled on the kibbutz.[45] According to Pawel, the plan was to build the first self-sustaining farm as a "mother house" and to "spin off" more communal farms in the future, "with an expansive goal of changing the world."[46] As far back as 1968, during his first fast, Chavez discussed plans for a UFW retreat based on the kibbutz that ultimately became the union's headquarters, La Paz.[47] Indeed, from the start the union had posited a privileged political relationship between Christianity and Judaism, as when "The Plan of Delano" claimed that the movement was not sectarian because it marched under the sign both of the "Sacred Cross" and "The Star of David."[48] This understanding of the special relationship linking farm workers and Jews ultimately extended to UFW support for the state of Israel.

The combination of "Sacred Cross" and "The Star of David," however, makes any symbol of Islam conspicuous in its absence, especially in light of the significant Yemeni presence in the farm worker movement, as well as the murder of Yemeni immigrant and striking union member Nagia Daifallah by the police, which occurred just four months before Chavez's 1973 statement in support of Israel. Despite claims it was "nonsectarian," the union's support for Israel blocked the development of a political relationship with forces of decolonization in the Arab world and helped drive a wedge between the UFW and the Black Panthers. Chavez's condemnation of the UN resolution also put him at odds with the Mexican state, which was one of the UN members that supported the measure (in response, Jewish organizations in the United States borrowed a UFW tactic and launched a tourism boycott of Mexico).[49] Chavez's comparison of farm workers and Israelis obscures Israel's status as a Cold War military ally of the United States and its occupation of Gaza and the West Bank. UFW Zionism also precluded the development of a comparative analysis of the occupied territories and the San Joaquin Valley's "farm fascism," and a critical juxtaposition of the situation of farm workers and Palestinians.[50]

In 1977 Chavez aligned himself with the anticommunist, antilabor dictator Ferdinand Marcos, accepting his invitation to visit the Philippines. Chavez made the trip despite the fact that delegates to the 1973 UFW convention had passed a resolution condemning the Marcos dictatorship and against the strong objections of Philip Vera Cruz, a Filipino activist and important union leader.[51] As reported by the *Washington Post* in a story headlined "Cesar Chavez Hails Philippines' Rule":

> Chavez, who was given an award yesterday by President Ferdinand Marcos for improving the lot of Filipino migrant workers in California, said that he had talked with almost 60 union leaders there, "and every single one of them said it's a hell of a lot better now (under martial law) than it was before." Asked in an interview if he had been told about approximately 130 strikes that had taken place despite the martial law ban on them or about the arrest of thousands of strikers, Chavez said, "I didn't know about that." . . . He said he had congratulated President Marcos on the country's land reform program under which 30,000 of the 1 million tenant farmers have begun buying land from their landlords.[52]

Ironically, the land reform for which Chavez congratulated Marcos actually favored big growers and corporate plantations in ways that recalled the agribusiness hierarchies of the San Joaquin Valley. Land reform potentially benefited only a relatively small number of peasants who were able to produce enough to pay the state back for land. Marcos further promoted "Green Revolution" technology and "miracle rice" requiring expensive chemical fertilizers that favored corporate agriculture and hurt small farmers. And Marco's land reforms did nothing for the mass of landless agricultural workers most resembling the UFW's constituency.[53]

Vera Cruz and others had opposed the UFW leader's trip to the Philippines precisely because Marcos had imposed martial law and clamped down on labor, so it is hard to believe Chavez when he pleads ignorance—which makes the photos he posed for in the Philippines seem especially striking. While perhaps the most photographed Chicano in history, Chavez was usually pictured in serious poses, rarely in light moments, and almost never "cutting up" for the camera. But during the Philippines trip he posed smiling for three photos while joining local workers in a rice field and for a fourth while straddling a large military cannon.[54] Upon his return to California, human rights and religious groups sent Chavez information about Philippine abuses under martial law and asked him to renounce the statements he made to the *Washington Post*. Chavez refused and even invited Marcos's labor minister, Blas Ople, to address the 1977 UFW national convention, leading Vera Cruz and others to break with the union.[55]

Narratives of decline notwithstanding, the UFW was founded on the contradictions and continuities between, on the one hand, Third Worldist revolutionary internationalism and, on the other hand, dominant Cold War nationalism of the sort promoted by corporate labor unions and agribusiness. Chavez and the UFW partly shared agribusiness investments in private property, patriarchal families, and anticommunism. *Fighting for Our Lives* could be reread in this light, highlighting the film's potential overinvestment in the power of visual technology to counter agribusiness violence. The UFW thus actually shared with agribusiness not only conservative investments in property and nationalism but also a fetishization of technology as a means for resolving labor conflict. As I argued in the introduction, agribusiness futurism included a faith in technological tools for containing labor conflict and was presented to the global South as a model of capitalist democratic progress implicitly defined over and against socialist and anticolonial alternatives. While obviously different from and in many ways antagonistic to agribusiness futures, the UFW's faith in visual technologies to overcome exploitation could be described in similar ways as suffering from a kind of instrumental rationality whereby technology promises to dissolve social contradictions without requiring the material transformations called for by anticolonial, anticapitalist movements of the global South, including Third Cinema.

Farm Worker Video

The UFW was an early and innovative adopter of new video technologies in the late 1970s and early 1980s. At the same time that it developed plans for constructing film production facilities around 1973, the union also investigated video. Film stock was expensive and, in addition to direct production costs, the union had to pay for the film to be developed before it could be edited. It also had to pay for the production of multiple prints of the completed film for distribution. Because of these expenses, union filmmakers had to carefully limit what they shot and then hope they had the footage they needed when it came time to edit. By contrast, video was relatively cheap, did not need to be developed, and could be reused. Video makers could afford to shoot large amounts of footage and view it immediately, making it easier to shoot more if necessary, which also meant more raw footage to recombine in the final edit. With video the union could record not only big dramatic moments but also the more mundane, quotidian aspects of union activity, including scenes of communal eating, singing, and simply joking around. UFW video was thus closer to the conventions of amateur photography or home video than it was to those of Hollywood film. And copying tapes for distribution was inexpensive, so the union could give thousands away for free.

Video thus enabled the UFW to potentially respond more quickly and creatively to the shifting terrain of immediate struggles than did older media such as film. Cheap, compact, and highly portable, videotapes were available for any group or individual to have and even hold in their hands, copy, and pass on to others, generating an almost tactile or haptic investment in the images on tape. The relative ease with which video could be integrated into the concrete practices of everyday life made it particularly apt for the UFW, which in the 1980s attempted to appeal to U.S. grape consumers by connecting their life worlds to the conditions of farm workers. For all of these reasons, Chavez wrote in an editorial for the UFW publication *Food and Justice* that video was "our most formidable boycott weapon."[56]

Chavez's description of video as a kind of weaponized media recalls not only the rhetoric of Third Cinema (Solanas and Getino's famous manifesto "Towards a Third Cinema" compares the film projector to "a gun that can shoot 24 frames a second")[57] but also the immediate historical context for home video's emergence in the 1970s and 1980s. Audio- and videocassettes were a prominent feature of the Iranian Revolution—for example, in recordings of speeches denouncing the U.S.-supported dictatorship of the shah and promoting the postrevolutionary government. The revolutionary deployment of video in Central America, moreover, was widely discussed in U.S. media. As part of their struggle against a U.S.-sponsored dictatorship, El Salvador's Frente Farabundo Martí para la Liberación Nacional (FMLN) made extensive use of video. The FMLN made videos depicting military victories and debunking anti-FLMN propaganda to screen in village plazas on VCRs powered by truck batteries. They also made training videos for guerrilla fighters and a video called *Time of Daring* for distribution in the United States.

Clips from FMLN videos were screened on *NBC Nightly News* and covered by the *New York Times* in an article titled "Salvadorans Use Video in

Propaganda War," which concluded that the FMLN was "combining the electronic revolution with political revolution." Meanwhile, the dictatorship attempted to claim video for the counterrevolution by making its own videos that the army then forced kidnapped groups of peasants to watch.[58] Similarly, in Nicaragua the Sandinista state "embraced video production, both for broadcast and VCR distribution/showing, as a primary means of communication," using it "to consolidate the revolutionary government and to keep people loyal, in the face of efforts by the *contras* to create a counterrevolution."[59]

The UFW partly drew on the radical cachet of video in its antipesticide documentary *The Wrath of Grapes* (1986), which was widely distributed on videocassette. The opening moments of the film alternate between brief interviews with farm workers and consumers who have been made sick by pesticides, and shots of a helicopter spraying pesticides on a field beneath an ominous, orange sky. These images are accompanied by the sound of dissonant piano music and the helicopter's whirring blades. The video freezes on the helicopter while the title—"The Wrath of Grapes"—is superimposed on it, and the sound of its blades are still audible as Chavez is heard saying "We're declaring war, war on the pesticides that are poisoning and killing our people." The history of agribusiness technology in general and aerial pesticide spraying in particular overlaps with the history of military weapons and warfare, a fact figured in El Teatro Campesino's play "Vietnam Campesino," where a plane sprays a California field in one scene and bombs a Vietnamese village in the next. The opening also recalls scenes of helicopters from Francis Ford Coppola's *Apocalypse Now* (1979) (in fact, the sound for *FFOL* was mixed at Coppola's studio, American Zoetrope) as well as images of the helicopters used by U.S.-backed forces to bomb El Salvador and Nicaragua. Framed in this way, Chavez's declaration of war implicitly suggests connections to Central American rebels and U.S.-based antiwar movements. From this vantage the video aligns the UFW with the kinds of revolutionary futurism associated with Latin American liberation theology that aim at transcending imperialist and capitalist violence.

But that declaration of war can also be read in relation to forms of U.S. nationalism. One informing model for the UFW's *Wrath of Grapes* video campaign was "Hands across America," a benefit and publicity event to combat hunger in which about more than six million people held hands, forming a human chain across the continental United States. The event was a follow-up to the earlier "USA for Africa" charity that produced the

Advertisements for cassette
copies of the UFW film
The Wrath of Grapes from
the pages of *Food and Justice*,
January and October 1988.

popular fundraising song "We Are the World," but as its title suggests, "Hands across America" represented a shift from foreign to domestic hunger. This inward turn presupposed a version of American exceptionalism I earlier attributed to Chavez and the UFW that asks "How can this happen in the United States?" Such questions ultimately reinvigorate nationalism, like the "American jeremiads" analyzed by Sacvan Bercovitch[60]— which in part explains the fact that even President Ronald Reagan, whose cuts in spending increased poverty and hunger, joined the route of handholders that passed through the White House. To promote the event, organizers produced a music video, broadcast on TV and distributed on videocassette, featuring scenes of people holding hands, including numerous celebrities, against iconic nationalist backgrounds (the Statue of Liberty, the Grand Canyon, etc.), intercut with patriotic images of eagles and flags. The UFW owned a copy of the tape, and the entire "Hands across America" campaign seems to have partly inspired the union's plans for distributing *The Wrath of Grapes*. In *Food and Justice* the UFW offered free tapes and urged its readers to call their local access cable channels to demand that the video be shown. The union also organized a staff of forty-five volunteers to travel to over a dozen cities in the United States and Canada to encourage unions, churches, minority leaders, and other community groups to screen the video. Volunteers met with local sympathizers and tapped into their organizational phone banks to promote the video. With its innovative telecommunications and video tactics, the UFW helped to pioneer a form of media activism that anticipated the use of the Internet and social networking media by contemporary political activists, including in the immigrants' rights movement. At the same time, however, the video campaign recalled "Hands across America" by tracing a map connecting major U.S. cities and centering Chavez as a kind of nationalist icon.

The focus on Chavez as nationalist icon is visible in video archived at the Reuther Library in Detroit from the 1988 "Fast for Life," the UFW president's thirty-six-day hunger strike in support of the grape boycott. The union pitched huge tents at its La Paz headquarters, where it had moved from Delano, to accommodate over eight thousand supporters and members of the international media for a series of public events during the final days of the fast. Meanwhile, UFW volunteers extensively videotaped all aspects of the fast, including a visit by a large group of celebrities from Los Angeles. The event was organized by Luis Valdez and featured many actors who had starred in his films, including Edward James Olmos,

Lou Diamond Phillips, Rose Portillo, and Tony Plana. After meeting with Chavez while he lay on his fasting bed, the celebrities held a press conference and attended a mass with the visibly weakened union leader. Finally, it was announced that Chavez was dangerously near death and would end the fast in a dramatic public ceremony. Surrounded by cameras and supported by two of his sons, Chavez labored to make his way into the tent, past the stage, to an empty chair in the front row, flanked by his wife, Helen Chavez, and his ninety-some-year-old mother, Juana Estrada Chavez. Twenty years earlier, in 1968, Chavez broke his first, twenty-five-day fast in a similar public ceremony in which he accepted a piece of bread from Robert F. Kennedy. In 1988 that earlier moment of nationalist iconicity was recalled when Kennedy's widow, Ethel Kennedy, also handed Chavez a piece of bread. Too weak to speak, Chavez's prepared statement was read by his son, Fernando; he explained that the fast represented "a declaration of noncooperation" with the growers and supermarkets, "those who grow and sell the poisoned food we all eat," and "an act of penance . . . for those who, by their failure to act, become bystanders in the poisoning of our food and the people who produce it."[61] Helping to provide a national frame to the event was Jesse Jackson, who was running for U.S. president at the time. At the end of the ceremony Chavez handed Jackson a small wooden cross, signifying the passing of the fast from union president to presidential candidate, who then fasted for three days before passing the cross to others in what became a "National Fast for Life," represented in a map from *Food and Justice* marking the national progress of the rolling fast initiated by the labor leader. Footage of the event was subsequently incorporated into UFW videocassettes promoting the boycott.[62]

While the fast and related videos helped communicate a critical perspective on pesticides to large numbers of people, it did not result in any significant victories for farm workers. Rather, UFW video campaigns substituted for direct organizing activities among farm workers. The hope that pressure from the consumer boycott would force growers to negotiate never materialized, and thus in a real sense the union's over-investment in the power of video to move consumers displaced attempts to build the farm worker's movement. This inflated faith in video is suggested by the UFW's obsessive taping of Chavez and all angles of the fast, including seemingly intimate scenes with family, celebrities, and doctors in his fasting bedroom at union headquarters. By connecting the production of agricultural products to farm worker death, the UFW used videos

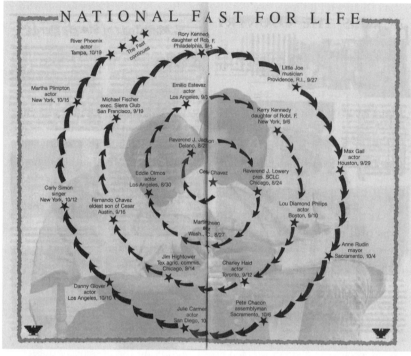

Mapping the "National Fast for Life." *Food and Justice,* October 1988.

to combat forms of commodity fetishism that obscured how agribusiness profits came at the expense of workers' lives. At the same time, however, the union ultimately engaged in its own fetishization of videos of Chavez in ways that increasingly substituted for and thereby partly foreclosed the organization of workers and other forms of material transformations aimed at producing better futures.

An overinvestment in video technology thus contributed to Chavez's politically debilitating iconicity. A popular poster depicting Chavez that the UFW advertised in *Food and Justice* shortly after the fast and in the middle of the boycott suggests some of the problems with iconicity. As the magazine explained, "At first glance the painting appears to be a simple portrait of Cesar but look closer . . . the clouds at the top become angels, with 36 crosses made of grapevines, symbolizing Cesar's 36-day fast last year; the mountains on the horizon are corpses on one side and fists raised in protest on the other; the skulls on the left are actually

Chavez become Leviathan. *Food and Justice,* September 1989.

workers and their children; in the center UFW supporters march, carrying flags and banners."[63] The poster recalls Hobbes's famous representation of Leviathan, in which an image of the sovereign was constructed out of innumerable smaller images of his devoted followers. As Michael Rogin argued, the image of Leviathan "absorbs viewers into the body politic and keeps them passive observers at one and the same time," making the image "a preview and ideal type of the relationship between modern mass society and the state."[64] In the twentieth century, according to Rogin, film and later television were the central media of mass culture, and they helped put "seeing and being seen at the center of modern political integration." Rogin came to that conclusion in the mid-1980s, at a time when mass media such as Hollywood films and network television increasingly came into competition with cable and home video, which seemed to provide greater diversity of images and greater viewer control and autonomy over when and under what conditions to watch them. Yet the political significance of the kind of iconicity Rogin associated with film does not disappear with new media; on the contrary, it becomes potentially even more limiting of political agency. The freedom of choice and autonomy promised by video, and more recently digital media, can take the place of transformative political activities. This at least is what seems to have happened in the present context, where video images of Chavez symbolically absorbed viewers into the body of the UFW, here represented by Chavez himself, while at the same time framing these relations of looking as self-sufficient forms of political intervention despite their disarticulation from the activities of union organizing. But regardless of audience response, it is clear that the union's leadership, including Chavez, placed too much faith in the power of media to transcend corporate agriculture, and were themselves too absorbed in video images of the iconic leader. The UFW's appropriation of video ultimately prepared the way for Chavez's incorporation into a pantheon of U.S. heroes, as suggested by the recent naming of a U.S. Navy weapons transport ship after the late labor leader. As we shall see in subsequent chapters, however, Chavez's media image has continued to be an object of struggle, and while it has been co-opted for conservative projects, it has also been remembered and resituated in ways that recall the radical revolutionary elements of UFW histories and that elaborate farm worker futurisms in new contexts.

3 Farm Worker Futurisms in Speculative Culture

George Lucas and Ester Hernandez

The technological visions of California agriculture represented in speculative visual culture reveal the historical connections between agribusiness and influential forms of white male agrarian populism that supported the Cold War militarism of the 1980s. Made by George Lucas, a native of the California agricultural community of Modesto, *Star Wars* provides a revealing speculative rendering of a dominant ideology in the recent history of California and national politics: a pastoral, free market, white individualism partly defined in dialectical relation to Mexican migrant labor. In other words, Lucas's work suggests that the Central Valley has been a key experimental laboratory for the development of forms of neoliberalism in which individual white market freedoms are engendered in opposition to racialized farm workers. By contrast, in her image in support of the UFW called *Sun Mad* and other works, Ester Hernandez, who is also from an agricultural community in California, linked Mexican workers and white consumers similarly affected by pesticides in ways that undermine nativist and corporate celebrations of whiteness. Her images of skeletons are part of a larger body of farm worker visual culture in the 1980s and 1990s that helps make visible the forms of violence and destruction that the articulation of white masculinity to high-tech agribusiness often obscures.

Not So Long Ago, in a Valley Nearby . . .

I situate *Star Wars* in relationship to the history of struggles between agribusiness and farm workers in California, arguing that the film's popularity both responds to and has helped to shape race and class formations in California that originate in its agribusiness economy. The epic battles between the UFW and agribusiness corporations have been a prominent feature of the regional mediascape; as Lucas's own early history overlaps and converges with the movement, its distorted remains are visible in his films. I focus on elements of Lucas's biography not only because they have been an important part of the way meaning has been made out of the *Star Wars* phenomenon, but also because they enable us to see the kinds of race and class subjectivities *Star Wars* presupposes and encourages. The film appeals to a broad audience in part because it provides resources for multiple, often contradictory interpretations and uses, but I emphasize its appeal to a form of free market white individualism connected to the agribusiness-dominated political economy of California's Central Valley. Lucas's early films in effect project the demise of the social movements of the 1960s and the morphing of countercultural critiques of state power into new forms of neoliberalism. Drawing both on insights generated by appropriations of *Star Wars* by digital artist and filmmaker Alex Rivera and on historical research into the UFW in California media and politics, I suggest that the film helps make visible the ideological and affective appeals of a kind of agrarian white populism identified with capitalism and against labor, the very formation that has helped empower right-wing politicians, from Ronald Reagan to George W. Bush. And traces of the historically sedimented race and class formations that crystallized in *Star Wars* are exposed and critically reenvisioned, I conclude, in recent digital filmmaking and cultural criticism based on Lucas's classic space opera.

In 2009 Lucas joined his friend Steven Spielberg to help dedicate a new building for the School of Cinematic Arts at the University of Southern California. Lucas is its most famous alumnus, and the school plays an important part in the familiar story about the Central Valley farm boy who became a famous director. Lucas contributed $75 million to the construction of the building, which is based on his design and includes a large "Spanish-style" courtyard, a tribute to old Hollywood's enthusiasm for Spanish revival architecture.[1] In the courtyard there is a life-size statue of school founder Douglas Fairbanks, who often played exotic "Latin" characters, including Zorro, a romantic hero of nineteenth-century "Spanish" California.[2] In keeping with that star image, the Fairbanks statue features the actor looking as though he is ready for one of his Latin roles, sporting a pencil-thin moustache and holding a scrolled document (a script?) in one hand and a sword (instead of a lightsaber?) in the other.

Historians and cultural critics have interpreted the California vogue for all things "Spanish," particularly in Hollywood, as part of a contradictory social formation that appropriated elements of a Spanish fantasy past while remaining indifferent or hostile to the contemporary Mexican working class, as if the fantasy helped California whites deny that part of their contemporary reality.[3] But rather than reading Lucas's design in relationship to the history of Hollywood, I wish to instead foreground another kind of historical juxtaposition involving the UFW. The new Lucas building is close to a small bronze plaque with a bas-relief bust of a smiling Cesar Chavez, commemorating his three visits to USC in 1982, 1986, and 1989 to promote the grape boycott. Los Angeles was the second-largest market for table grapes in the world, and as a result, in the 1970s and 1980s, Chavez and the UFW were highly visible in and around Hollywood, where they cultivated the support of entertainment industry liberals and others. Chavez's final visit to USC occurred when he was recovering from his longest fast ever, part of a renewed push to publicize the dangers of pesticides and, through the boycott, force agribusiness to negotiate with the union. The plaque is inscribed with a quotation from Chavez: "The end of all education should surely be service to others."

The Chavez memorial at USC, along with the establishment of a Chicano/Latino major there, was partly a response to demands by Latino students in the wake of the 1992 Rodney King uprisings near campus, at a time when the public image of the university with respect to race relations was undergoing scrutiny. The memorial was announced in 1994; by the time it was completed in 1998, USC was involved in a dispute with a largely Latino labor union that self-consciously invoked the memory of Chavez. Maria Elena Durazo, the president of the Hotel Employees and Restaurant Employees (HERE) Local 11, led the union in a conflict with USC that started when the university refused to guarantee that the jobs of HERE's 350 workers would not be subcontracted out. After a year of negotiations without an agreement Durazo expanded the struggle by building an alliance with a newly formed student group, the Student Coalition against Labor Exploitation (SCALE). The faculty adviser to SCALE was Professor Laura Pulido, a USC geographer and historian of the UFW's battles against pesticides. In the spring of 1998, workers protested at the USC graduation and students staged an alternative graduation in solidarity with HERE. That fall there was a large march of students, workers, and clergy in support of the union, while 135 national religious leaders signed a statement critical of USC for "valuing the bottom line over and above human dignity." When still no progress was made, Durazo, who as a child had worked in the fields of Oregon and California with her migrant farm worker parents, borrowed Chavez's tactic of the rolling hunger strike. On May 10, 1999, with the help of veteran UFW organizers, she and forty other people began a fast that, according to Randy Shaw, was "likely the most highly publicized such event since Chavez's 1988 effort." On the eleventh day, she passed the fast on to California state assemblyperson Gilbert Cedillo, who passed it on to Los Angeles County Federation of Labor head Miguel Contreras, and so on. The rolling fast ultimately involved over 200 participants and lasted for 150 days. According to Shaw, students "would pass the fast to each other in a ceremony at the statue of Tommy Trojan, the symbol of USC."[4]

When UFW cofounder Dolores Huerta attended the dedication of the Chavez memorial on campus, she blasted the university for its hypocrisy.[5] Huerta's daughter with Cesar Chavez's brother Richard, Maria Elena Chavez, was a USC film student at the time who studied with Mark Harris, the producer of *Huelga* (see chapter 2), by then a USC professor. Maria Elena Chavez was also involved in campus activism supporting the union, and she even made a short film about the strike.[6] USC finally agreed to safeguard the union members from subcontracting in October 1999, leading Shaw to conclude that "Durazo's spiritual fast had changed the momentum of the struggle, and proved decisive in changing her adversary's position."[7]

In light of this backstory, the Cinematic Arts building, with its "Spanish" courtyard and statue of a white actor in Latin drag, almost seems to mock the Chavez memorial. But what if we read this strange juxtaposition differently, as the sign of a secret connection? What if we imagined that the Chavez memorial was part of the unconscious or the suppressed of the new Lucas building? What if the Lucas world was linked to the history of Chavez and the UFW, the absent presence distantly animating the drama of *Star Wars*?

What at first seems an unlikely comparison becomes plausible when we consider in greater detail where the two histories meet. *Star Wars* emerges from a regional history in which agribusiness has been a dominant political, economic, and cultural force since the early decades of the twentieth century, roughly paralleling the history of the development of the film industry in Southern California. During the 1930s there were hundreds of agricultural strikes in the state among male and female farm and cannery workers, strikes often led by Mexicans, which partly inspired John Steinbeck's famous novel *The Grapes of Wrath*.[8] But the strikes also helped inspire forms of "farm fascism" that combined violence with domination of local movie screenings and the press, not to mention Associated Farmers of California propaganda.[9] In response, farm worker unions struggled to organize workers and produce their own media—press, photography, and film—to combat the agribusiness media monopoly.[10] As we have seen, in the post–World War II context, media technology became increasingly important to farm worker struggles, not only to combat agribusiness propaganda but also to intervene in a civil society dominated by state institutions aligned with agribusiness and actively hostile to farm worker interests. This is the world into which Lucas and other California baby boomers were born, where conflicts between agribusiness and labor loomed large in the local visual field.

1944

In his earliest recorded act of civil disobedience, a teenage Cesar Chavez is arrested at a movie theater in the Central Valley town of Delano after refusing to move from the "whites only" section to the section reserved for blacks, Filipinos, and Mexicans.[11]

George Lucas is born in Modesto, another segregated Central Valley town, to George Sr., who owns a local stationery store and walnut ranch, and Dorothy Bomberger, the daughter of a prominent local family.[12]

1948

Chavez joins an automobile caravan of support for a strike against the mammoth DiGiorgio Fruit Company by the National Farm Labor Union, led by Ernesto Galarza. The union collaborates with Hollywood unions to make a documentary about the strike, *Poverty in the Valley of Plenty*, but is ultimately bankrupted when the company successfully sues for libel and the film is banned (see chapter 1).[13]

1952–1962

Chavez becomes a community organizer in San Jose, near what will become Silicon Valley. At the end of this period he returns to Delano and, along with Dolores Huerta, founds the National Farm Worker Association, an immediate precursor to the UFW.

During the same years Lucas reads comic books and ultimately tinkers with cameras and cars on his family's walnut farm.

1963

A teenage Lucas begins to frequent bohemian San Francisco, including countercultural film screenings at City Lights Bookstore and San Francisco State University.[14] The following year, after two years at Modesto Junior College, he transfers to USC to study film.

1965

The Delano grape strike begins with farm workers demanding they be paid the federal minimum wage. It lasts five years and results in agreements with major growers.

1966

Farm workers walk three hundred miles north from Delano to the state capital in Sacramento as part of a pilgrimage that ends on Easter Sunday. The pilgrims walk through downtown Modesto, past its iconic civic archway celebrating agribusiness prosperity with the slogan "Water, Wealth, Contentment, Health." Seemingly overnight Chavez becomes a huge media celebrity and *Huelga,* the first documentary about the UFW, is produced and broadcast on public TV.

In the same year Lucas returns to USC as a graduate film student, where he begins making short experimental films.

1967

Striking farm workers and supporters begin a national boycott of California table grapes. The pro-UFW documentary *Decision at Delano* is released and plays on college campuses and in public schools. It features a satiric performance by El Teatro Campesino lampooning a cowboy hat–wearing labor contractor and a grower.

Lucas completes several student films including *The Emperor,* which is about a Los Angeles disc jockey who, at one point, delivers an ad for the United Fruit Company, which leads to a surreal scene, set in a cornfield, where two Latino characters, "Rodriguez" and "Dominguez," have just executed someone. Rodriguez is dressed as Che Guevara while Dominguez is outfitted like Pancho Villa.[15]

Mirror inversions. On the left, members of El Teatro Campesino perform as a grower and a labor contractor in a scene from *Decision at Delano* (1967); on the right, actors in George Lucas's USC student film *The Emperor* (1967) impersonate Latino revolutionaries.

1968

In the face of suggestions from some strikers that the union consider adopting violent tactics, Chavez rededicates the movement to nonviolence by fasting for twenty-five days. When he finally breaks his fast he is joined by Robert Kennedy, who hands Chavez a piece of bread, resulting in some of the most iconic visual images of the 1960s.

1969

Francis Ford Coppola founds the production company American Zoetrope in San Francisco. Imagined as an alternative to the Hollywood studios, this filmmaking "commune" is where Lucas will do postproduction work on his first feature film, *THX 1138*.[16]

1970

Chavez is jailed for fourteen days in Salinas, California, for refusing to obey a court order to end a boycott, an incident that is widely reported in the media. Coretta Scott King and Ethel Kennedy visit him in his cell. Kennedy is greeted by protesting Teamsters and a group from the local John Birch Society, who wave flags and shout "Ethel, go home!" She is reportedly surrounded and physically threatened by members of the crowd, much of which was captured for broadcast on the national evening TV news. At the same time the growers and their allies, the Teamsters, employ thugs to menace and beat picketers and their supporters.[17] Released after winning an appeal, Chavez tells TV reporters that the prison was a "disgrace" that reminded him of farm labor camps.[18]

1971

Lucas releases *THX 1138*, a futuristic drama about a white man called THX (Robert Duvall) who rebels against a totalitarian society and ultimately escapes from one of its prisons. Lucas says it is about situations where people are "in cages with open doors" and that its theme is "the importance of self and being able to step out of whatever you're in and move forward rather than being stuck in your little rut."[19]

In June the UFW establishes a film department and begins to build its own film and video production facilities. They also help produce the film *Nosotros Venceremos* about the Delano grape strike, the march to Sacramento, Chavez's first fast, and the union's first victorious contracts.

1972

Chavez once again fasts for twenty-five days, this time in Phoenix, in opposition to an Arizona law that effectively prevents farm workers from organizing, striking, and boycotting. During the fast he utters the now famous phrase "Sí se puede" (Yes we can), which Huerta takes up as a rallying slogan in the concurrent protests.[20]

1973

The UFW begins filming *Fighting for Our Lives*. The sound for *FFOL* is ultimately mixed at American Zoetrope, and the film includes dramatic footage of police beating farm workers in scenes that echo images from *THX 1138*. The UFW also launches a highly publicized boycott of the E & J Gallo Winery of Modesto.

Lucas releases *American Graffiti,* a nostalgic film about white teens cruising the streets of Modesto in 1962, the year Chavez and Huerta established their first union in the Central Valley. Lucas says that the film celebrates "all that hokey stuff about being a good neighbor, and the American spirit" and that the heroes of both *THX 1138* and *American Graffiti* show that "anybody who wants to do anything can do it. It's an old hokey American point of view, but I've sort of discovered that it's true."

Police violence in the future and the present. Scenes from *THX 1138* (George Lucas, 1971) and from *Fighting for Our Lives* (Glen Pearcy, 1975).

1975

The UFW releases *FFOL* and organizes a march of a few thousand union members and supporters from San Francisco to Modesto in order to pressure Gallo to come to the bargaining table. By the time they arrive, over fifteen thousand people have joined them. The march is widely covered in the media, including the national TV news, and helps to build support for passage of the California Agricultural Labor Relations Act, which establishes the right of farm workers to collective bargaining.[21]

Lucas founds Industrial Light and Magic and writes the first draft of *Star Wars*.

1976

Amid celebrations of the U.S. bicentennial, *FFOL* is nominated for an Academy Award for best documentary.

1977

Twentieth Century Fox releases Lucas's *Star Wars* on May 25 in the United States.

This partial parallel history indicates that Chavez and the UFW were vital actors in regional and national media in ways that would be hard to ignore, particularly for an aspiring filmmaker from a California agricultural community. Moreover, my time line suggests that both Lucas and Chavez were directly involved in alternative 1960s film cultures that, while distinct in many ways, partly converged in others. The audience members for the kinds of experimental films Lucas watched in San Francisco, a center of UFW support, would also have been likely to attend UFW screenings and events. And yet there are also many differences between the Lucas universe and the UFW, starting with the distinction between the collective address implicit in "Sí se puede" (Yes we can) and the individualist cliché that "anybody who wants to do anything can do it"—which is to say that the Lucas trajectory combines the countercultural affiliations and rebellious impulses of the San Francisco scene, on the one hand, with the kinds of middle-class white individualism characteristic of nearby agricultural towns such as Modesto, on the other.

This combination of counterculture rebellion and conservative individualism is well represented by *THX 1138*.[22] In its mode of production the film constitutes a rebellion against the Hollywood studio system, which is how Lucas described it both then and subsequently.[23] The counter-cultural ethos of the production context is suggested by Lucas's short film about the making of *THX 1138* called *Bald*. Filmed in San Francisco, *Bald* begins with the bearded and longhaired Coppola and Lucas drinking wine and discussing Lucas's plan for all the characters to sport bald heads, followed by footage of the actors and actresses having their heads shaved.[24] The title character of *THX 1138* also rebels against an oppressive system, figured by a futuristic totalitarian state. The film is a reactionary dystopia that melds a Cold War demonology of Soviet society with a kind of anti–big government white male individualism defined in opposition to women, homosexuals, black people, and farm workers. One sign of state oppression in the film is the erasure of gender differences—men and women have identical uniforms and shaved heads and answer to unisex codes in place of gendered names. The state forcibly separates THX and his pregnant wife, LUH (Maggie McOmie), and seemingly murders her. At the same time, THX must resist the sexual advances of a male superior, SEN (Donald Pleasence), who attempts to arrange it so that the two men will be forced to live together in state-controlled housing. This is in fact why SEN is ultimately imprisoned, where he continues to pursue THX. There the men are joined by a black male figure named SRT (Don Pedro Colley), who turns out to be a hologram. SRT recalls an earlier scene where, as a sign of his debasement within a mass society, THX masturbates while watching the hologram of a naked black woman dancing to the sound of drums. The bizarre implication is that the state uses pornographic racial representations to control the white hero in ways that alienate him from himself and from "real" human relationships, defined as heterosexual relations with his white wife.

Ultimately THX escapes the tyranny of mass society and becomes a free man only after losing LUH and literally racing away from the film's gay and black characters. The gay character is the first to fall by the wayside, when the robot police arrest him. SRT is next: together he and THX steal police cars, but the black hologram quickly crashes whereas the white male hero outdistances both him and the police. In the concluding scenes THX eludes the police and climbs up a long ladder, out of what is revealed to have been a society constructed underground, and into the light and fresh air of the "real" world on the surface. The final shots suggest the quasi-religious resurrection of the white male hero: the silhouette of a lone individual is defined against the background of the setting sun, while the solemn choral music of Bach's *St. Matthew Passion* plays on the sound track. In these ways the film uses countercultural tropes of resistance to state power to deify a lone white man in rebellion against a government that violates his personal freedom by treating everyone— white men, women, gay people, and people of color—the same.

In the present context, the most uncanny figures in the film are the "shell dwellers" who live on the edge of the underground world. The film's sound editor and cowriter Walter Murch explains that the human characters have moved underground in response to "some kind of radiological or ecological disaster," and they are surrounded by a "society of dwarf people who live at the outer edges of society in the shell, which means up near the surface of the earth and presumably they're closer to whatever troubles have beset the surface of the earth and they're looked upon as a nuisance by the rest of society."[25] As THX makes his escape he must evade a group of shell dwellers that attack him and momentarily impede his progress. Their role in the narrative, combined with their depiction as grotesque and animalistic, suggest that the shell dwellers are fictionalized versions of farm workers. Their marginal social status and proximity to ecological disaster recalls farm worker vulnerability to pesticide poisoning and the UFW's highly visible campaigns against the chemicals' use in California agriculture. The fact that the characters are played by little people with dark hair and beards recalls racist representations of Mexican farm workers as small in stature and hence constitutionally well suited for "stoop labor." Similarly, the shell dwellers are dehumanized within the film's narrative (human characters react with visceral disgust to their perceived smell) and sound design (their voices are supplied by recordings of bears and apes) in ways that recall racist depictions of farm workers as dirty and animalistic. Ultimately the freedom and individuality of the film's white male hero depend on the distance he puts between himself and the shell dweller as farm worker.

Lucas compared the character of THX to Curt from *American Graffiti*, claiming that both represent the "American point of view" where "anybody who wants to do anything can do it," which he refers to elsewhere as the "Horatio Alger myth" of pulling yourself up by the bootstraps.[26] In interviews then and later, Lucas narrates his own life in similar terms. He has often, for example, figured himself as a rebel and an outsider, striving for freedom of expression.[27] "Freedom" is a keyword for Lucas, particularly individual freedom, but "equality" is not, perhaps because he associates it with a kind of state-imposed uniformity as in *THX 1138*.[28] The arc of Lucas's early career thus describes an ideological shift analyzed by

In police custody: a shell dweller from *THX 1138*.

David Harvey in his *Brief History of Neoliberalism*. Harvey argues that the social movements of the 1960s represented an unstable combination of struggles against structural inequalities and for individual freedom, and that over the course of the 1970s such tenuous coalitions were broken as countercultural individualism morphed into neoliberalism: "For almost everyone involved in the movement of '68, the intrusive state was the enemy and it had to be reformed. And on that, the neoliberals could easily agree. But capitalist corporations, business, and the market system were also seen as primary enemies requiring redress if not revolutionary transformation: hence the threat to capitalist class power. By capturing ideals of individual freedom and turning them against the interventionist and regulatory practices of the state, capitalist class interests could hope to protect and even restore their position."[29] Lucas, I would argue, is a key figure in this history, and his career makes visible the conflicted emergence of neoliberalism in relationship to the political economy of California's Central Valley, where individual white market freedoms are defined in relationship to Mexican farm workers.

In his autobiographical recollections, Lucas focuses on individuals proving themselves in a free market, thereby obscuring raced and gendered material inequalities. He expresses such sentiments in the formula that people are in "cages with open doors," prisons of their own making that can be transcended through individual initiative. This kind of facile idealism forcibly disappears otherwise highly visible counterevidence of material inequalities (low wages, the absence of rights and legal protections, the prevalence of state and vigilante violence) and the necessity of a collective response. And yet traces of such inequalities remain in the form of Latino characters in Lucas's early films that indirectly reference the UFW and its struggles with agribusiness. In two instances Latino characters symbolically mediate the countercultural rebelliousness of 1968 and the emergent neoliberal individualism of the 1970s. On the one hand, his student film *The Emperor* suggests an identification between film school rebels and Latino revolutionaries fighting against an agribusiness corporation. On the other hand, the film also others the Latino characters, who speak in exaggerated Spanish accents, wear theatrical costumes, and execute another character. From this perspective *The Emperor* screens like a demeaning parody of the Latino and Latin American movements of the period, including the UFW and Chavez.

Similarly, in *American Graffiti* Curt at first partly identifies with, but then ultimately distances himself from, Latino gangsters. During his last night in Modesto before leaving for college, Curt is kidnapped by three "hoods" from a car club called the Pharaohs—made up of Joe Young (Bo Hopkins) and two Latinos, Carlos (Manuel Padilla) and Ants (Beau Gentry)—when he mistakenly sits on the car of an absent fourth Pharaoh, Gil Gonzales.[30] The group gives Curt a choice: either destroy a police car or Ants will drag him behind *his* car. After he successfully demolishes the cop car the hoods offer to make him a member, but since he is bound for college in the morning Curt declines, leaving behind those, like the Latino gangsters, who cannot escape the "cage" of rural life. In the end Curt boards a "Magic Carpet Airlines" plane, and as it takes off the view from his window fills the screen with an aerial image of brown and gold agricultural fields, bisected by a freeway. The scene recalls films and photos of UFW marches like those analyzed in the previous chapter—only minus the farm workers—suggesting that it is in part the farm worker movement that the upwardly mobile Curt must transcend.

While images of Latino revolutionaries and gangsters may seem far removed from Chavez and the UFW, conservative and agribusiness media in fact represented them in just such terms. During the 1960s and 1970s, agribusiness and its allies produced a constant stream of press releases, pamphlets, and books suggesting that Chavez was an authoritarian dictator, the leader of a gang of thugs, a revolutionary, a communist, and a crook.[31] Perhaps most famously, Governor Ronald Reagan, a staunch supporter of agribusiness, announced in a 1968 press conference that the boycott was "illegal," "immoral," and "attempted blackmail." Using the rhetoric of Cold War anticommunism, he further called it the "first

Curt and the Pharaohs sitting on Gil Gonzalez's car, listening to "The Great Pretender" on the radio while watching *The Adventures of Ozzie and Harriet* on a TV in a storefront window in *American Graffiti*, directed by George Lucas (1973). The scene suggests that Curt is a white middle-class pretender among the racialized Valley hoods.

Adopting an agribusiness gaze: the view from Curt's vantage point as he flies away from the Central Valley.

domino" threatening to spread labor unrest throughout California agriculture. In order to demonstrate his opposition to the boycott, he publicly ate grapes for the news cameras.[32] Like other conservatives, Reagan represented the UFW as a kind of subversive criminal conspiracy in ways that are echoed by Lucas's Latino rebels and hoods.

Lucas's Latino characters thus partly represent fictional versions of Chavez and the UFW that serve to mediate a decisive shift from counterculture to neoliberalism, San Joaquin Valley style. With this last phrase I mean to suggest a regional social formation, with national influence, that combines myths of white male individualism, agrarian values, and market freedoms in opposition to farm workers of color. While by the 1940s corporate agriculture had largely destroyed the material preconditions for agrarian populism in the West, images of the yeoman farmer have continued to play an influential role within right-wing political discourses in California and other parts of the United States. More recently, with his fishing trips, cowboy boots, and bouts of brush clearing on his Texas ranch, George W. Bush aimed to repeat the similar performances of both his father and Ronald Reagan in their attempts to appeal to white male voters in the South and West within a tradition of agrarian populism.

And while agrarian populism has historically been associated with men, the George W. Bush administration's secretary of agriculture, Ann Veneman, described herself as "a poor little peach farmer's daughter" from the Central Valley. Born and raised in Modesto and reportedly Lucas's second cousin, Veneman began her career working as a lawyer for the local firm representing Gallo in its battle with the UFW; according to journalist Laura Flanders, she has "spent her entire adult life taking big business's side in a battle that pits the largest corporations in the world against the smallest farmer."[33] As Bush's agrarian political style and Veneman's reference to her father suggest, even though agribusiness threatens small farmers, images of the white male farmer as the bedrock of democracy have helped reinforce the conflicted alliance between white populism and corporate capitalism.

One of the most influential proponents of such an alliance is Victor Davis Hanson, onetime Bush administration adviser, emeritus Fresno State classicist specializing in agrarian communities, Hoover Institute fellow, and former employer of Mexican farm workers. Hanson's personal history as a farmer is often cited as lending credibility to the anti-immigrant views articulated in his popular books, *National Review* columns, and blog. He is "a classicist, but also a farmer, who was born, lives, and works on a family farm in California's Central Valley," and in his writings Hanson attempts to "make sense" of the world from an "agrarian vantage point" that has been "handed down from some five previous generations."[34] In his book *Fields without Dreams: Defending the Agrarian Ideal* he argues that the small family farm is the "foundry of the country—its values, its militia, its very resilience." The life of a farmer, who is generally male in this account, is "a struggle with a purpose, where self and family have clear roles prescribed by the wisdom of the ages," while farms "forge family ties, the notion that blood above all is to be honored and protected, feuds, divorces, and alienation to be avoided." Farmers are "natural bedrock conservatives" who distrust "fashion and trend—whether it be multiculturalism or leveraged buyouts."[35]

While he is sometimes critical of the way agribusiness corporations have undermined family farms, Hanson bridges the gap between agrarian populism and corporate power by demonizing Mexican farm workers. In *Mexifornia: A State of Becoming,* his paranoid, dystopian account of the near-future immigrant takeover of California, he forecloses a broader, critical discussion of corporate capitalism by instead blaming migrants for a host of social problems, including violent crime, theft, sexually transmitted diseases, drunk driving, monopolizing emergency medical resources, littering, abandoning dogs and cats on his farm, and even stealing a copy of one of his book manuscripts from his rural mailbox. Echoing a familiar conservative narrative of countercultural disenchantment, Hanson notes that when he was an adolescent he secretly put pro-UFW bumper stickers on his uncle's farm truck and later he and his brother attended a UFW rally. But as he got older and wiser he started to question the heroic image of Chavez presented in the public schools, claiming to discover that the UFW leader was an ambitious opportunist, a sort of "Mexican George Meany, in charge of a vast empire of stoop laborers," who, in combination with liberal politicians, helped "loot" union dues.[36] Here the figure of the Mexican farm worker anchors a neoconservative psychobiography, a racist Valley variation on neoliberalism that attacks state tyranny but embraces the tyranny of the market.

Hanson represents an influential kind of Valley Republicanism, where Mexicans are hyper-visible as phobic objects that organize nativist political projects and subjectivities. By contrast, Lucas has been more closely aligned with liberal Democrats, while Latinos are marginal to his films. Even so, the comparison with Hanson is revealing, since Hanson renders in explicit and extreme terms the relationship between white farm boy and Mexican farm worker that is also represented, although in much more implicit and indirect ways, in *Star Wars,* to which I now turn.

The Migrant Farm Worker in *Star Wars*

There are no farm workers in *Star Wars,* but their power as an animating absence is still important. The UFW challenged a hegemonic white agrarianism in the Valley by foregrounding images of farm workers rather than romantic images of a white yeomanry. UFW media implicitly negated the figure of the white farmer that helped shore up corporate agribusiness, and I would argue that Luke Skywalker represents the negation of the negation and *Star Wars* the reactionary return of the white farm boy. At the same time, traces of Chavez and the UFW are disseminated across the landscape of the Manichean world the film imagines.

Alex Rivera's film *Sleep Dealer* (2008) makes visible the ways *Star Wars* mediates farm worker narratives. *Sleep Dealer* develops a scenario Rivera first presented in *Why Cybraceros?* (1997), a short film in which a fictional corporation promises to use new computer technology to solve the "immigration problem" by enabling Mexicans to operate, from Mexico, farm worker robots in the United States. A satiric response to the Internet utopianism of the late 1990s, it incorporated footage from the UFW's *Fighting for Our Lives* showing police and Teamsters attacking strikers. Building on his earlier work, *Sleep Dealer,* Rivera's first feature film, focuses on the character of Memo (Luis Fernando Peña), a young peasant farmer living in the interior of a near-future Mexico where water has been privatized and a large pipeline has been built to transport it to the United States. When a group of rebels—dubbed "aqua-terrorists" in the media—emerge to fight water privatization, the United States launches a war on terror in Mexico, including attacks on suspected rebel strongholds by automated drones like those used in today's actual war on terror. Near the beginning of the film, a military drone, remote-controlled from the United States by a Chicano soldier named Rudy Ramirez (Jacob Vargas), destroys Memo's home and kills his father. This tragedy turns Memo into a migrant who travels from his rural home to the border city of Tijuana. There he meets Luz, a sort of futuristic media maker who downloads other people's memories and sells them on the equivalent of the Internet; she introduces Memo to a brave new world of work, helping him implant electronic nodes all over his body so that he can perform remote labor. Soon he has a job working for a company called Cybraceros Inc., where he is hooked up to cables and a sort of virtual reality mask, enabling him to operate, from Tijuana, construction 'bots in the United States. Meanwhile, Luz has been selling Memo's memories on the Internet, where they come to the attention of Rudy the drone pilot, who, consumed with guilt, migrates to Mexico to find Memo and make amends. Together, the three characters break into a Cybraceros facility and commandeer the technology in order to fly a drone to Memo's village and destroy a massive, heavily guarded dam.

As Rivera has explained, *Sleep Dealers* is partly a reworking of *Star*

Recalling the Royal Chicano Air Force: rebel drone pilot Rudy Ramirez *(above)* flies his drone toward the "Death Star" dam *(below)*.

Wars, with the destruction of the dam standing in for the destruction of the Death Star. Moreover, Memo's character arc, in which an imperial army destroys his family's farm and initiates his migration toward the center of the empire, recalls Luke's odyssey.[37] Rivera's reappropriation of *Star Wars* in turn suggests that the Skywalker story borrows the structure of a migrant worker narrative for the story of the white farm boy, but rather than being based in the fields of Mexico, the imaginary world of *Star Wars* begins in the farmland of California. According to *Wired* writer

Steve Silberman, though filmed in Tunisia, the scenes of Luke's home planet of Tatooine, where he initially lives on a small family farm with his aunt and uncle, were modeled on "the dusty Central Valley flatlands."[38] In the film's fantastic, revisionary reversal, however, the figure of the white farm boy occupies a position that more closely resembles that of a migrant farm worker. Landless and dispossessed, vulnerable to extreme forms of militarized police power, and forced by material conditions to leave home in order to survive, Luke's story sounds like that of many farm workers. And yet recalling Heinlein's *Farmer in the Sky* (see chapter 2), in *Star Wars* the noble white farm boy appropriates for agrarian populism the pathos of exploitation and marginalization that was previously attached to the farm worker movement. Or more precisely, Luke's fate at the start of the film is made more tragic, and his ultimate rise more heroic, in part because he is a white farm boy who has fallen to the level of a migrant farm worker. This reading is supported by the analysis of *THX 1138,* which suggests a similar kind of racialized reversal, whereby the film's white male hero experiences extreme forms of police violence that recall period images of black and Chicana/o civil rights protesters being beaten by the police. And substituting an oppressed white farm boy for oppressed people of color recalls the contemporaneous emergence of discourses of reverse discrimination, which rearticulated civil rights rhetoric in order to argue that state efforts to redress prior histories of inequality violated the rights of white men.[39] The early films of Lucas thus help make visible an influential historical shift from the social movements for radical transformation of the 1960s to an emergent neoconservative and neoliberal reaction of tactical reversals.

Displacing migrant farm workers by mimicking them, the white farm boy proceeds to fight a brutal empire represented by a ruthless "black" villain. A number of critics have argued that the Darth Vader character is shaped by ideas about racialized blackness, and I would suggest that the figure references Latinos as well.[40] Just as Chavez was symbolically and practically linked to civil rights and anticolonial leaders (Gandhi, Martin Luther King, Huerta, Bobby Seale), I would speculate that Vader condenses a variety of racialized or Third World movements for social transformation, including the UFW, that are often represented by the shorthand of "1968." And the *Star Wars* villain is contradictory in ways that recall Chavez's conflicted public image. On the one hand, with his disfigured body and audibly labored breathing, Vader seems to require the life support of his elaborate costume. On the other hand, he speaks in a powerful, commanding voice and exercises a charismatic, quasi-religious power over a vast army of minions. Similarly, many of the famous media images of Chavez from the 1960s represent him weakened by one of his fasts and being supported by other people, and yet at the same time agribusiness interests and their allies used hyperbolic rhetoric and imagery in order to demonize the UFW. Whereas McWilliams had argued that agribusiness was fascist, conservatives constructed a counter-narrative in which Chavez's public commitment to nonviolence and self-sacrifice was a sham that masked a charismatic dictator's will to power. And in ways even more extreme and explicit than Reagan's language about falling dominos, right-wing books with titles such as *Little Cesar: The Farm Worker Movement* (1971) and *Little Cesar and His Phony Strike* (1974) compared Chavez to an imperial dictator and a Mafia don.[41] Hanson recently echoed such period pieces when he claimed that the union leader's public image was at odds with his ambition to control "a vast empire of stoop laborers"—which is to suggest that Darth Vader can be read as a demonological rendering of Chavez as dictatorial union boss.

And yet, recalling Milton's Satan, Darth Vader has perhaps proven to be the most interesting character to viewers and consumers of *Star Wars,* and I would wager that the villain has sold more merchandise, inspired more imitations, and generally generated more global cultural attention than any of the heroes. Michael Rogin's claims about the forms of political demonology that have dominated California and ultimately the United States are helpful for understanding the Vader effect. Taking Ronald Reagan as exemplary, Rogin analyzes a conservative political formation that has historically demonized people of color, radicals, and labor unions in its devotion to "counter-subversion." He identifies a counter-subversive tradition in U.S. politics and films that project forms of violence and aggression onto social groups that challenge the status quo and then promotes the use of their own vilified tactics against them. From this perspective, the threat posed by subversive others licenses government officials to mimic the demons they have created.[42] All of this seems like a revealing gloss on *Star Wars,* where the figure of the white farm boy, threatened with displacement by the UFW and other forces of transformation, serves to energize investments in Darth Vader. How else can we understand the narrative of Lucas's transformation from rebellious farm boy to the head of a vast corporate empire? As he explained on a 2004 DVD release of *Star Wars,* "I'm not happy that corporations have taken over the film industry, but now I find myself being the head of a corporation, so there's a certain irony there. I have become the very thing that I was trying to avoid. That is Darth Vader—he becomes the very thing he was trying to protect himself against."[43]

According to USC film scholar David James, Lucas re-created his film school experience in grandiose ways, first with major donations to USC and then "in the idealized version of film school at the Skywalker Ranch, with its own offices, editing, and post-production facilities. Here the conditions of USC in the 1960s were replicated on a corporate scale, and here he made his own hypertrophied experimental films. So *Star Wars* reads as the projection of a childhood fantasy and also an allegory of his own career: Luke and Lucas get to play with the toys of Industrial Light and Magic, destroy the bad boys from Hollywood, and return the movies to the mentality of pubescence."[44] As James persuasively argues, Lucas's ideal is a corporate one, with origins in his own history and self-narration. Based on my research, I would add that the corporate ideal represented by Skywalker Ranch is imaginatively based in agribusiness. The ranch, which cost over $100 million and sits on over four thousand acres of land in rural Marin County, is anchored by a massive Victorian farmhouse with an expansive front porch and surrounded by a grape vineyard. In 2012 the website for Skywalker Sound at the ranch prominently featured images of the vineyards (minus workers), including a QuickTime film that presents a panoramic view of fields.[45] The grapes are harvested (presumably by farm workers of color) and used to make wine, and the Skywalker Vineyard website describes the history of the enterprise in ways that recall San Joaquin Valley styles of neoliberalism. "The genesis of Lucas' vintner dreams," according to the website, "can be traced back to his childhood in Modesto, California. Surrounded by vineyards—the fragrance of fermenting grapes permeating the air—the small Central Valley community was imbued with the culture of grape growing and wine making." Although historically the ranch's location has been viewed as inhospitable for grapes, Lucas possessed grand "vintner ambitions" and "embraced the frontiersman mentality," "relishing the challenge and committing himself to the cause," becoming "among the first to pioneer plantings in the Marin region." Recalling the director's own self-narration as filtered through a heroic agribusiness perspective, the site concludes that Lucas "aimed to push the envelope, defying the odds as well as conventional wisdom" to make wine that is "a victory over nature and a testament to tenacity."[46] Skywalker Ranch is thus not just a corporate fantasy of the family farm on steroids; it also represents Lucas's media empire as an

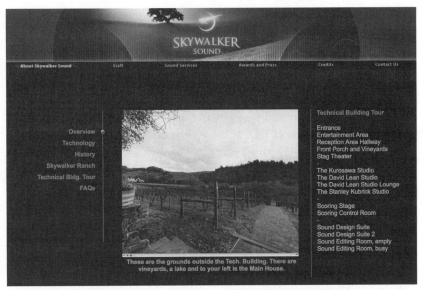

Skywalker Ranch grape vineyard, as presented on the Skywalker Sound website.

idealized version of the E & J Gallo Winery, the Modesto company that fought the UFW for so long.

All of which is to suggest that the history of pre-digital race and labor formations continues to influence contemporary culture, starting with Lucas's own digital filmmaking. Lucas is deeply invested in his corporate history, and to that end he has released digitally revised versions of almost all of his major, pre-digital films—much to the chagrin of many fans and critics.[47] In 2004 he released into theaters and on DVD *THX 1138: The George Lucas Director's Cut,* which made a number of digital additions, many of which serve to intensify the kinds of racial representations analyzed earlier. The white hero now masturbates to a digitally enhanced hologram of the naked black dancing woman, for example, while the shell dwellers that attack him have been replaced by dark CGI apes.[48] This last change has contradictory implications since, on the one hand, it obscures the connections between Lucas and the UFW suggested by the shell dwellers in the original version of *THX 1138,* while on the other hand, the very substitution of digital monkeys seems to recall the more recent past of anti-immigrant discourse in California and the United States more generally. The 1980s and 1990s saw the rearticulation of older race and class ideologies in the form of white anti-immigrant nativism directed at workers from Latin America and often framed in the language of animality (especially parasites and vermin), filth, waste, and other expressions of racialized disgust. At the same time, and partly in response to such populist nativism, state and federal immigration enforcement became increasingly militarized, incorporating high-tech military weaponry and surveillance equipment (including flying drones). And so the 2004 director's cut of *THX 1138* roughly coincided both with Hanson's nativist best seller *Mexifornia* and the establishment of U.S. Immigration and Customs Enforcement, which has unleashed what Rachel Buff calls a new "deportation terror" against migrant workers.[49]

While historically CGI has been used to create a variety of effects, it has often been deployed in figural ways to represent exotic or fantastic characters and creatures. This practice has lent itself to the creation of racialized digital characters, most infamously the figure of Jar Jar Binks for the first *Star Wars* prequel (1999), which was widely criticized for being a CGI version of a blackface minstrel.[50] Jar Jar Binks recalls the black holograms of *THX 1138,* suggesting that Lucas has used CGI not only to produce a kind of enhanced realism but also as a means of derealizing race and class conflict—which is to shift focus away from whether this or that use of CGI is realistic or persuasive and to instead ask what it means to render race and class differences as special effects.[51] In the case of *THX 1138,* the original had already represented farm workers in fantastic terms; when new digital tools became available they were used in ways that made the shell dwellers even more "unreal," like the holograms. Here, however, the substitution of digital apes for human actors displaces workers literally and symbolically. Or more precisely, in the director's cut, figures representing farm workers are digitally incorporated into the film in ways that drain them of humanity and disconnect them from political economic contexts. Analyzing Lucas in relationship to the UFW thus suggests the extent to which he has increasingly used digital technology to create compelling fictional worlds that draw on the "real world" but ultimately secede from it. We might thus say that the corporate development and deployment of CGI sublates social and material histories of race and class, simultaneously preserving and canceling them out, in ways that ultimately deny their reality. Meanwhile, cultural criticism celebrating the centrality of *Star Wars* to a new participatory digital culture risks reproducing the ideologies encoded in its source material.[52]

Seeing Skeletons: The Work of Ester Hernandez

Since the 1970s, the greater San Joaquin Valley has been home to a group of Chicana/o writers and artists who critically reflect on the history of farm labor. The most well-known figure is perhaps Richard Rodriguez, the conservative gay writer and critic whose prominence as a pundit in both print and electronic media makes him the most visible "Hispanic" public intellectual in the United States. Other writers from the region include Oscar Zeta Acosta, Gary Soto, and Helena María Viramontes. Valley visual art is represented by the agitprop *actos* of El Teatro Campesino and the plays and films of Luis Valdez, as well as the paintings, sculptures, and UFW graphics produced by the Royal Chicano Air Force. Many of these artists grew up working in the fields and they have produced a rich collection of work reflecting on such contexts. In the rest of this chapter I focus especially on the career of Ester Hernandez, whose images of skeletons are part of a larger body of farm worker visual culture in the 1980s and 1990s that helps bring into stark critical relief the connections between white masculinity and corporate agriculture.

During the Chicano/a movements of the 1960s and 1970s, activists and artists appropriated images from the popular broadsides of Jose Guadalupe Posada, a Mexican graphic artist who used skeletons to satirize the wealthy and the powerful and to represent the travails of the common people on the eve of the revolution. Posada's work informed the use of *calaveras* or images of skulls (and by extension, skeletons) in Chicano/a art protesting the wars in Vietnam and Central America as well as in pieces about the struggles of farm workers. Activist artists further drew on the visual practices of mourning and memory associated with the "Day of the Dead." As documented in Lourdes Portillo's film *La Ofrenda: The Days of the Dead* (1988), during the 1980s Chicanos/as and others used skeletons in altars and in public parades partly to protest the death and destruction caused by the Reagan administration's inaction in response to the AIDS epidemic, as well as its military interventions in Central America.

Hernandez is an important figure in that tradition. The child of Mexican farm workers and a farm worker herself for a while, she grew up in the agricultural community of Dinuba in the San Joaquin Valley and her life and work have been closely linked to the UFW. Hernandez partly traces her interest in visual technology to a complex family history of migration and labor: "My mother carried from her birthplace in North Central Mexico the ancient Mexican traditions of embroidery and gardening. My grandfather was a master carpenter who built religious sculptures in his spare time. On my paternal side, my Yaqui and Mexican father was an amateur photographer."[53] As a child, her art combined these influences and an engagement with mainstream U.S. and Mexican media: "My main interest was portraiture, using school models as well as my own family and friends. For an additional bag of French fries, I was always more than willing to add an Elvis Presley hairdo or Elizabeth Taylor eyebrows or a Maria Felix *lunar* for my family and friends. I also created designs for embroidery, as well as homemade tattoos."[54] Her artistic aspirations, however, were discouraged by the agribusiness economy that dominated the Valley. As Hernandez explains, "My high school counselors told me that my only possibility for becoming an artist was drawing facial composites for the police, who were constantly looking for Mexicans and Indios from the surrounding areas." In the Valley, the policing of Mexicans and Indians was often performed on behalf of agribusiness. After she graduated from high school in 1965, UFW protestors came to her town as part of the march to Sacramento but "were greeted by the police, and the ranchers and their dogs . . . The only thing I had seen that resembled it was the Civil Rights Movement in the South. Yet it wasn't African Americans, it was us. That was a turning point in my life."[55] At about the same time Hernandez was inspired by the UFW performance collective El Teatro Campesino. Later, she recalled that it impressed her and gave her strength when the group "blatantly made fools of the police and ranchers, right in front of them."[56]

In the early 1970s Hernandez moved to the Bay Area, attended Grove Street College and Laney College in Oakland, and joined a Latina mural collective in San Francisco. She ultimately enrolled in the Berkeley art department, but her experience there "was like stepping back into the institutions I had grown up with. The art department was, for the most part, filled with white, tenured, elderly men who were more interested in the past and academic trends than the present. They couldn't even pronounce my name, so they called me Chiquita or Rosarita. I quickly realized that my involvement and commitment to being a Latina artist was not valued by the Euro-centric, elitist establishment, especially those images that asserted the power and creativity of Latina women."[57] In addition the art school's celebration of individual white male artistic genius, and of abstract art over figurative art, clashed with Hernandez's often collaborative art projects that engaged concrete political contexts and struggles. A good example of such work from these years, and one of her most well-known images, is titled *La Virgen de Guadalupe defendiendo los derechos de los Chicanos / The Virgin of Guadalupe Defending the Rights of Chicanos* (1975) and was published on the cover of a Berkeley newspaper produced by a Third World feminist collective.[58]

In contrast to Lucas, who was also interested in painting but ultimately chose special effects–laden films as his medium, Hernandez favored the "low" technology of silkscreening, a choice that put her at odds both aesthetically and politically with the commercial art world. As she suggests, silkscreening "is great for getting my prints in numerous places at one time, as well as for making the price of my work accessible to the community. But commercial galleries tend to prefer originals simply because they are more valuable moneywise. Also, the political nature and subject matter of my art, mainly Latina–Native women, does not lend itself to the largely conservative commercial art galleries."[59] Dominant artistic institutions such as universities and art galleries celebrate the autonomy of the artistic field and its disengagement from politics; individual white male artists; and the unique work of art with high market value. Confronting the art world reminded Hernandez of "stepping back into the institutions [she] had grown up with" because, I would argue, they shared with agribusiness an investment in white male possessive individualism and private property. By contrast, her own work is linked to feminist, anti-racist, and anti-agribusiness movements.

The *calaveras* in Hernandez's posters and paintings assume multiple forms that, when taken together, undermine agribusiness efforts to appeal to a wholesome whiteness by revealing the face of death behind the industry's self-promotional mask. Hernandez sometimes uses skeletons as icons of corporate greed and destruction. Her silkscreen print for *Heroes and Saints* (1992), Cherríe Moraga's play about pesticide poisoning in a farm worker community, includes just such a corporate *calavera* (Plate 3).[60] The central portion of the poster appears to be based on an aerial photograph of a crop duster spraying a field with pesticides. The plane is captured as it flies across the field of the image, from left to right, and trails a widening stream of pesticides, tinted a bright chemical orange. Hernandez places the *calavera* in the top right hand corner of the poster, seemingly trailing the chemical current the plane leaves in its wake. In my reading, the skeleton partly represents the corporate officials who comfortably glide through life, skimming off the top, while standing on the backs of working people. The skeleton can also be read as an image of white nativism, or more precisely, of white nativism in tandem with agribusiness.

Recalling the scene she described above of ranchers, police, and dogs, in her artwork titled *The Beating of Dolores Huerta by the San Francisco Police* (1988), Hernandez uses a skeleton to represent politicians who attempt to mobilize police power and white male populism in support of corporate agendas.[61] It memorializes the nearly fatal beating that UFW Vice President Dolores Huerta received while protesting U.S. Vice President George H. W. Bush's fund-raising visit to San Francisco on September 14, 1988, during his presidential campaign against Massachusetts Governor Michael Dukakis. At the time the UFW was in the middle of a grape boycott in order to publicize the dangers of pesticides, and Chavez had recently completed the thirty-six-day fast discussed in the previous chapter. Three years earlier, Chavez had joined Dukakis in Boston for the governor's signing of a proclamation in support of the UFW boycott. During the presidential campaign, Bush attempted to capitalize on the proclamation by traveling to the Sun Maid raisin factory in the San Joaquin Valley town of Kingsburg to denounce the boycott and secure agribusiness support, no doubt aided by his campaign communications director, a Washington lobbyist who had represented Sun Maid.[62] He had already made two previous campaign trips to the area in which he participated in media events calculated to underline his commitment to agribusiness interests, including performances by "The California Raisins," a troupe of minstrel-like singers and dancers, sponsored by the California Raisin Advisory Board, that promoted the industry while dressed as giant raisins. In one campaign visit, Bush witnessed a California Raisin performance at a Sun Maid raisin plant near Hernandez's home (although outside the plant several people wearing homemade California Raisin costumes gathered to protest the Reagan–Bush administration's support for the Nicaraguan contras).[63] But on the day before his speech to wealthy donors at the St. Francis Hotel in San Francisco, Bush stopped at Sun Maid, where he condemned the boycott and, along with California Governor George Deukmejian, dramatically ate grapes for the cameras.[64]

During his presidential campaign, Bush attempted to represent a combination of conservative ideologies of free enterprise, anti-unionism, and a muscular law and order conservatism, all imaginatively bound together by appeals to white male populism. Anticipating his son's performances of agrarian whiteness, Bush Sr. attempted to distance himself from his Yale pedigree and privileged class background by telling reporters about his taste for country music and fried pork rinds. Just as his widely reported distaste for broccoli was framed as a sort of masculine protest against

Ester Hernandez, *The Beating of Dolores Huerta by the San Francisco Police* (1988), charcoal on pastel paper; courtesy of Ester Hernandez and Department of Special Collections, Cecil H. Green Library, Stanford University Libraries.

nagging wives and mothers, Bush's public ingestion of pesticide-sprayed grapes represented a "regular guy" protest against a radical Mexican union.[65] Indeed, young Republicans attending the September rally at Sun Maid carried signs reading "Real Men Eat Grapes."[66] The significance of the gesture was further reinforced by the way Bush self-consciously repeated a similar anti-union media event staged by Ronald Reagan, that icon of white populism in alliance with corporate power. Recalling and amplifying San Joaquin Valley styles of white male neoliberalism, Bush successfully appealed to many voters in the area, ultimately winning the Valley and the state. While accounting for a relatively small percentage of California voters, the agribusiness-dominated San Joaquin Valley often bears a disproportionate electoral influence, serving as a swing region between the northern and southern parts of the state.[67] The 1988 presidential campaign thus reminds us of the historical influence of agribusiness futurisms in dominant politics.

In an effort to counter Bush's pro-agribusiness publicity, Huerta followed him to San Francisco to join a protest of over a thousand people, "organized by a coalition of groups calling for everything from a non-interventionist policy toward Central America to more funding for AIDS research," where she planned to distribute a UFW press release.[68] Titled "Union Responds to Bush Attack on Grape Boycott," it included the following quotation from Huerta: "Cesar Chavez was willing to risk his life in a 36-day water-only fast to protect farm workers and consumers from poisonous pesticides. What does George Bush offer other than empty political rhetoric? Mr. Bush's statement demonstrates, once again, that he is simply wealthy, comfortable and insensitive to the needs of poor working people in our country. It also reveals his ignorance of the pesticide threat to the public and our environment."[69] Whereas Bush had attempted to paint himself as a conservative populist, Huerta emphasized his wealth and distance from the concerns of working people. The slight, fifty-eight-year-old labor leader was apparently trying to disseminate the press release when a policeman in riot gear lunged at her several times with his club, breaking several ribs and rupturing her spleen in the near-fatal attack.

The scene was partly captured on film by a local TV news camera positioned behind the policeman, and Hernandez reproduced this perspective in *The Beating of Dolores Huerta*. Pushing into the frame from the left and right, the heads and shoulders of two policemen press in on Huerta, whose face, shielded by her hand, appears between them, in the center of the image. The officers' helmeted heads loom large and phallic, visually reinforcing the long club that one of them raises against the union leader. In the top right corner is a small *calavera* that, like a puppet master, manipulates a web of bone-white strings attached to the attacking officer. Intervening between the skeleton and the scene of violence below, however, is a stylized image of the black UFW thunderbird, familiar from flags and other union graphics, which breaks the club with its talons and cuts some of the strings with its beak. Given the context that inspired the work, the skeleton that pulls the policeman's strings would seem to reference politicians like Bush, who placed the real and symbolic power of the state behind agribusiness. And more broadly, I read the menacing skeleton that pulls the policeman's strings as the face of white populism in partnership with corporate conservatism.

In her most famous work, the silkscreen print called *Sun Mad,* Hernandez helps make visible the consequences for women of color of the alliance between white nativism and agribusiness (Plate 4).[70] Historically, many agribusiness ads and labels have featured images of attractive young white women who imaginatively "come on" to the viewer, smiling and seeming to offer themselves, or at least their fruit, to the consumer. These flirtatious farmers' daughters are complemented by the many images of rosy-cheeked farm children that have also adorned agribusiness products. Such images represent agribusiness as though it were the small family farm of white agrarianism, not a transnational network of corporate connections. Recalling the idealized image of the family within discourses about the family farm, fruit and vegetable labels featuring young white women and children harvesting crops serve to disappear women's work by naturalizing it as a contribution to the family farm. Such representations also whitewash the labor of the many women of color who work in the fields of the Valley.

One such image, and the source for Hernandez's *Sun Mad,* is of course the label found on Sun Maid raisins. In its genesis, the corporate trademark seems calculated to make the product appear as an innocent member of the small farm family. In 1915 the eventual model for the image, Lorraine Collett Petersen, worked at a raisin-packing house in Fresno when she was hired for fifteen dollars a week by the California Associated Raisin Company to serve as the corporation's "ambassador" to the Panama–Pacific International Exposition. Dressed in a blue bonnet and a white blouse, she strolled among the fairgoers and passed out samples of raisins from a large wooden platter. In one promotion Petersen even rode in an airplane over the fair and dropped raisins from the sky. Midway through the exposition she returned to Fresno to participate in a local "Raisin Day Parade," where she was spotted by a visiting Sun Maid executive. Taken by her substitution of a red bonnet for the blue one provided by the company, he asked Petersen to sit for an oil painting that would ultimately serve as the basis for the famous trademark. Although the image has been altered over the years, its basic elements have remained constant, forming one of the world's most widely recognized corporate logos: backlit, as it were, by the stylized rays of the sun, a smiling, rosy-cheeked young white woman in a red bonnet holds an ornate wooden tray overflowing with grapes. The image is so iconic that in 1988, the same year as Bush's campaign visits to the Sun Maid plant, the company donated Petersen's original bonnet to the Smithsonian Institute, which also holds a copy of Hernandez's *Sun Mad*.[71]

One striking aspect of the Sun Maid trademark is the way it appropriates women's labor and converts it into an advertisement. Part of the reason Petersen was picked to represent the company's product was because she actually worked in a packing shed. She was featured with the costume and tools of her job, including a bonnet for protection from the sun and the wooden platter used to hold grapes. Large numbers of women worked for agribusiness companies, and by the 1930s many of them were Mexicans who engaged in union organizing and strikes. But as transmuted by corporate commodity aesthetics, the image of the raisin worker becomes an ad for white nativism. Recalling the conventions of backlighting in Western art analyzed by Richard Dyer, the bright yellow sun that imaginatively lights the "Sun Maid" from behind serves to foreground her whiteness. Even the grapes she holds are Thompson or "white" grapes. The trademark, moreover, represents the figure of the female worker within the naturalizing framework of the patriarchal family farm. Although in 1915 Petersen was an adult woman of marriageable age, in the label she became a "maid," an unmarried girl presumably still living at home and contributing her labor to her family. The phrase "Sun Maid" further naturalizes and idealizes the process of corporate agriculture, suggesting that it is the heat of the sun, and not low-wage workers, that makes raisins.

As Hernandez explains, she began thinking about *Sun Mad* when she learned about dangerous levels of pesticides in the water tables of her hometown. On stationery emblazoned "City of Dinuba, Raisinland U.S.A.," the director of public works informed Hernandez's mother that four of the city's eight wells were contaminated by dibromochloropropane, a pesticide used in agriculture. As she explains:

> *Sun Mad* has to do with going home to visit my mother in 1979. My mother saved articles out of the newspaper and notices from the mail that talked about the water contamination by pesticides in the San Joaquin Valley, especially in our barrio. For two years I thought about it. Then my mind went back to the work that I did when I was a farm worker and to the work that was still going on in that immediate area—growing grapes for the raisin industry. I focused on something personal, the Sun Maid box. Slowly I began to visualize how to transform the Sun Maid and unmask the truth behind the wholesome figures of agribusiness.[72]

The Sun Maid label is "personal" for Hernandez because it pretends to represent the kinds of farm labor that she and her community had actually performed—and continue to perform. In one sense, then, recalling *ofrendas* and related rituals of mourning and memory, Hernandez's *calaveras* memorialize the exploited, the damaged, and the dead, farm workers who have been beaten by the police, poisoned by pesticides, or simply worked to death—which in part explains why Hernandez incorporated *Sun Mad* into a memorial to her father in the form of an installation for a 1989 Day of the Dead exhibition at the National Museum of Mexican Art in Chicago. As art critic Amalia Mesa-Bains explains, in front of the *Sun Mad* image:

> this *ofrenda* included a circle of stones enclosing a mound of dirt. In the center of the offering was the farmworker's hat and scarf, a poignant reminder of a life of toil and dignity in one of America's most shamefully exploitative industries. . . . Despite its direct social commentary, *Sun Mad* implies through its specter of death a melancholy remembrance of all those whose suffering has gone unrecognized. Hernandez's work is a mournful homage to the losses in her own family and to the children of farm workers whose birth defects and illnesses remain the unacknowledged price of agricultural profit.[73]

In my reading, *Sun Mad* also satirizes the Devil's bargain between patriarchal white nativism and corporate conservatism. Hence in her revision of the corporate logo, Hernandez de-fetishizes agribusiness representations by connecting them to material labor conditions. In Marx's famous account, commodity fetishism refers to the ways in which the symbolic attractions of commodities take on an imaginary life of their own that partly displaces from public view and reflection the human labor that produced them. By contrast, in examples like the Sun Maid raisin trademark, the labor of making raisins is not hidden; rather, the representation of labor itself becomes a fetish, constructed from the image repertoire of white nativism and abstracted from the actual labor conditions of corporate agriculture. *Sun Mad* undermines that fetish by making visible the human costs of agricultural production. Hernandez thus employs a rigorously de-reifying gaze, revealing the racialized and gendered forms of exploitation obscured in corporate advertising.

By basing her image on the Sun Maid label, Hernandez is able to take advantage of its high visibility, and by extension the corporation's vast publicity machine, to further the visibility of her critical image. Hernandez's use of visual technology is formally complex and experimental in ways that contradict dominant assumptions about those aesthetic qualities, in part because she participates in a larger field of politically engaged farm worker visual culture. *Sun Mad* started as a silkscreen print, and large numbers of prints have been made, often finding their way into UFW marches and other protests. *Sun Mad* has been extensively reproduced on postcards and T-shirts that have been incorporated into protests as well as the marches and ceremonies memorializing Cesar Chavez after his death, but such reproductions have also served to disseminate the image in everyday contexts and spaces. In this way *Sun Mad* infects Sun Maid, so that once you have seen Hernandez's image it is impossible not to think of it whenever you see an ad for raisins. And to the extent that commodity images like the Sun Maid ad represent congealed labor time, by effectively diverting a portion of the corporation's advertising budget for her anticorporate image, Hernandez effectively reappropriates a portion of surplus value in order to help make labor exploitation visible. With this mode of satire, Hernandez uses corporate visual culture against itself, leading Dolores Huerta to write that "*Sun Mad* is made memorable by Ester's use of artistic vengeance—a vengeance without hatred or violence."[74] Whereas Lucas employs an idolized image of the white farm boy in the service of a Vader-like corporate empire, Hernandez appropriates an agribusiness image for the farm worker movement. Recalling the martial artist of *La Virgen de Guadalupe defendiendo los derechos de los Chicanos,* the militant *virgen* defending the rights of Chicanos with a karate kick, Hernandez's *Sun Mad* counters the agribusiness domination of the visual field by using the force and momentum of San Joaquin Valley neoliberalism against itself.

Afterword
Farm Worker Futurism Now

Like other critics of the UFW, journalist and activist Randy Shaw partly
narrates the history of the union in terms of decline, but as the title of his
book suggests—*Beyond the Fields: Cesar Chavez, the UFW, and the Struggle
for Justice in the 21st Century*—the story he ultimately tells is more complicated. Shaw documents how the UFW produced several generations
of organizers and activists who have been central to the contemporary
global labor movement represented by immigrants' rights organizations
and unions such as UNITE HERE and the Service Employee International
Union (SEIU), the union that represented the striking janitors and that
organized the rolling hunger strike at USC discussed in the previous chapter. All of which suggests that farm worker futurisms have been widely
disseminated in a variety of influential forms. I thus conclude by analyzing
legacies of the historical farm worker movement beyond the fields, in the
context of new labor systems and new labor movements. In what follows I
focus on the dissemination of farm worker futurism in three arenas: speculative fictions that view racialized, low-wage-labor exploitation as central to
new forms of empire partly modeled on forms of farm fascism; the use of
mobile phones in the organization of the immigrants' rights movement as
an echo of the farm worker appropriation of technology from below; and
the history of struggles over the production and use of computer hardware
in relationship to conflicts over technology in agricultural production.

Speculative Fictions of Labor, Empire, and Farm Worker Futurity
A trio of twenty-first-century speculative fictions suggest that farm worker
futurisms serve as a powerful critical matrix for thinking about contemporary imperialism as based in modes of labor exploitation with historical

antecedents in corporate agriculture. All three works in effect extrapolate from the farm worker critique of farm fascism in order to understand neoliberal imperialism.

The independent film *The Gatekeeper* (2002) presents a dystopian narrative about undocumented Mexican workers in the context of the U.S. "war on terror" that builds on the longer history of farm fascism. Made on the cheap for around $200,000, the film was written and directed by John Carlos Frey, who also stars as Adam Fields, a self-hating half–Mexican U.S. citizen who passes as white and who works as a Border Patrol agent. Set in San Diego, the film opens with images of migrants crossing the border at night as seen through the green light of night-vision goggles. At the same time, an anti-immigrant talk show called *The National Radio Patrol: Defending America from the Mexican Invasion* can be heard on the sound track. It soon becomes apparent that agent Fields is watching the migrants as he talks on his mobile phone with the host of the show. He ultimately alerts a group of nativist vigilantes and joins them in attacking the migrants. Deciding that his group of vigilantes needs to launch a broader offensive, Fields subsequently comes up with a sensational scheme to draw attention to the inadequacies of border enforcement. Equipped with a GPS device, a miniature digital camera, and a mobile phone, he proposes to go undercover and join a group of immigrants illegally entering the United States on the Fourth of July; as part of their celebration of national independence, his vigilante friends will then swoop down, apprehend the migrants, and film the caper for broadcast.

Throughout his odyssey, we see repeated shots of the migration process from the perspective of Fields's hidden camera, footage presumably to be used in the vigilante video. His plan backfires, however, when two white drug traffickers intervene and kill the vigilantes. Fields's fate is sealed when he loses his mobile phone and, along with the other migrants, is captured by the drug traffickers and made to carry gallon jugs filled with the chemicals used in making methamphetamine. He is then transported to a heavily fortified and electronically surveilled ranch on the U.S. side of the border, where he is forced at gunpoint to manufacture meth in a makeshift lab. Departing dramatically from the hispanophilic/hispanophobic film conventions for representing drug traffickers, the villains of *The Gatekeeper* are instead represented as a sadistic white father and son team who recall the patriarchal corporate agriculture of California history. The white meth ranchers, moreover, resemble the members of Fields's nativist vigilante group, suggesting the ways that

Farm worker meth lab. *The Gatekeeper* (John Carlos Frey, 2002).

forms of racialized fascism have mediated between nativism and corporate agriculture. Finally, as a post-9/11 film, the premise of *The Gatekeeper* anticipates the embedding of journalists among military units during the Bush administration invasion of Afghanistan and Iraq, and thus suggests parallels between the war on terror and the history of agribusiness militarization.

Sleep Dealer (2008) also draws connections between the history of agribusiness domination and the contemporary war on terror. At the start of the film Memo and his father must purchase water from a reservoir in Oaxaca enclosed by barbed wire and chain-link fence and patrolled by automated drones and paramilitary "frogmen." Here two icons of agribusiness technological "progress," the dam and the plane, are represented as weapons of a U.S. empire enforcing the privatization of common resources. The initial drone attack that kills Memo's father is part of a larger U.S. offensive directed at "aqua terrorists" opposed to a massive private dam and water pipeline owned by the "Del Rio Water Inc." The private water company figures not only contemporary efforts to privatize water in Latin America but also the large-scale, state-sponsored water projects such as dams and canals that have historically fed California agribusiness. Recalling *Star Wars* and the destruction of the Death Star, in the climax of *Sleep Dealer* Memo and Luz help Rudy, the Mexican American soldier from San Diego, access an automated drone and fly it across the border to destroy the dam. The film thus concludes with a utopian fantasy of seizing technology from below, in opposition to state-supported corporate enclosures, as water streams through a rift opened in the dam by the rebel drone pilot. (A related fantasy of technology takeover from below animates Rivera's Internet-based project *LowDrone,* which invites visitors to remotely control "the world's first aerial lowrider armed with video surveillance capabilities" and fly it over the border fence from Tijuana to the U.S. side.)[1] The break in the dam is revealed to Memo (and the audience) in a digital video booth—a near-future technology of time–space compression that recalls migrant uses of telegraphy to communicate and wire money—where Memo visits with his mother and brother in Oaxaca via a screen in Tijuana. When Memo's brother directs a camera at the dam outside, the sight and sound of rushing water fills Memo's booth. By incorporating footage of water into an immersive, aural and visual sensorium surrounding a migrant worker, *Sleep Dealer* projects a utopian vision of de-privatization and equal access to common resources such as water.

In a similar vein, Rosaura Sánchez and Beatrice Pita's novella *Lunar Braceros, 2125–2148* extrapolates from agribusiness histories of exploitation and farm worker disposability to project a future where low-wage workers of color are forced to migrate to the moon to contain radioactive corporate waste. The world is partly ruled by "Cali-Texas," a police state incorporating northern Mexico and the U.S. Southwest plus Alaska and Hawaii, and representing the interests of "the transnational agri-business corporations and the four big bio-techs, companies that controlled anything and everything that had to do with technology transfer, informatics, and any kind of power generation."[2] The agricultural and other exports of Cali-Texas enable it to dominate the south by destroying Latin American industries, although trade confederations and indigenous groups in South America fight back, claiming a tenuous and embattled relative autonomy. The novel is largely composed of dispatches in the form of "nanotexts" from a "lunar bracero," a Latina named Lydia, to her son, Pedro, living in an indigenous community in the jungles of Ecuador. Implicitly referencing the history of carceral farm worker camps and, more recently, the conversion of agricultural land to prisons in the San Joaquin Valley, Lydia explains that she was born and raised on a razor-wire "reservation" in Fresno, one of many "internal colonial sites" created to contain "expendable . . . surplus population[s]." In a kind of internalization of the speculative labor scenario in *Sleep Dealer,* on the Fresno rez the "new

A migrant video booth and a projection of the commons. Memo
surrounded by water in *Sleep Dealer* (Alex Rivera, 2008).

'vagrants' or 'migros'"—the homeless and the unemployed—"became a
controlled laboratory labor force" and "produced not only the usual goods
that had formerly been shipped south to sweatshops and assembly plant,
but also . . . weapons, secret surveillance instrumentation, robotic instruments, and new telecommunications systems . . . Bio-labs seeking to create
artificial organs, new medications, enhanced bodies, and to artificially
develop new species had free rein in the Reservation."[3] Lydia is among
a small number of rez residents whose scientific and technical aptitudes

make them useful to the transnats and who are thus provided university educations and required to work in jobs off-rez. After joining a group of "anarchos" protesting the Fresno rez, Lydia is imprisoned but offered a reduced sentence if she agrees to become a "techo" on the moon disposing of radioactive waste. Reassured that her wages will be transferred to an account for her parents that will enable them to purchase their release from the reservation, Lydia agrees to join a "motley crew" of seven other "lunar braceros."

At the center of the novella is a story of lunar bracero disposability and insurrection that combines conventions from science fiction film and literature with histories of agricultural labor exploitation and resistance. While examining a suspicious waste container Lydia and her partner, a Mexican Chinese techo named Frank, discover that it is filled with the corpses of other lunar braceros. Rather than transporting workers back to earth at the end of their contracts, the corporation kills them instead and disposes of the bodies in the waste containers. They further learn that in anticipation of their deaths the company has kept their wages rather than transferring them to their reservation families. Lydia, Frank, and the other techos rebel against their manager, hijack a spaceship, and make an armed escape from the moon to Tierra del Fuego, where they stage a UN press conference on the Cali-Texas–controlled territories of the moon. Hounded by the lethal forces of the transnational corporation, the group of rebel lunar braceros scatter and some are killed or disappear, but Lydia and Frank ultimately free Lydia's sister, Leticia, and along with Leticia's lover, Maggie, and others they live and work on a collective indigenous farming community in the Amazon. Lydia leaves her "nanotexts" for Pedro as she and Frank make their trip north to raise a rebellion against the reservations. As the novella ends, the future remains open to possibility but also to great danger and loss; Pedro writes that "we've all heard about the social upheaval that broke out three years after they left," but his parents have "disappeared and we haven't had any communication" from them since then. Pedro resolves to join a small group of former lunar braceros and their families and friends as they travel north, to search for his parents and "join them in their struggle."[4]

In contrast to *The Gatekeeper,* which ends with the funeral of a migrant worker, both *Sleep Dealer* and *Lunar Braceros* remain guardedly open to alternate possibilities, speculative forms of futurity supported by recent popular movements in Latin America against neoliberal privatization, especially of water, that threaten subsistence agriculture. Indeed, both *Sleep Dealer* and *Lunar Braceros* draw on concepts of the "new en-closures" as theorized by the Midnight Notes Collective (MNC). The "new enclosures" is the term the MNC uses to describe the privatization of common land and resources in contexts of neoliberal globalization. It is derived from a history of the old enclosures, "a counter-revolutionary process whereby after a century of high wages and breakdown of feudal authority, beginning in the late 1400s, farmers in England were expropri-ated from their land and commons by state officials and landlords. They were turned into paupers, vagabonds and beggars, and later into waged workers, while the land was put to work to feed the incipient international market for agricultural commodities." At the same time one could de-scribe European conquest and colonization in the Americas in similar terms, and the MNC extends its analysis to the Third World "debt crisis" and bank-imposed "structural readjustment" of the 1980s and 1990s that in many ways anticipated the more recent emergence of a debt crisis in Europe and the United States.

From there it is not hard to imagine agribusiness as a crucial part of the ongoing history of enclosure that continues to inform the new enclo-sures of neoliberalism. *Sleep Dealer* and *Lunar Braceros* draw on the col-lectivist futures projected by the farm worker movement but also, more precisely, on forms of farm worker futurity like those represented by the NFLU banner with the slogan "To the Disinherited Belong the Future" (see chapter 1). Both works represent the speculative labor of imagin-ing a future as such, not an accomplished alternative future but rather the future as possibility, the expectation of an unknown and uncertain "future space of time." In *Sleep Dealer* the rogue drone pilot Rudy boards a Mexican bus headed south, while Luz and Memo face an uncertain fu-ture; in *Lunar Braceros* the fate of Lydia and the forces of opposition she represents are unknown. In neither case is utopia achieved or a definitive future won, and the prospects for transformation remain fleeting and fu-gitive, but both narratives close with openings, positing futurity, or the pressing but unfulfilled desire for a future.

Lunar Braceros, in particular, opens the future to possibilities be-yond the enclosures of patriarchy and the privatization of reproduction. In contrast with the mutually reinforcing ideological embrace between property and patriarchy as analyzed in chapter 2, where fatherhood is made natural and sacred by its association with private property and vice versa, *Lunar Braceros* depicts a kind of queer reproduction in common. Lydia's first love was Gabriel, another tech from the Fresno rez who was ultimately killed by the corporation but not before freezing one of her fertilized eggs, which is ultimately implanted in Lydia's lesbian sister, and together their respective partners and other family and friends raise Pedro and another adopted child in the jungle before migrating north. By thus positing the possibility of the future as such within the brutal limits of imperial labor exploitation, *Sleep Dealer* and *Lunar Braceros* ask how material conditions and social relations would have to be transformed in order to support global expectations of the future, or the future as commons.

Technology from Below: Migrant Workers and Mobile Phones

Recalling agribusiness contexts where technology became objects and means of struggle, mobile phones have proven central to recent struggles over nativism and immigrant rights. Victor Hanson, the influential nativist and former employer of Mexican farm workers in the San Joaquin Valley whom I discussed in the previous chapter, has complained that with their easy access to TVs, cell phones, and other cheap electronics, Mexican immigrants contribute to the increasing immorality and dumbing down of U.S. culture.[5] Similarly, a widely circulated nativist YouTube video for a song called "Press One for English" vilifies the influence of Mexican immigrants on U.S. communications technologies.[6] Meanwhile, nativist vigilantes such as the Minutemen have armed themselves with cell phones, digital cameras, and aerial drones in order to stop the movement of people and drugs across the border, performing the kind of techno-nativism referenced in *The Gatekeeper*.

At the same time, pro-immigrant organizations have increasingly used new media technology to combat both vigilante and state-sponsored forms of nativism that would criminalize the undocumented. Protests against 2005's "Border Protection, Anti-terrorism, and Illegal Immigration Control Act" (H.R. 4437), for example, included extensive use of new media technology. While the massive national pro-immigrant rallies of 2006 were largely organized "in traditional fashion with unions, churches, Hispanic organizations and Spanish-language radio . . . there were [also] hundreds of smaller protest actions happening without the input of any centralized organization. They happened almost simultaneously across the nation and involved hundreds of cities and tens of thousands of mostly high school students driven by Internet networks and mobile text messaging."[7] In contrast with nativists like Hanson, who interpret migrant appropriations of technology in dystopian terms, scholars of mobile phones describe migrant "mobile swarms" or "smart mobs" as both "a milestone

Hackear para Principiantes by R. Dominguez. *Sleep Dealer* (Alex Rivera, 2008).

of what is already here" and "a 'beta test' of what is coming."[8] Despite their differences, both narrative framings fetishize technological novelty in ways that obscure longer social histories in which migrants have made critical and creative uses of new technologies of time–space compression.

Ricardo Dominguez is a key, mediating figure in the history connecting farm worker futurism to what he calls electronic civil disobedience (ECD). Dominguez is one of the cofounders of Electronic Disturbance Theater (EDT), an activist art group that in 1998 created virtual sit-in technology or "denial of service" computer protests in solidarity with the Zapatistas. In homage to that work, *Sleep Dealer* includes a scene where Memo hacks into military communications networks on a makeshift computer using a book titled *Hackear Para Principiantes (Hacking for Beginners)* by "R. Dominguez." With his digitally based performances or what he calls "gestures," Dominguez has effectively recast prior articulations of civil disobedience—from Thoreau to Gandhi, Martin Luther King, and Cesar Chavez—for contemporary, Internet-based projects for social justice. As the leading theorist and practitioner of ECD, Dominquez helped to invent and deploy a conception of the Internet not simply as a mode of communication about inequality and social injustice but as itself a site of struggles against oppression. His gestures reveal how power changes with computer networks, compelling artists and activists to combine both actions in physical space such as traditional protests and marches, with related kinds of interventions in digital spaces, including virtual sit-ins.

Just as more familiar forms of protest slow the city traffic surrounding them, or just as sit-ins disrupt the regular flow of activity in buildings and other public places, virtual sit-ins are organized efforts to slow or in some cases briefly stop the workings of a website. With the other members of the Electronic Disturbance Theater, Dominquez developed and creatively and effectively used "FloodNet," an Internet application that enables hundreds and often thousands of users to request from large Internet servers information that they do not contain, thus triggering the server to repeatedly post error messages that both slow down its functioning (and in some cases cause a server to briefly stop, but without permanently damaging it) while at the same time lodging symbolic protests in the heart of power. One of Dominguez's most well-known and creative applications of FloodNet was in 1998, in support of the Zapatista movement in Chiapas, Mexico, in its efforts to draw attention to the dispossession and displacement of indigenous peoples that resulted from NAFTA. In one gesture he orchestrated, FloodNet users were able to upload messages to the server logs of the Mexican government's website by purposely asking for a nonexistent URL titled "justice" or "human rights," leading the server to repeatedly return messages like "justice_ not found" or "human rights_not found." In another Dominguez application of FloodNet, users effectively uploaded to the Mexican state server the names of indigenous people who have recently been massacred by the military. Dominguez has organized similar forms of electronic civil disobedience directed at Lufthansa Airlines for its work with the German government to deport immigrants (as a result, the airline ended its collaboration with the state) and at the World Economic Forum.

Dominguez builds on farm worker traditions of civil disobedience in the sense that FloodNet performances are nonviolent (they do not materially damage networks or harm people) and radically transparent (performances are publicly announced and participants identify themselves). Building on so many of the great twentieth-century movements for social justice, ECD dramatizes inequality for the digital age, drawing attention to the disparity between powerful institutions and the everyday and symbolic forms of resistance wielded by the relatively powerless. Dominguez's work with the Zapatistas, for example, was at first imagined as a virtual companion to the Zapatista Air Force. Recalling the Royal Chicano Air Force, the Zapatista Air Force was a form of political theater in which rebels bombarded Mexican military barracks with paper airplanes inscribed with messages like "Soldiers, we know that poverty has made you sell your lives and souls. I also am poor, as are millions. But you are worse off, for defending our exploiter." Shortly thereafter EDT released its software so that, in the words of Jill Lane, "activists could mount their own aerial attack on any web site." As Lane continues, such gestures ultimately reveal "the incommensurate force and aggression that underwrites the policies of the government and military; thousands of armed troops and real airplanes are dispatched to 'fight' communities armed with little more than paper" and code.[9]

In 2008 Dominguez participated in "The Port Huron Project," a series of performances of antiwar speeches from the 1960s and 1970s by Coretta Scott King, Howard Zinn, Angela Davis, Stokely Carmichael, and others organized by artist Mark Tribe. As his contribution Dominguez delivered the antiwar speech by Cesar Chavez analyzed in chapter 2, which focuses on the social and cultural forces that support gendered technologies of violence—including the use of guns by the big growers, the police, and private security forces—in ways that encourage young male farm workers to "find their manhood at end of a gun" by "kill[ing] other poor farm workers in Southeast Asia." Like Chavez, Dominguez performed the speech in LA's Exposition Park, in the shadow of USC, to a clapping audience cheering "Sí se puede!" The performance was captured on digital video and displayed on MTV's oversized HD screen in Times Square, playing every hour, Monday through Friday, for about a month in 2008. It has since screened as part of museum installations and is widely available on the Internet.[10]

At nearly the same time, starting in 2007, Dominguez, working as an associate professor with researchers at b.a.n.g. lab at the University of California, San Diego's CALIT2, created the "Transborder Immigrant Tool," an application enabling migrants to use inexpensive mobile phones to find water between northern Mexico and the U.S. Southwest and to access "survival poetry." As Dominguez explains it:

> With the Transborder Immigrant Tool, we are taking a technology, the GPS system and a cell phone system, which, again, are very attuned, at this moment in time, to attachment to the body. And so the Transborder Immigrant Tool does continue the history of electronic civil disobedience in creating a code that basically performs the belief that there is a higher law that needs to be brought to the foreground:

Farm worker futurism on the Jumbotron. Ricardo Dominguez performing
Cesar Chavez (2008).

a universal *common* law of the rights of safe passage. And so the tool
calls forth this sense that there is a community of artists who are
willing to foreground the higher law. We connect to the histories of
higher law within the US, from civil disobedience to the underground
railroad. So, the performative matrix that b.a.n.g. lab and Electronic
Disturbance Theater has always tried to establish is indeed a deep
connection between code and the body—a deep connection between
code and those bodies that are outside of the regime of concern in
terms of rights, in terms of consideration, in terms of being a community worthy of some sense of universal rights. (emphasis added)[11]

With its emphasis on common rights of safe passage, Dominguez's theory
and practice of electronic civil disobedience builds on ideas about the
commons crystallized by the UFW. The Transborder Immigrant Tool, in
other words, is a technology of futurity, which asks how would the world
need to be different in order to sustain the universal expectation of a future as such, including for undocumented border crossers.

Farm Worker Futurism and the Production of Computer Hardware
The UFW's contradictory, early adoption of new computer technology
helped directly and indirectly shape labor organizing in the computer industries of Silicon Valley. By the mid-1970s the UFW had taken a decid-

edly computational or cybernetic turn and increasingly invested in systems theory, communications technology, and computers in ways that coincided with the historical emergence of what Manuel Castells calls "The Internet Galaxy." According to Miriam Pawel, in those years "Chavez became intrigued by the science of 'management,' and saw salvation in a retired navy management guru" and "systems design expert" named Crosby Milne, who offered his help to the union in 1976 as part of "his patriotic duty in the nation's bicentennial year." Milne promoted a theory popular in corporate business literature since the mid-1960s called "Management by Objective," a system in which managers and subordinates identify and graph the progress of SAMs, or Strategic, Achievable, and Measurable objectives. With "its neat charts and boxes" and "clear lines of authority," the use of the SAM system to organize the work at union headquarters was further complemented and supported by the UFW's construction of a federally supported microwave communications network that broadcast "Radio Campesino" and linked union headquarters to a clinic and farm worker social services center. By the 1980s the UFW had not only adopted the relatively new technology of home video but also home computers for producing donor databases and mass mailings as well as for designing pro-union visual images.

The UFW's appropriation of new computer technologies was contradictory. On the one hand, it combined the kind of fetishization of technology's ability to supposedly resolve social contradiction that partly characterized the early history of the Internet, with a Cold War mania for systems of technocratic organization and control. On the other hand, artists working with the UFW such as Barbara Carrasco employed new computer software to produce challenging new images, including a piece of computer-generated animation highlighting the dangers of pesticides. Anticipating Dominquez's Times Square project, Carrasco's piece was produced in support of the UFW boycott in New York, one of the largest markets in the world for California table grapes. It was screened every twenty minutes during the month of July in 1988 on the giant "Spectacolor" billboard atop 1 Times Square, in between ads for Raid's "Max Roach Bait" and director James Cameron's underwater alien film titled *The Abyss*.[12] Since the early twentieth century Times Square has been the world epicenter of dazzling forms of commodity fetishism, culminating in electric "spectaculars," giant animated billboards including "a blinking penguin for Kool cigarettes, a clown tossing quoits in the shape of the Ballantine ale logo . . . an animated cartoon for Old Gold cigarettes," a steaming coffee cup advertising A & P Coffee, and, most famously, a billboard for Camel cigarettes "which puffed out five-foot-wide smoke rings of steam."[13] By 1961 the iconic 1 Times Square, formerly home of the *New York Times,* was emptied of tenants and largely turned into a giant hollow advertisement platform for electronic billboards that converted "dead labor" into mesmerizing spectacles of seemingly living, breathing commodities. By contrast, Carrasco's animated billboard symbolically reverses that process: it begins with a pesticide-spraying biplane flying toward the viewer, which leaves the word "PESTICIDES!" in its wake; cuts to a scene of a farm worker picking grapes who falls prone in the fields as a fine LED pesticide spray rains on the body; and ends with an image of a cluster of grapes made out of human skulls. Carrasco thus used the technologies of computer animation and e-commodity fetishism to de-reifying effect by visualizing the dependence of grape production on farm worker death.

This history of the UFW's cybernetic turn extends to the labor politics of California's Silicon Valley, which is itself built on a longer history of agribusiness domination in the region. The future home to high-tech industry was previously a center of agricultural production and hence the employment of farm workers, which is why Galarza worked there in the 1950s and in part why Chavez began his life as a community organizer in nearby San Jose. These connections between agribusiness and the computer business, moreover, are visible in the recent history of Silicon Valley and the "dot-com" boom of the 1990s.

Many Silicon Valley companies have taken an active interest in archiving and presenting their corporate histories, but perhaps none more than the Intel Corporation, the world's largest maker of semiconductor chips, the inventor of the microprocessors in most personal computers, and a digital pioneer in the fabrication of historical memory. It operates the Intel Museum and Intel Corporate Archives, which includes both online components and a material incarnation at company headquarters in Santa Clara, California. As articulated on its website in 2009, the museum's mission is to collect, preserve, and exhibit "Intel corporate history for the purpose of increasing employee, customer and public awareness of Intel innovations, technologies and branding in an interactive and educational manner." It is geared toward parents and children as well as teachers and students, thousands of whom every year visit the museum where, among other things, they get to simulate the experience of working at Intel. A multimedia presentation in the "Intel Culture Theater" promises

PESTICIDES! Computer animation by Barbara Carrasco, Times Square (1988).

to let visitors "see what it's like to work at the world's largest computer chip manufacturer, and learn more about Intel's risk-taking and results-oriented—yet fun—business environment." The "fun" part is represented by the figure of the worker wearing what in the industry is called a "bunny suit." The white bunny suits, which cover workers from head to toe and include a visored helmet with a battery-operated air filter unit, are worn in the company's large white clean rooms or microchip fabrication facilities. In the gift store one can buy plush dolls representing clean room workers and T-shirts decorated with dancing employees. An interactive exhibit devoted to the company's "Brand Program" prominently features its successful trademark image of an excited bunny-suited worker jumping in the air with upstretched arms and splayed fingers. One particularly popular exhibit presents a simulated employee locker room where adults are invited to help children "try on a bunny suit and imagine you are going to work in an Intel fab." The museum's website depicts a little girl of color being helped into a bunny suit. A subsequent photo shows a bunny-suited child, body and face obscured by the costume, leaping in the air in imitation of the Intel trademark. While it is not surprising that a corporation would attempt to persuade people to identify with its products, Intel encourages museum visitors to interact with both Intel hardware and a virtual version of the work process, inviting people to take pleasure in performing an Intel "brand" based on images of happy workers.[14]

In contrast with conventional theories of fetishism in which commodities obscure the labor of the workers who produce them, like the Sun Maid raisin company (see chapter 3), Intel incorporates its workers into its advertising, making an idealized image of its labor relations part of the pitch for its products in ways that displace the material costs and consequences of working in such clean rooms. The image of the little girl of color in the bunny suit is part of a corporate memory-making machine that disappears the work-related illnesses and injuries of low-wage Asian and Latin American migrant workers in Silicon Valley, not only in the clean rooms but also among the poorly paid janitors and service workers who support the regional high-tech economy.[15] The company's positive spin on Valley labor relations forms part of a broad cultural offensive against organized labor. The Intel Museum and Intel Corporate Archives are self-consciously aimed at (re)producing a historical memory of Intel innovation in labor relations, and visitors are repeatedly informed about how the company was founded in opposition to hierarchical, East Coast firms and hence developed in a more open and egalitarian manner that supported both teamwork and a meritocratic system of individual achievement. Although the benefits of this unique business culture have not extended to low-wage workers of color, their images and simulated experiences are nonetheless incorporated into the museum in ways that make labor appear to be a kind of playful risk-taking or heroic play, and suggest that labor unions are unnecessary relics of the past. Intel's self-representation recalls agribusiness futurism, where technology and the rationalization of labor promises to make labor conflicts a thing of the past.

Even though, or perhaps *because,* low-wage clean room workers are relatively marginalized within the material process of production, they have been symbolically central to the way Intel reconstructs its history, and by extension, to the historical origins of the digital "revolution."[16] Intel founder Robert Noyce, himself an amateur photographer, worked closely with several commercial photographers who produced images for ads, annual reports, and celebrations of company anniversaries, many of which prominently featured bunny-suited employees.[17] For example, a glossy 1984 magazine marking Intel's fifteenth anniversary titled *A Revolution in Progress . . . A History of Intel to Date* included a portrait of a bunny-suited worker on its cover and a section about the history of the bunny suit inside. The magazine also included a 1977 photo of a "start-up team" of fab workers in white bunny suits and Stormtrooper masks surrounding their "leader," a computer engineer wearing a Darth Vader mask.[18]

Why would the company want to dress up its history in *Star Wars* costumes? From one perspective this choice suggests that, like Lucasfilm or Industrial Light and Magic, Intel is a dominant corporate empire. Indeed, the photo illustrates a story about the history of the company's international expansion titled "The Sun Never Sets on Intel." But here the blunt celebration of corporate imperialism is softened by association with a nostalgic image reminiscent of boyish fun. At the same time the image tells us something about the corporation's historical view of its labor relations. In a section titled "Inside Intel: The Evolution of a Culture," Intel's "corporate values" of openness, individual meritocracy, and teamwork are enumerated in ways that seemingly dissolve differences between management and labor. Similarly, in the caption to the *Star Wars* photo, workers become members of a "start-up team" and the manager becomes "team leader." The magazine thus displaces an actual history of labor struggles in Silicon Valley, first in agriculture and then in more recent high-tech industries, with an image representing the mythic struggles in *Star Wars.*

As this example suggests, *Star Wars* has become an important reference point for corporations and workers in Silicon Valley. As Michael Kanellos, a journalist who covers Valley IT industries, argues, the film "stands as perhaps one of the greatest influences, if not the greatest force, on the development of the high-technology industry. Released in 1977, the original *Star Wars* inspired thousands with the belief that a better life lay beyond the junior high school cafeteria. The trickle down effect can be seen all over Silicon Valley."[19] This fascination with the space opera among Silicon Valley companies and IT enthusiasts more generally is extensively represented in the pages of *Wired* magazine and elsewhere; recalling the analysis of how Lucas's films mediate the conflict between agribusiness and labor (chapter 3), I would argue that the popularity of *Star Wars* in Silicon Valley suggests that the labor relations there are built on the remnants of agribusiness futurisms. Like Lucas's corporate empire, Silicon Valley originated out of an agribusiness culture and economy. And according to Castells, Silicon Valley companies developed a new work model, limited to their more privileged employees, that drew on elements of the 1960s countercultures but melded them to capitalist entrepreneurship in ways that recall Lucas's similar historical morphing from counterculture to San Joaquin Valley neoliberal.[20]

Like agribusiness, starting in the Cold War period high-tech companies in Silicon Valley, including Intel, have been aggressively devoted to combating organized labor, becoming what David Bacon has called "laboratories for developing personnel-management techniques for maintaining a union-free environment." Along with older tactics of incorporating sham company unions in order to displace independent union organizing, new union-busting techniques have been created, including the "team method" of organizing workers on plant floors, represented by the "team" of workers in *Star Wars* masks. As a result of such efforts, IT industries in the Valley remain largely un-unionized. The force of corporate antiunionism is suggested by the fact that many clean room workers are paid low wages and made vulnerable to premature death because of toxic chemicals in ways that most people would do everything they could to avoid if they had other options.[21] As David Naguib Pellow and Lisa Sun-Hee Park argue in *The Silicon Valley of Dreams: Environmental Injustice, Immigrant Workers, and the High-Tech Global Economy,* immigrant women workers in the "core jobs" of semiconductor production struggle to make a living while dying due to high exposure to toxic, carcinogenic chemicals (not to mention the even more precariously situated workers in the "periphery jobs in printed circuit board, printer, and cable assembly, including home-based piecework and prison labor," disposable workers doing dangerous work).[22] The dot-com bubble of the late 1990s depended on an expansion of low-wage jobs and the employment in particular of migrant women in Silicon Valley, the U.S.–Mexico border region, and other parts of the world. Many low-wage jobs in IT production are dangerous, exposing workers to highly toxic chemicals. Moreover, during the bubble Silicon Valley was highly segregated, and Mexican and Asian workers lived in poor neighborhoods vulnerable to the dumping of toxic waste generated by IT industries.

For those who profited, the growth of the Silicon Valley high-tech economy sustained an optimistic ideology of progress through information technology. Its promoters projected that the IT economy would transcend many of the limitations of the old, industrial age of capitalism it promised to supersede. Silicon Valley companies claimed that theirs was a "clean," "postindustrial, post-smokestack" enterprise representing progress over the past, including the region's agricultural and canning industries.[23] As Pellow and Park point out, however, both farm workers and high-tech workers are similarly vulnerable to exposure to toxic chemicals, suggesting that farm worker critical perspectives on agribusiness futurism can be usefully transposed to digital futurism, in part because—corporate claims to a historic, revolutionary break notwithstanding—the two have overlapping origins.

The entwined origins of agribusiness and digital futurisms are further suggested by representations of workers in Silicon Valley popular culture. The last decade or so has witnessed an explosion of collectable plastic figurines for sale on the world market. Leading the way have been the Homies, a popular line of small, plastic figurines representing the largely Chicana/o inhabitants of an imaginary barrio somewhere near Silicon Valley. These finely detailed and painted figures of various barrio "types," with names such as "Smiley," "Shy Girl," and "Spooky," are widely sold in gumball machines, at swap meets, on eBay, and on the Homies official website. Each of the almost two hundred Homies has a name and a brief biographical sketch, and together over one hundred million have been sold. Homies creator David Gonzales works on the expanding Homies merchandising empire from his office in Oakland, and he has based many of the figures on people from his hometown of San Jose, the Chicano metropolis directly adjacent to Silicon Valley. In this context the Homies have emerged as revealing iconic responses to the history

The Homies website.

of the Silicon Valley bubble and the euphoric fantasies of technological progress that accompanied it. In contrast with period studies of IT and cyberspace that focused on their transcendence of time, space, and materiality, the Homies invite us to reconsider the ways in which ideas and fantasies about social media emerge in relationship to material conditions of production that depend on the exploitation of racialized and gendered migrant labor.

The Homies express the contradictions between capital and labor by alternatively undermining and reproducing industry fantasies of technological progress. In recent history, the increasing speed and shrinking size of new communications technologies have been represented as signs of technological progress, the commodity fetishes of the information age. This emphasis on speed and size tends to symbolically dematerialize communications commodities and the labor that produced them. In the first instance, the speed of information flows promises to melt formerly solid geographical distances into thin air, enabling consumers to communicate in real time with people in vastly distant places. Moreover, this manner of fetishizing the new technology tends to displace alternative representations of space, such as the segregated work sites and neighborhoods in and around Silicon Valley. In the case of size, the style and form of shrinking computers and cell phones suggests commodities that are so high-tech that their thin margin of materiality is on the verge of vanishing, leaving no trace of the labor that made them. In these ways, narratives of technological progress contribute to forms of reification that obscure the labor of the women of color who built Silicon Valley and other nodes in the high-tech economy.

Collectively, the Homies gave three-dimensional shape to these contradictions. From one perspective, they effectively leveraged counterimages of the micro that, instead of obscuring labor, actually foregrounded racialized working classes, especially Latinos. From this vantage point, the figures represent the return of the oppressed workers rendered invisible in dominant depictions. From another perspective, however, as commodities themselves, the Homies replicated the reifications of shrinking cell phones and computers. Individual Homies recalled the icons and avatars of cyberspace, whereas prepackaged Homies, geometrically arranged and covered in modular clear plastic, resembled computer disks and microchips. All of which reminds us that Gonzales is himself a sort of information capitalist who markets the Homies brand to manufacturers and other licensees. Recalling the horizontal disintegration of production characteristic of post-Fordism, Gonzales in effect subcontracts with other companies to produce the Homies. But if the Homies represent the occluded working class of Silicon Valley, who makes the Homies? All the figures in my collection have "Made in China" stamped on their backs, suggesting that the Homies have followed the strategy of the many IT companies that have turned to manufacturing zones on the coast of China in search of cheap labor.

Similarly, the Homies also represent contradictory responses to influential discussions of speed and new media technology. Whereas discourses of speed promise to enable the users of new technologies to compress time and space and transcend temporal and geographic boundaries, the Homies are imaginatively rooted in a barrio with well-defined borders. By focusing on the distinctiveness of the barrio, the Homies' neighborhood marks the forms of segregation and uneven development that have characterized information capitalism. In contrast to a progressive narrative of technological speed triumphing over space, the Homies' barrio reminds us that the digital age has also reproduced local, geographic differences. Rather than simply compressing time and space, information capital reproduces differences between, on the one hand, the exclusive neighborhoods of Silicon Valley millionaires and, on the other hand, the working-class barrios near one of the many regional Superfund sites produced by the high-tech industry's dumping of toxic waste. The Homies also indirectly reference the race and gender segregation within the industry. Whereas Silicon Valley companies expressly target immigrant women for low-wage jobs, the Homies' neighborhood includes more men, a number of whom are involved in activities in the informal sector of the economy, including petty crime. Many Homies thus represent the reserve army of male lumpenproletariat who are excluded from low-wage work in the formal sector.

A good example is the Homie called "Wino." According to his online biography, "Wino" used to own a "Dot-Com website company" but he returned to the barrio and became an alcoholic when his company failed: "He used to drink Crystal and Dom now it's Ripple and T-Bird."[24] In contrast with the upward arc of conventional narratives of technological progress and boom-time upward mobility, Wino's story is circular, returning to the same limited barrio conditions and prospects with which it began. By representing a perspective on Silicon Valley from below, figures like Wino undermine fantasies of technological progress by suggesting that developments in IT industries coincided with older forms of barrio segregation and poverty.

While the Homies seem to represent the intractability of spatial segregation and inequality in the face of the digital compression of time and space, their own mode of production presupposes just such time–space compression. Gonzales developed his products on the margins of the new economy and ultimately mimicked some of its central practices. He markets the Homies on the Web and presumably takes advantage of the forms of "just-in-time" production that the Internet and subcontracting with Chinese manufacturers enable. As these examples suggest, at one and the same time the Homies undermine and reinforce the ideas and practices associated with IT industries in Silicon Valley, combining the perspective of the worker with that of the capitalist.

A dialectical materialist interpretation of the Homies, then, focuses on how they represent the labor relations that have characterized the recent history of new media, contexts that are often discussed as if they had little to do with labor. On the one hand, the Homies bring into critical relief the phantasmagoria of information technology, defetishizing the dreamworlds it conjures by representing people and places exploited or rendered disposable within IT economies. On the other hand, the Homies also reproduce ideologies of technological progress that obscure the labor that produces the plastic figures themselves. Icons with two hands, the Homies are what Walter Benjamin called "dialectical images" that express the raced and gendered contradictions between capital and labor that have informed an IT economy with agribusiness origins—which is finally to say that the Homies are contradictory because the contradictions between capital and labor that have defined agribusiness continue to shape even a world of virtual realities.

The agribusiness-informed conflicts between capital and labor are finally represented in the history of the successful unionization efforts of the Latino immigrant janitors who clean Silicon Valley buildings and offices. For decades tech companies there contracted outside firms to provide cleaning services, and so janitors have not been part of the company "team." Although this arrangement favors corporations because it relieves them of responsibility for providing benefits to the janitors and because competition among janitorial subcontractors keeps costs (and hence wages) low, the janitors' exclusion from a corporate work culture organized around labor control has perhaps contributed to the success of the "Justice for Janitors" movement. "Justice for Janitors" is an ongoing campaign to organize janitors in various locations, including Silicon Valley, where it began in 1988 as an organizing drive by the Service Employees International Union, led by several former UFW organizers. Recalling histories of farm worker futurism, SEUI successfully intervened in an IT-dominated visual field, notably by disrupting Apple CEO John Sculley's speeches at the 1991 Macworld Expo in San Francisco and at an Apple shareholders meeting in protests that garnered the union extensive media publicity. Throughout the 1990s, striking janitors could be seen wearing red T-shirts to protest their invisibility to employers and the broader public. The union, in other words, attempted to make visible the labor and living conditions disappeared in digital futurism.

On November 12, 1991, the union held a rally of over two hundred people at Apple headquarters in Cupertino to launch a hunger strike, including SEIU president Mike Garcia and six janitors. The strikers demanded that Apple require its janitorial subcontracting company, Shine Building Maintenance Inc., to recognize and negotiate with the union, pointing out that most of the workers cleaning Apple buildings made only $5.25 an hour and worked without health care benefits. UFW cofounder Dolores Huerta spoke at the rally and claimed that the plight of the janitors was the same as farm workers. In response, Apple released a statement saying, "We are concerned that the service employees union would go to these drastic measures to gain publicity on this issue," and took the opportunity for the first time during the strike to publicly support Shine.[25] Six days later the janitors ended their strike in a ceremony at Sacred Heart Church in San Jose. Chavez addressed the crowd alternatively in English and Spanish, leading them in the chant "Abajo con Apple" ("Down with Apple"), promoting the SEIU boycott of Apple products, and concluding, "All the struggles are the same. Farm workers, janitors . . . it's the same cause." At the end of the ceremony twenty people agreed to continue the fast in a rolling hunger strike like the one that concluded Chavez's 1988 "Fast for Life" (chapter 2).[26] The strike was ultimately a success and SEIU negotiated a contract with Shine, including a raise and benefits.

In the wake of the janitors' hunger strike, and as if to symbolically ward off future labor problems, in 1997 Apple incorporated an image of Chavez into its highly successful "Think Different" advertising campaign. The series of ads included iconic images of mostly male, twentieth-century visionaries such as Albert Einstein, Pablo Picasso, and Martin Luther King, and figures from the world of 1960s counterculture such as Muhammad Ali, Bob Dylan, and John Lennon. In ways that resemble agribusiness commodity aesthetics that sell products with images of farm workers and their tools, the photo of Chavez used by Apple shows him balancing a shovel and rake on his shoulder. And recalling agribusiness relations of looking where corporate heads impose the power of their privileged gaze on farm workers, Apple appropriated a high-angle shot of Chavez with downcast eyes, as if in symbolic deference to the gaze of the computer giant. By contrast, other figures in the campaign are represented in photos where they seem to return the spectator's gaze, including icons of nonviolence like MLK and the Dalai Lama. Even Jim Henson and Kermit the Frog look back at the viewer. Apple's Chavez ad was displayed in various media, including, like Carrasco's electronic billboard, on the sides of large buildings.

But whereas Carrasco's computer-animated billboard focused a dereifying gaze on agricultural commodities, Apple used the image of Chavez on its billboard to sell its brand. Given the contemporary dominance of Apple it is easy to forget that in the 1990s its success was far from certain, and the "Think Different" campaign was widely regarded as key to helping to save the company from ruin. As the *San Jose Mercury News* reported in 1998, while Apple had been "widely derided just one year ago as the technology world's latest road kill . . . the new iMac computer propelled the company to its first profitable year since 1995," and the "Think Different" campaign contributed to its renewed success. "A jubilant Steve Jobs," according to the newspaper, "announced the numbers in front of a crowd of more than 1,500 employees, investors, analysts and media" in an auditorium decorated with banners of Chavez and John Lennon while music from the Grateful Dead played.[27] In this context, the Chavez "Think Different" ad represents a contradictory kind of corporate counterculture that resembles George Lucas's agribusiness-inflected neoliberalism with its similar combination of countercultural and corporate individualism (chapter 3).

The speculative history reconstructed in *Farm Worker Futurism,* starting in the aftermath of World War II but stretching back to nineteenth- and early twentieth-century contexts, continues to inform the present. Looking back on recent Silicon Valley labor struggles reminds us of the multiple direct and indirect connections between the United Farm Workers and the emergence of global high-tech powers like Intel and Apple. The UFW/SIEU engagement with the high-tech industry further serves as an informing precursor to more recent discussions of Intel's toxic waste dumping in and around communities of color in New Mexico and Arizona, as well as the seeming disposability of the Chinese workers and high levels of suicide in factories that supply Apple.[28] Similarly, the recent appropriation of mobile phones by immigrants' rights protestors is part of a longer history of vernacular migrant techno cultures of time–space compression. And finally, in contemporary speculative fiction historical forms of farm worker futurity have influenced the political imagining of prospects for social transformation under neoliberalism.

Throughout this work, I have argued that the agricultural valleys of California, often dismissed in dominant imaginings as the "flyover" parts of the state, are in fact hubs of farm worker futurism and its radical speculative practices. The study of futurist farm worker interventions in a corporate-dominated visual field reveal California's agricultural valleys as laboratories for the development of contemporary forms of neoliberalism. The tyranny of the free market, the competitive war of all against all, and the festishization of police power over social welfare all partly originate in the ideologies and practices of farm fascism. Historically, the future starts in the valleys of California, and that continues to be true today. The dystopian near futures of contemporary speculative fictions, for example, represent the San Joaquin Valley's contemporary reality. The climate disasters projected in science fiction have already happened in the Valley, where drought and the absence of state regulations have made many people vulnerable to shortages and created new classes of the water-poor. Near Delano, where the UFW was founded, the town of Porterville recently ran out of water. According to the 2010 U.S. census, the town is over 70 percent Latino with a per capita income of $11,315 (compared to $29,551 for the state as whole) and 35.8 percent of its residents below the poverty line (over twice the California wide percentage).[29] Like the unincorporated Valley towns of the 1930s and 1940s effectively run by local elites without interference from elected officials (chapter 1), East Porterville is a U.S. "census designated place" with no municipal government. And recalling prior periods of farm fascism when farm workers were subject to evictions and police violence, according to local news reports poor residents of East Porterville "aren't reporting their wells have gone dry out of fear their landlords will evict them, or their children will be taken away."[30] Meanwhile, in the wake of the drought and in the absence of state regulations, agribusiness companies have dramatically expanded their tapping of groundwater in ways that are consistent with the longer history of the corporate efforts to privatize water by capturing state water projects. In what one area hydrologist compares to a new "arms race," corporate growers have expanded production of lucrative but thirsty crops like almonds, walnuts, and pistachios by drilling deeper and deeper wells—in some cases as deep as two Empire State Buildings—and depleting thousand-year-old reserves in an instant.[31]

In addition to water shortages, the San Joaquin Valley is home to the worst pollution in the country, much of it generated by agricultural production. In 2014 the list of the ten most polluted U.S. cities included three there and one in the Sacramento Valley.[32] Researchers believe that pollution is responsible for the disproportionately high infant mortality rate among Latinos in Kern County, the region of the Valley where farm worker unions have been most active.[33] In general, life expectancy rates in the San Joaquin Valley are about five to seven years less than the state average.[34] Key institutions consistently underserve populations in the agricultural valleys of California, including educational institutions. Out of the ten least educated U.S. cities four are in the San Joaquin Valley and a fifth is in the Salinas Valley.[35]

Anticipating the Fresno rez future represented in *Lunar Braceros,* starting in the 1980s the San Joaquin Valley became home to thirteen prisons and numerous other corrections facilities, including two ICE detention centers. Delano, the former headquarters of the UFW, is home to two prisons. In a chapter titled "Crime, Croplands, and Capitalism" of her book *Golden Gulag: Prisons, Crisis, and Opposition in Globalizing California,* Ruth Wilson Gilmore asks why so many Valley towns have become prison sites; while it's complicated, she persuasively argues that the answer has to do with the agribusiness control over the regional political economy. The Valley town of Corcoran—home to two prisons—has long been dominated by the Boswell cotton empire: "Corcoran's quality as a place was shaped by agribusiness oligopolies that had worked closely with, and exploited rivalries within, the state government at different levels over the century to achieve land and labor control, resource subsidies, and other forms of economic power, and that now sought a transformation of the local geography of investment that would complement, not compete with, cotton's continued dominance."[36] Prison building thus effectively served as a spatial fix for the contradictions of agribusiness. The first prison built in Corcoran in 1985, for example, was sited on almost two thousand acres of poor, idle agricultural land purchased from the Boswell Company for an estimated ten times its value as farmland.[37] Moreover, prisons are in the interest of agribusiness because even though their economic benefits have rarely materialized, the promise of more jobs serves to deflect from agribusiness's responsibility for structural inequality, such that the San Joaquin Valley is one of the most productive agricultural regions in the United States but with the lowest per capita incomes.[38] In such a context, overly optimistic visions of their supposed advantages encouraged Valley residents to believe that prisons were the best way "to secure the future."[39] The longer history of farm fascism also helped shape and reinforce commonsense ideas that took mass incarceration for granted and shielded prisons from critical scrutiny. Recalling Chavez's claim that agribusiness weaponry and violence encouraged even farm workers to "seek their manhood at the end of a gun," Gilmore argues that the siting of a prison in Corcoran effectively educated people "for surveillance and deferral to authorities—an old story in an agricultural community threatened by 'farm fascism' during the labor wars of the 1930s."[40] Unfortunately, then, many of the residents of Corcoran and other Valley towns failed to ask questions about futurity, or how their world would have to be different in order to sustain a widespread expectation of the future as such; instead, they succumbed to a partly agribusiness-derived futurism that defines utopia with razor wire.

At the same time, however, resistance to the prison–industrial complex in California partly depends on the farm worker movement. Many of the towns in the "prison alley" of the San Joaquin Valley, are peopled by farm workers, who have often helped lead the opposition. As Gilmore notes, efforts in 1999 to build a prison in the Valley town of Farmersville were foiled by a seemingly unlikely coalition of growers and farm workers organized under the flag of the UFW. About twenty UFW members joined high school students and ranchers in testifying, in English and Spanish, at a city council meeting to consider a proposal to build a private 550-bed prison in the town. They successfully argued not only against forms of prison futurism that predicated economic prosperity on expanded incarceration, but also that prisons produced their own dystopias, aggravating "race and class inequalities by fixing into the city's landscape under night-polluting lights the heightened expectations of racialized, impoverished criminality that U.S. prisons symbolize."[41] Farm workers saw, in other words, how prison futurism was built on agribusiness futurism, including dramatic transformations in the visual field aimed at controlling land and labor. San Joaquin Valley prisons radiate 24/7, illuminating the fixed architecture of the here and now and waging war against the nighttime sky and the dreams of a different world it inspires. To revise Oscar Wilde's famous aphorism for the denizens of farm worker futurism—all of us are in the dirt, but some of us are looking at the stars.

Notes

Preface and Acknowledgments

1. Walter Benjamin, *The Arcades Project,* ed. Rolf Tiedeman (New York: Belknap Press, 2002).

Introduction

1. Interview with Alex Rivera, *The Reeler,* January 23, 2008, http://www.thereeler .com/sundance_features/alex_rivera_sleep_dealer.php.

2. Both films can be viewed online. For *Why Cybraceros?* see the director's website, http://www.invisibleamerica.com/movies.html. For *Why Braceros?* see the Internet Archive, http://www.archive.org/details/WhyBrace1959.

3. All quotations in this paragraph are from Ernesto Galarza, *Farm Workers and Agri-business in California, 1947–1960* (Notre Dame, Ind.: University of Notre Dame Press, 1977), 66–69. The final quotation is Galarza quoting from a February 1960 U.S. Department of Labor Employment Security Review. The accompanying photograph is from the Wisconsin Historical Society, McCormick-International Harvester Collection, "Experimental Cotton Harvester," 49907.

4. See the following examples from issues of the International Harvester publication titled *International Trail*: 24, no. 1 (1954): 2; 25, no. 1 (1955): 2; 29, no. 6 (1959): 23; 30, no. 5 (1960): 15; 54, no. 3 (1963): 10.

5. Wisconsin Historical Society, International Harvester, "Futuristic International 'Powermatic' Tractor," 11325.

6. I define "agribusiness" as the combination of large-scale corporate growers and agricultural technology companies that are subsidized by research and development at state experiment stations and public colleges and universities. See R. Douglas Hurt, *Agricultural Technology in the Twentieth Century* (Manhattan, Kans.: Sunflower University Press, 1991). As early as 1939 C. Horace Hamilton argued that "farm machinery manufacturers and the large oil companies are engaged in the process of agricultural production, without having to take nearly so many of the risks as does the farmer." See Hamilton, "The Social Effects of Recent Trends in the Mechanization of Agriculture," *Rural Sociology* 4, no. 1 (1939), reprinted in *The Social Consequences and Challenges of New Agricultural*

Technologies, ed. Gigi M. Berardi and Charles C. Geisler (Boulder, Colo.: Westview Press, 1984), 68.

7. Nicholas Mirzoeff, *The Right to Look: A Counterhistory of Visuality* (Durham, N.C.: Duke University Press, 2001).

8. Carey McWilliams, "The Rise of Farm Fascism," in *Factories in the Field: The Story of Migratory Farm Labor in California* (Berkeley: University of California Press, [1935] 1990), 230–63.

9. Ruth Wilson Gilmore, *Golden Gulag: Prisons, Surplus, Crisis, and Opposition in Globalizing California* (Berkeley: University of California Press, 2007).

10. For photography, see the two volumes by Richard Steven Street, *Photographing Farm Workers in California* (Stanford Calif.: Stanford University Press, 2004), and *Everyone Had Cameras: Photography and Farm Workers in California, 1850–2000* (Minneapolis: University of Minnesota Press, 2008). While there is a vast amount of film and video depicting California farm workers, and in particular the UFW, large collections have not been gathered together and made readily accessible. For samples of relevant film and video clips, see the Farm Worker Movement Documentation Project, https://libraries.ucsd.edu/farmworkermovement/media/video/index.shtml. The largest collection of UFW-related film and video is at the Walter P. Reuther Library at Wayne State University in Detroit. More generally, the most iconic footage of the march to Sacramento, for example, and of Chavez and Robert Kennedy, has been used repeatedly in documentaries and on television, so that anyone with even a passing familiarity with the UFW has probably seen some of the images.

11. John Smythies, "A Note on the Concept of the Visual Field in Neurology, Psychology, and Visual Neuroscience," *Perception* 25, no. 3 (1995): 369–71.

12. W. J. T. Mitchell, "Showing Seeing: A Critique of Visual Culture," *Journal of Visual Culture* 1, no. 2 (2002): 170.

13. Jacques Lacan, *The Seminar of Jacque Lacan, Book XI: Four Fundamental Concepts of Psychoanalysis,* ed. Jacques-Alain Miller, trans. Alan Sheridan (New York: Norton, 1998), 86–87.

14. Ibid., 88.

15. Frantz Fanon, *Black Skin, White Masks* (New York: Grove Press, 2008); Judith Butler, "Endangered/Endangering: Schematic Racism and White Paranoia," *Reading Rodney King, Reading Urban Uprising,* ed. Robert Gooding-William (New York: Routledge Press, 1993), 15–24.

16. Kodwo Eshun, "Further Considerations of Afrofuturism," *CR: The New Centennial Review* 3, no. 2 (2003): 287–302.

17. Catherine S. Ramírez, "Afrofuturism/Chicanafuturism: Fictive Kin," *Aztlán: A Journal of Chicano Studies* 33, no. 1 (2008): 187–88. See also Ramírez, "Deus ex machina: Tradition, Technology, and the Chicanafuturist Art of Marion C. Martinez," *Aztlán: A Journal of Chicano Studies* 29, no. 2 (2002): 55–92.

18. Jayna Brown and Alexis Lothian, "Speculative Life: An Introduction," *Social Text: Periscope,* January 4, 2012, http://socialtextjournal.org/periscope_article/speculative_life_introduction/. Recent scholarship in literature and cultural studies organized around the critical concept of "Afrofuturism" has focused on race and labor in speculative figurations of African chattel slavery and Jim Crow. Liter-

ary works by Octavia Butler and Samuel Delany, as well as John Akomfrah's 1996 documentary about futurism in African diasporic literature and music titled *The Last Angel of History,* have helped galvanize a range of related artistic and critical projects based in representations of race, labor, and technology, and while it is a varied and multiform intellectual and cultural formation, my own study has been particularly informed by the historical perspectives of Afrofuturism, notably in anthologies edited by Sheree R. Thomas, *Dark Matter: A Century of Speculative Fiction from the African Diaspora* (New York: Warner Books, 2000) and *Dark Matter: Reading the Bones* (New York: Warner Books, 2004); and "Afrofuturism," a special issue of *Social Text* edited by Alondra Nelson, *Social Text* 71 (2001). Finally, a recently published volume edited by Walidah Imarisha and Adrienne Maree Brown titled *Octavia's Brood: Science Fiction Stories from Social Justice Movements* (Oakland, Calif.: AK Press, 2015) provides a complementary counterpart to my own efforts to connect speculative fiction and farm worker movements.

19. Kodwo Eshun, "Further Considerations of Afrofuturism," 293.

20. In contrast with Muñoz, who uses the phrase "reproductive futurity," I instead use "reproductive futurism" to suggest the linear, ends-oriented future logics of heteronormative reproduction, reserving "futurity" for formations that oppose such logics.

21. Despite the futurist arc of the farm worker movement, the more familiar and influential historical narratives depict it as an artifact of the past, remote from speculative thought and action about the future. The dominant account of twentieth-century California agriculture combines a narrative of technological progress in the fields with one of decline or a series of declines for the farm worker movement. Some of the first efforts to organize farm workers, leading to a series of partly communist-led agricultural strikes in the 1930s, were crushed by agribusiness before decade's end; a successful organizing drive after World War II was similarly destroyed; finally, the UFW emerged to great initial success in the 1960s only to precipitously decline in influence and power in the 1980s. My own study takes issue with such narratives of decline, which I understand as the inverse of the linear narrative of progress criticized by Walter Benjamin for obscuring contradiction and conflict. Narratives of declension make it more difficult to see and appreciate the critical edge of farm worker efforts to imagine and construct better worlds in opposition to corporate plans for the future, while at the same time obscuring farm worker investments in notions of progress that dovetailed with agribusiness. For examples of declension historiography, see Matthew Garcia, *From the Jaws of Victory: The Triumph and Tragedy of Cesar Chavez and the Farm Worker Movement* (Berkeley: University of California Press, 2014); and Miriam Pawel, *The Union of Their Dreams: Power, Hope and Struggle in Cesar Chavez's Farm Worker Movement* (New York: Bloomsbury, 2012).

22. José Muñoz, *Cruising Utopia: The Then and There of Queer Futurity* (New York: New York University Press, 2009), 30.

23. Ibid., 49, 55–56.

24. Hamilton, "Social Effects of Recent Trends in the Mechanization of Agriculture," 70.

25. Wisconsin Historical Society, International Harvester, "Farm Machinery Hall at Century of Progress," 49742.

26. Luis Hochman, "Man of the Monsters," *Mechanix Illustrated,* May 1947, 52; Wisconsin Historical Society, International Harvester, "Century of Progress Queen Feeds Mechanical Cow," 29131.

27. *International Harvester Exhibits,* A Century of Progress, Chicago, May 26– October 31, 1934, souvenir program, 33–34.

28. "Robot Plows while Farmer Rests," *Popular Science,* September 1934.

29. Wisconsin Historical Society, International Harvester, "Girl Standing with Harvey Harvester," 59238.

30. *Harvester World,* September–October 1938, 17.

31. Wisconsin Historical Society, International Harvester, "Girl Standing with Harvey Harvester," 59238.

32. Wisconsin Historical Society, International Harvester, "Farmall Tractor Advertising Poster," 4727, 4726.

33. Jeffrey L. Meikle, "From Celebrity to Anonymity: The Professionalization of American Industrial Design," in *Raymond Loewy: Pioneer of American Industrial Design,* ed. Angela Schönberger (Munich: Prestel–Verlag, 1990), 56. In the same volume, see "Raymond Loewy and the World of Tomorrow: New York's World Fair, 1939" by Donald J. Bush, who argues that "the result of a fully streamlined environment would be the disallowance of regional, ethnic, popular, or class variations" in favor of a "planned, rationalized, uniform national aesthetic" (96).

34. Joshua C. Taylor, *The Designs of Raymond Loewy,* Renwick Gallery of the National Collection of Fine Arts (Washington, D.C.: Smithsonian Institution Press, 1975), 7.

35. Christina Cogdell, *Eugenic Design: Streamlining America in the 1930s* (Philadelphia: University of Pennsylvania Press, 2010), 4.

36. McWilliams, *Factories in the Field,* 5.

37. Ibid., 56. See also Deborah Fitzgerald, *Every Farm a Factory: The Industrial Ideal in American Agriculture* (New Haven, Conn.: Yale University Press, 2010), 16.

38. Karl Marx and Frederick Engels, "Preface to the 1882 Russian Edition," *Manifesto of the Communist Party,* https://www.marxists.org/archive/marx/works/ 1848/communist-manifesto.

39. Fitzgerald, *Every Farm a Factory,* 75–105.

40. McWilliams, *Factories in the Field,* 273–75.

41. Galarza, *Farm Workers and Agri-business in California, 1947–1960,* 71.

42. Raymond Loewy, *Industrial Design* (Woodstock, N.Y.: Overlook Press, 1979), 127.

43. *Harvester World,* March 1948, 20.

44. Wisconsin Historical Society, International Harvester, "IH Prototype Dealership Building Image," 25180.

45. *Harvester World,* March 1948, 15.

46. "Millions for Modernization," *Harvester World,* June–July 1946.

47. *Roots in Chicago, One Hundred Years Deep,* International Harvester commemorative book, 1947, 48.

48. *Harvester World,* March 1948, 14.

49. *Harvester World,* June 1949, 23.

50. "New IH Plan and Building Design Leaps U.S. Border into Other Countries," *Harvester World,* October 1946, 9–10. See also the photo essay titled "Progress . . . Below the Rio Grande," about the mechanization of agriculture in Mexico and the building of the first IH manufacturing plant in Saltillo; and "Dedicated to Mexico's Farmers," a *Harvester World* cover story about festivities surrounding the inauguration of the new plant. *Harvester World,* June–July 1946, 2–6; *Harvester World,* October 1947, 8.

51. "Way Out West in the Land of Cotton," *Harvester World,* September–October 1951, 19–20.

52. Miriam J. Wells, *Strawberry Fields: Politics, Class, and Work in California Agriculture* (Ithaca, N.Y.: Cornell University Press, 1996), 23.

53. See Hurt, *Agricultural Technology in the Twentieth Century,* 7. He details in particular how the spread during 1930s and 1940s of tractors (27–28), cotton harvesters (39–40), and irrigation systems (75–76) led to the expansion of production in ways that favored large corporations and drove small farmers out of business.

54. Wells, *Strawberry Fields,* 24.

55. Galarza, *Farm Workers and Agri-business in California,* 71.

56. Ibid., 97–202.

57. Ibid., 86.

58. According to Mai Ngai, Galarza and other union critics of contract labor used "slavery and concentration-camp metaphors" to emphasize "the unfree nature of contract labor," and yet "that discourse also had the effect of constructing braceros as a foreign element entirely outside the American labor force and society" in ways that presaged his ultimate identification with the interests of citizen over non-citizen workers. See Ngai, *Impossible Subjects: Illegal Aliens and the Making of Modern America* (Princeton, N.J.: Princeton University Press, 2003), 141.

59. Ernesto Galarza, *Strangers in Our Fields* (Washington, D.C.: Joint United States–Mexico Trade Union Committee, 1956), back cover.

60. Ibid., 32–35.

61. Ernesto Galarza, *Merchants of Labor: The Mexican Bracero Story* (Santa Barbara, Calif.: McNally and Loftin, 1964), 16.

62. Galarza, *Farm Workers and Agri-business in California,* 67.

63. Ibid., 61.

64. Ibid., 67.

65. On the racialization and gendering of technology see Michael Adas, *Machines as the Measure of Men: Science, Technology, and Ideologies of Western Dominance* (Ithaca, N.Y.: Cornell University Press, 1989); Adas, *Dominance by Design: Technological Imperatives and America's Civilizing Mission* (Cambridge, Mass.: Belknap Press of Harvard University Press, 2009); Rebecca Herzig, "The Matter of Race in Histories of American Technology," 155–70, and Bruce Sinclair, "Integrating the Histories of Race and Technology," 1–17, in *Technology and the African-American Experience: Needs and Opportunities for Study,* ed. Bruce Sinclair (Cambridge, Mass.: MIT Press, 2004); and Venus Green, *Race on the Line: Gender,*

Labor, and Technology in the Bell System, 1880–1980 (Durham, N.C.: Duke University Press, 2001).

66. Galarza, *Farm Workers and Agri-business in California,* 91.

67. Ivette Perfecto and Baldemar Velasquez, "Farm Workers: Among the Least Projected," *EPA Journal* 18, no. 1 (1992): 13–14, cited in David Naguib Pellow and Lisa Sun-Hee Park, *The Silicon Valley of Dreams: Environmental Injustice, Immigrant Workers, and the High-Tech Global Economy* (New York: New York University Press, 2002), 50.

68. Edmund P. Russell III, "'Speaking of Annihilation': Mobilizing for War against Human and Insect Enemies, 1914–1945," *Journal of American History* 82, no. 4 (1996): 15058–59.

69. In 1957, in response to the question "How Do You Spot Tomorrow's Trends?" International Harvester Vice President Eugene F. Schneider answered that one of the most promising future trends is "chemical farming," including "more liquid fertilizers and insecticides." See "How Do You Spot Tomorrow's Trends?" *Harvester World,* November–December 1957, 10.

70. *The Big Land* (1967), David L. Wolper Collection, Cinema Library, University of Southern California; Mark Arax and Rick Wartzman, *The King of California: J. G. Boswell and the Making of a Secret American Empire* (New York: Public Affairs, 2003), 344–45. For similar photographic images and related text see *DiGiorgio Corporation 1965 Annual Report,* Ernesto Galarza Papers, Special Collections M0224, Stanford University Libraries, Department of Special Collections and University Archives, Box 35, Folder 1.

71. Donna Haraway, *Modest Witness@Second_Millenium.FemaleMan©_Meets_ OncoMouse™* (New York: Routledge, 1997), 32.

72. Juanita P. Ontiveros, *Pilots of Aztlán: The Flights of the Royal Chicano Air Force* (KVIE 5, Sacramento, written and directed by Steve LaRosa, 1994), VHS tape, Ester M. Hernandez Papers, M1301, Stanford University Libraries Department of Special Collections and University Archives, Box 51, Folder 6. See also Eldon W. Downs and George F. Lemmer, "The Origins of Aerial Crop Dusting," *Agricultural History* 39, no. 3 (1965): 123–35.

73. Ricardo Favela, *Royal Chicano Air Force Piñata Biplane,* and Esteban Villa, *5 de mayo con el Royal Chicano Air Force Arte Musica Poesia,* Royal Chicano Air Force Archives, California Ethnic and Multicultural Archives (CEMA), University of California, Santa Barbara.

74. Adas, *Machines as the Measure of Men;* Adas, *Dominance by Design;* Chandra Mukerji, "Intelligent Uses of Engineering and the Legitimacy of State Power," *Technology and Culture* 44, no. 4 (2003): 655–76. As Sinclair writes of the African American context, "Defining African Americans as technically incompetent and then—in a kind of double curse—denying them access to education, control over complex machinery, or the power of patent rights lay at the heart of the distinction drawn between black and white people in this country . . . This deeply ingrained and long perpetuated myth of black disingenuity has been a central element in attempts to justify slavery." See "Integrating the Histories of Race and Technology," 2.

75. Adas, *Machines as the Measure of Men,* 223–25; Adas, *Dominance by Design,* 5, 14, 67–128, 82, 97, 179. For accounts of the telegraph and British imperialism see John Tully, "A Victorian Ecological Disaster: Imperialism, the Telegraph, and Gutta-Percha," *Journal of World History* 20, no. 4 (2009): 559–79; Robert W. D. Boyce, "Imperial Dreams and National Realities: Britain, Canada and the Struggle for a Pacific Telegraph," *English Historical Review* 115, no. 460 (2000): 39–70; Daniel Headrick, "A Double-Edged Sword: Communications and Imperial Control in British India," *Historical Social Research* 35, no. 1 (2010): 251–65. In the mid-nineteenth-century United States, according to David E. Nye, the telegraph was "celebrated as a force that would help realize 'manifest destiny.'" See "Shaping Communication Networks: Telegraph, Telephone, Computer," *Social Research* 64, no. 3 (1997): 1075. Paul Gilmore concludes that the technology "was celebrated for extending the conquest of a disembodied white mind over both the globe and the bodies of inferior, primitive peoples." See "The Telegraph in Black and White," *English Literary History* 69, no. 3 (2002): 806. See also Jeffery K. Lyons, "The Pacific Cable, Hawai'i, and Global Communication," *Hawaiian Journal of History* 39 (2005): 35–52; Yakup Bektas, "Displaying the American Genius: The Electromagnetic Telegraph in the Wider World," *British Journal for the History of Science* 34, no. 12 (2001): 199–232; Norman L. Rue, "Pesh-Bi-Yalti Speaks: White Man's Talking Wire in Arizona," *Journal of Arizona History* 12, no. 4 (1971): 229–62; Charles Vevier, "The Collins Overland Line and American Continentalism," *Pacific Historical Review* 28, no. 3 (1959): 237–53; James Lewallen, "Wired Wild West: The U.S. Army and the Telegraph in the Trans-Pecos Region of Texas, 1870–1891," *Journal of Big Bend Studies* 15 (2003): 101–14. Finally, for a study of trains, telegraphs, and U.S. financial imperialism in Mexico see John Mason Hart, "Building the Railroads," in *Empire and Revolution: The Americans in Mexico since the Civil War* (Berkeley: University of California Press, 2002), 106–30.

76. See Elizabeth Jean Norvell, "Syndicalism and Citizenship: Postrevolutionary Worker Mobilization in Veracruz," 98, and Emilio Zamora, "Labor Formation, Community, and Politics: The Mexican Working Class in Texas, 1900–1945," 141, in *Border Crossings: Mexican and Mexican-American Workers,* ed. John Mason Hart (Wilmington, Del.: Scholarly Resources, 1998); C. López, M. Rafel-Morales, J. Cervantes-de-Gotari, and R. Colás-Ortiz, "Steam Locomotives in the History of Technology of Mexico," in *The International Symposium on the History of Machines and Mechanisms,* ed. H. S. Yan and M. Ceccarelli (Dordrecht, Neth.: Springer, 2009), 152–64.

77. George Sanchez, *Becoming Mexican American: Ethnicity, Culture, and Identity in Chicano Los Angeles, 1900–1945* (New York: Oxford University Press, 1995), 35.

78. Sinclair, "Integrating the Histories of Race and Technology," 7. See also Judith Carney, "Landscapes of Technology Transfer: Rice Cultivation and African Continuities," 19–48, and Barbara Garrity-Blake, "Raising Fish with a Song: Technology, Chanteys, and African-Americans in the Atlantic Menhaden Fisher," 107–18, both in the same volume, *Technology and the African-American Experience,* ed. Sinclair. For the African American labor context see also Venus Green's *Race on the Line* and Joel Dinerstein, *Swinging the Machine: Modernity, Technology, and*

African American Culture between the World Wars (Amherst: University of Massachusetts Press, 2003). Also relevant is Alexander Saxton's discussion of Chinese miners' innovative use of dynamite in *The Indispensable Enemy: Labor and the Anti-Chinese Movement in California* (Berkeley: University of California Press, 1975), 58.

79. Vicki L. Ruiz, *Cannery Women, Cannery Lives: Mexican Women, Unionization, and the California Food Procession Industry, 1930–1950* (Albuquerque: University of New Mexico Press, 1987); Patricia Zavella, *Women's Work and Chicano Families: Cannery Workers of the Santa Clara Valley* (Ithaca, N.Y.: Cornell University Press, 1986). More recently, Catherine S. Ramírez analyzes religious sculptures by New Mexican artist Marion C. Martinez that were composed out of discarded computer hardware and partly inspired by work experiences at the Los Alamos National Laboratory. See Ramírez, "Deus ex machina," 69.

80. See Carla Freeman's study of women data-entry workers in Barbados, *High Tech and High Heels in the Global Economy: Women, Work, and Pink-Collar Identities in the Caribbean* (Durham, N.C.: Duke University Press, 2000).

81. José Limón, *Mexican Ballads, Chicano Poems: History and Influence in Mexican-American Social Poetry* (Berkeley: University of California Press, 1992), 12–13.

82. Brian Larkin, *Signal and Noise: Media, Infrastructure, and Urban Culture in Nigeria* (Durham, N.C.: Duke University Press, 2008); Derek W. Vaillant, "Sounds of Whiteness: Local Radio, Racial Formation, and Public Culture in Chicago, 1921–1935," *American Quarterly* 54, no. 1 (2004): 26–66; Heather Hendershot, "God's Angriest Man: Carl McIntire, Cold War Fundamentalism, and Right-Wing Broadcasting," *American Quarterly* 59, no. 2 (2007): 373–97.

83. Barbara Dianne Savage, *Broadcasting Freedom: Radio, War, and the Politics of Race, 1938–1948* (Chapel Hill: University of North Carolina Press, 1999).

84. Sinclair, "Integrating the Histories of Race and Technology," 10.

85. Pellow and Park, *Silicon Valley of Dreams*.

86. Stephen J. Pitti, *The Devil in Silicon Valley: Northern California, Race, and Mexican Americans* (Princeton, N.J.: Princeton University Press, 2003), 199.

87. Alicia Schmidt Camacho, *Migrant Imaginaries: Latino Cultural Politics in the U.S.–Mexico Borderlands* (New York: New York University Press, 2008), 5.

88. Darko Suvin, "Estrangement and Cognition," in *Metamorphosis of Science Fiction: On the Poetics and History of a Literary Genre* (New Haven, Conn.: Yale University Press, 1979), 3–15.

89. For examples of agribusiness futurism in popular media see "Cotton Picker Does Work of Gang," *Popular Science,* March 1931, 39; Sterling Gleason, "Better Farm Animals Promised by New Tests," *Popular Science,* April 1937, 56–57; "Big-Business Farmer," *Popular Science,* April 1942, 87–89; "Farmers Turn Mechanics to Feed America," *Popular Science,* January 1945, 204–6; Ladd Haystead, "Fantastic Farm Machines Turn Fields into Factories," *Popular Science,* May 1948, 129–34; Robert E. Martin, "Amazing Machine Picks Seeds That Will Grow," *Popular Science,* January 1940, 108–10; "Moon Farms to Banish Starvation," *Mechanix Illustrated,* May 1954, 72–75, 216–17. For historical studies of science fiction literature that engages histories of settler colonialism and empire see Istvan Csicsery-

Ronay Jr., "Science Fiction and Empire," *Science Fiction Studies* 30, no. 2 (2003): 231–45; Carl Abbott, "Homesteading on the Extraterrestrial Frontier," *Science Fiction Studies* 32, no. 2 (2005): 240–64; Patricia Kerslake, *Science Fiction and Empire* (Liverpool, U.K.: Liverpool University Press, 2007); and John Rieder, *Colonialism and the Emergence of Science Fiction* (Middletown, Conn.: Wesleyan University Press, 2008).

90. On the notion of Foucauldian reordering see Roderick Ferguson, *The Reorder of Things: The University and Its Pedagogies of Minority Difference* (Minneapolis: University of Minnesota Press, 2012).

91. Curtis Marez, *Drug Wars: The Political Economy of Narcotics* (Minneapolis: University of Minnesota Press, 2004), 185–224; Marez, "Subaltern Soundtracks: Mexican Immigrants and the Making of Hollywood Cinema," *Aztlán* 29, no. 1 (2004): 57–82.

92. Clyde Woods, "Neo-plantation, Neo-liberalism," unpublished talk, Reimagining the Hemispheric South Conference, Department of English, University of California, Santa Barbara, January 21, 2011.

93. Fredric Jameson, *Postmodernism, or, The Logic of Late Capitalism* (Durham, N.C.: Duke University Press, 1990), 294.

94. Muñoz, *Cruising Utopia.*

1. "To the Disinherited Belongs the Future"

1. H. Bruce Franklin summarizes the author's accomplishments and influence in this way: "In 1939, Heinlein published his first story, and within two years was already being acclaimed by some as the most popular living writer of science fiction. By the mid-1960s, Heinlein had an audience of millions. His works have been translated into twenty-eight languages. All but one of his thirty-five published books (twenty-six novels and nine collections of shorter fiction) is presently in print in mass-market paperbacks. He is customarily called 'the Dean of science fiction.' Heinlein is the only author who has won the Hugo Award (the World Science Fiction Convention's prize for the best novel of the year) four times. He was the first writer of hardcore science fiction to break into general circulation magazines. He is a leading figure in the development of the modern science-fiction movie, science-fiction television serials, and the modern science-fiction juvenile novel. Words coined in Heinlein's fiction have become part of our language . . . Heinlein is also a respected figure in military circles, chosen to address the United States Naval Academy and to fly in the B-1 bomber." See Franklin, *Robert A. Heinlein: America as Science Fiction* (New York: Oxford University Press, 1980), 4–5.

2. Ibid., 6–7.

3. Ibid., 11.

4. Ibid., 18.

5. Mike Davis, "'What Is a Vigilante Man?': White Violence in California History," in *No One Is Illegal: Fighting Racism and State Violence on the U.S.–Mexico Border,* ed. Justin Akers Chacón (Chicago: Haymarket Books, 2006), 53, 57.

6. Ibid., 57.

7. William H. Patterson Jr., *Robert A. Heinlein: In Dialogue with His Century,* vol. 1: *1907–1948: Learning Curve* (New York: Tom Doherty Associates, 2010), 187.

8. Ibid., 190.

9. "Water Is for Washing" was originally published in the science fiction pulp magazine *The Argosy* in 1947 but was subsequently reprinted in Robert A. Heinlein, *The Menace from the Earth* (New York: Signet, 1959). Page numbers in subsequent notes refer to this edition.

10. Ibid., 183.

11. The novel was originally published as a serial titled "Satellite Scout" in the magazine *Boys' Life* (1950) and subsequently republished as *Farmer in the Sky* (New York: Charles Scribner's Sons, 1950). Page numbers in subsequent notes refer to this edition.

12. Franklin, *Robert A. Heinlein*, 74.

13. Heinlein, *Farmer in the Sky*, 104.

14. Ibid., 105.

15. Ibid., 130.

16. Ibid., 202.

17. Ibid., 211.

18. As Franklin argues, "Heinlein, who began life as a boy in rural Missouri, here projects an imaginary future that resurrects one of the most cherished symbols of the American past, the family farm . . . Heinlein seems to relish the switch in values that comes from projecting the past into the future." See *Robert A. Heinlein*, 8.

19. Two films Heinlein wrote, *Voyage to the Moon* and *Project Moon Base*, represent white voyagers who travel to the moon in ways that recall transborder migrant workers. See "Strangers in a Strange Land" in Curtis Marez, "Cesar Chavez's Video Collection," *American Literature* 85, no. 4 (2013): http://scalar.usc.edu/nehvectors/curtis-marez/strangers-in-a-strange-land-farm-workers-in-heinlein.

20. Heinlein, *Farmer in the Sky*, front cover.

21. The illustration depicting the white boys' mastery of the alien tractor is reproduced in Marez, "Cesar Chavez's Video Collection," http://scalar.usc.edu/nehvectors/curtis-marez/alien-tractor.

22. Ernesto Galarza, *Spiders in the House, Workers in the Field* (Notre Dame, Ind.: University of Notre Dame Press, 1970). See also Richard Steven Street, "*Poverty in the Valley of Plenty*: The National Farm Labor Union, DiGiorgio Farms, and Suppression of Documentary Photography in California, 1947–66," *Labor History* 48, no. 1 (2007): 25–48.

23. This narrative of Chavez's earliest known act of civil disobedience is based in his own account in Jacques E. Levey's *Cesar Chavez: Autobiography of La Causa* (Minneapolis: University of Minnesota Press, 2007), 84–85. Miriam Pawel claims that Chavez joined the navy in 1946 and that she could not find documentation for his arrest. See *The Crusades of Cesar Chavez: A Biography* (New York: Bloomsbury, 2014), 20, 488.

24. Curtis Marez, *Drug Wars: The Political Economy of Narcotics* (Minneapolis: University of Minnesota Press, 2004).

25. Walter Goldschmidt, *As You Sow* (Glencoe, Ill.: Free Press, 1946), 117–19.

26. Ibid., 110–12, 214–15.

27. Street, "*Poverty in the Valley of Plenty*," 30–31.

28. Carey McWilliams, *Factories in the Field: The Story of Migratory Farm Labor in California* (Berkeley: University of California Press, [1935] 1990), 234–37; Galarza, *Spiders in the House,* 54; Goldschmidt, *As You Sow,* 181–83.

29. Galarza, *Spiders in the House,* 54.

30. McWilliams, *Factories in the Field,* 123.

31. Galarza, *Spiders in the House,* 14–15.

32. Ernesto Galarza, *Farm Workers and Agri-business in California, 1947–1960* (Notre Dame, Ind.: University of Notre Dame Press, 1977), 94.

33. Galarza, *Spiders in the House,* 84–85. For an image of the "Jolly Farmer" see the DiGiorgio advertisement in Box 36, Folder 2 of the Ernesto Galarza Papers, Special Collections M0224, Stanford University Libraries, Department of Special Collections and University Archives (hereafter Galarza Papers).

34. See Goldschmidt, who cites texts from the 1930s to this effect by Paul S. Taylor, Tom Vasey, Varden Fuller, and McWilliams. His own book, *As You Sow,* is of course an important contribution to this literature as well.

35. David R. Roediger, "Du Bois, Race, and Italian Americans," in *Are Italians White? How Race Is Made in America,* ed. Jennifer Guglielmo and Salvatore Salerno (London: Routledge Press, 2003), 260.

36. Thomas A. Guglielmo, "'No Color Barrier': Italians, Race, and Power in the United States," in *Are Italians White?* ed. Guglielmo and Salerno, 36–38.

37. Stuart Hall, "Gramsci's Relevance for the Study of Race and Ethnicity," in *Stuart Hall: Critical Dialogues in Cultural Studies,* ed. David Morley and Kuan-Hsing Chen (London: Routledge Press, 1996), 416. See also Giuliana Bruno, *Streetwalking on a Ruined Map: Cultural Theory and the City Films of Elvira Notari* (Princeton, N.J.: Princeton University Press, 1993), 17, 331.

38. Jennifer Guglielmo, "White Lies, Dark Truths," in *Are Italians White?* ed. Guglielmo and Salerno, 9–10.

39. See Mathew Frye Jacobson, *Whiteness of a Different Color: European Immigrants and the Alchemy of Race* (Cambridge, Mass.: Harvard University Press, 1998), 56–62; and Vincenza Scarpaci, "Walking the Color Line: Italian Immigrants in Rural Louisiana, 1880–1910," in *Are Italians White?* ed. Guglielmo and Salerno, 60–76.

40. Caroline Waldron Merithew, "Making the Italian Other: Blacks, Whites, and the Inbetween in the 1895 Spring Valley, Illinois Race Riot"; Michael Miller Topp, "'It Is Providential That There Are Foreigners Here': Whiteness and Masculinity in the Making of Italian American Syndicalist Identity"; Salvatore Salerno, "I Delitti Della Razza Bianca (Crimes of the White Race): Italian Anarchists' Racial Discourse as Crime," all in *Are Italians White?* ed. Guglielmo and Salerno. Salerno notes that in the 1910s, *Regeneración,* the Spanish-language newspaper published in the United States by the Mexican anarchist Ricardo Flores Magón, included a column in Italian written by the immigrant anarchist Ludovico Caminita, and according to the column a number of other Italian immigrants joined Mexican anarchists fighting in the revolution (120).

41. Paola A. Sensi-Isolani and Phylis Cancilla Martinelli, "Historical Perspective," in *Struggle and Success: An Anthology of the Italian Immigrant Experience*

in California, ed. Sensi-Isolani and Martinelli (New York: Center for Migration Studies, 1993), 11.

42. Joseph Giovinco, "'Success in the Sun?' California's Italians during the Progressive Era," in *Struggle and Success,* ed. Sensi-Isolani and Martinelli, 20–37.

43. Robert DiGiorgio and Joseph A. DiGiorgio, "The DiGiorgios: From Fruit Merchants To Corporate Innovators," an oral history conducted in 1983 by Ruth Teiser, Regional Oral History Office, Bancroft Library, University of California, Berkeley, 1983–84, 7–8, 11; "DiGiorgio Corp.—Company Profile," http://www.referenceforbusiness.com/history2/46/Di-Giorgio-Corp.html; Miriam Hansen, *Babel and Babylon: Spectatorship in American Silent Film* (Cambridge, Mass.: Harvard University Press, 1994), 243–96.

44. Thomas A. Guglielmo, *White on Arrival: Italians, Race, Color, and Power in Chicago, 1890–1945* (New York: Oxford University Press, 2003).

45. Rose D. Scherini, "Executive Order 9066 and Italian Americans: The San Francisco Story," *California History* 70, no. 4 (1991–92): 366–77; and Stephen Fox, "The Relocation of Italian Americans during World War II," in *Struggle and Success,* ed. Sensi-Isolani and Martinelli, 199–213.

46. Isami Arifuku Waugh, Alex Yamato, and Raymond Y. Okamura, "Japanese Americans in California: Historic Sites—Kawasaki Labor Camp," Five Views: An Ethnic Historic Site Survey for California, California Department of Parks and Recreation, 1988, http://www.nps.gov/; DiGiorgio Oral History, 120.

47. "Joseph DiGiorgio," *Fortune,* August 1946, 96–103, 205–8. The quotations in this paragraph are on pages 99, 100, 103, 207, and 208, while the photo of DiGiorgio in front of a Sicilian backdrop is on 97.

48. "This World," Sunday supplement, *San Francisco Chronicle,* June 26, 1948, cover, 2–3.

49. "Joseph DiGiorgio," *Fortune,* 96.

50. Ibid., 97.

51. "The Fruit King," *Time,* March 11, 1946, http://www.time.com/time/magazine/article/0,9171,776733,00.html.

52. Laura Pulido, *Environmentalism and Economic Justice: Two Chicano Struggles in the Southwest* (Tucson: University of Arizona Press, 1996), 67.

53. See, e.g., "Joseph DiGiorgio," *Fortune,* 99.

54. The quotations in this paragraph are from Michael Rogin, *Black Skin, White Noise: Jewish Immigrants in the Hollywood Melting Pot* (Berkeley: University of California Press, 1996), 78, 85, 80.

55. As Galarza argues, even though it often required great skill, farm labor was generally defined as unskilled, particularly when performed by women. See *Farm Workers and Agri-business in California,* 29.

56. See Stuart Hall, "Toad in the Garden: Thatcherism among the Theorists," in *Marxism and the Interpretation of Culture,* ed. Cary Nelson and Lawrence Grossberg (Urbana: University of Illinois Press, 1988), 35–57. Even after DiGiorgio's death his image remained central to company media. See *The DiGiorgio Story* (San Francisco: DiGiorgio Fruit Company, 1959), http://etgdesign.com/family/digiorgio/.

57. "This World," *San Francisco Chronicle,* 3.

58. Galarza, *Farm Workers and Agri-business in California.*

59. Kern County Special Citizens Committee, *A Community Aroused* (1947), Galarza Papers, Box 35, Folder 4. See also Galarza, *Spiders in the House,* 25. In a major publicity coup, the *Los Angeles Times* made the pamphlet the subject of a piece called "Kern County Farm Pictures Refute 'Serfdom' Charges," December 17, 1947.

60. "Citizen's Committee on the DiGiorgio Strike," press release, 14, 1948, 7, Galarza Papers, Box 35, Folder 3.

61. Galarza Papers, Box 36, Folder 5.

62. Ibid.

63. Michael Denning, *The Cultural Front* (New York: Verso, 1997), 93.

64. Still, *Photo-History* had limitations that Galarza subsequently strove to overcome. The magazine, for example, focused almost exclusively on white workers in ways that Galarza saw as barriers to the kinds of interethnic, transnational organizing that would help to empower Mexican farm workers. According to Stephen J. Pitti, Galarza's efforts in the 1930s and 1940s "seem to anticipate patterns of transnational political activism now emerging in the twenty-first century." See Pitti, "Ernesto Galarza, Mexican Immigration, and Farm Labor Organizing in Postwar California," in *The Countryside in the Age of the Modern State: Political Histories of Rural America,* ed. Catherine McNicol Stock and Robert D. Johnston (Ithaca, N.Y.: Cornell University Press, 2001), 163. Galarza was committed to crossing color and citizenship lines, working to organize black, white, Filipino, and Mexican farm workers. As we shall see, he also worked to include women both in union struggles and in union publicity.

65. Galarza, *Farm Workers and Agri-business in California,* 9–10.

66. "Southern Tenant Farmers' Union, Living and Working Conditions in the South, ca. 1940s," Galarza Papers, Box 65, Folder 10.

67. See Pitti, "Ernesto Galarza."

68. Ernesto Galarza, "Not Tobacco Road," *Kern County Union Labor Journal,* October 17, 1947, Galarza Papers, Box 35, Folder 13

69. Galarza, *Farm Workers and Agri-business in California,* 64–65.

70. Ibid., 128.

71. Ibid., 107.

72. Ernesto Galarza, "A 'Twenty-Mile' Picket Line: Ranch Workers Organize to End 'Grapes of Wrath' Era," *Trade Union Courier,* May 17, 1948, Galarza Papers, Box 35, Folder 14.

73. "Court Injunction Hits Agricultural Workers' Long Strike," *Businessweek,* July 31, 1948, 74–76, Galarza Papers, Box 35, Folder 14.

74. Ernesto Galarza, "DiGiorgio Strikers Face Guns, Eviction," *Seafarers Log,* June 4, 1949, Galarza Papers, Box 35, Folder 14.

75. *Union Reporter,* May 1948, Galarza Papers, Box 35, Folder 14.

76. Galarza Papers, Box 36, Folder 5.

77. Galarza, *Spiders in the House,* 33.

78. Ibid., 33.

79. Roy Brewer, "Movies for Labor: Hollywood Film Council Leads the Way," *American Federationist,* July 1948, 11, Galarza Papers, Box 35, Folder 14.

80. Galarza, *Spiders in the House,* 32.

81. George Lipsitz, *The Possessive Investment in Whiteness: How White People Profit from Identity Politics* (Philadelphia: Temple University Press, 1998).

82. Galarza, *Farm Workers and Agri-business in California*, 68–69, 67.

83. Mae Ngai, *Impossible Subjects: Illegal Aliens and the Making of Modern America* (Princeton, N.J.: Princeton University Press, 2014), 128, 149.

84. Galarza, *Spiders in the House*, 97.

85. Dennis Hevesi, "Roy Brewer, 97, Labor Chief in Blacklist-Era Hollywood, Dies," *New York Times,* September 23, 2006, http://www.nytimes.com/2006/09/23/obituaries/23brewer.html. Brewer's central role in the attack on *Salt of the Earth* is extensively documented by James J. Lorence in *The Suppression of Salt of the Earth: How Hollywood, Big Labor, and Politicians Blacklisted a Movie in the American Cold War* (Albuquerque: University of New Mexico Press, 1999). For a discussion of Brewer and Reagan, see Michael Rogin, "Ronald Reagan, the Movie," in *Ronald Reagan, the Movie: And Other Episodes in Political Demonology* (Berkeley: University of California Press, 1987), 28–29.

86. Galarza, *Spiders in the House*, 96.

2. From Third Cinema to National Video

1. Philip K. Dick, "Strange Memories of Death," in *The Shifting Realities of Philip K. Dick: Selected Literary and Philosophical Writings,* ed. Lawrence Sutin (New York: Vintage Books, [1984] 1995), 39. Dick completed the story in 1979, but it was first published after his death.

2. "You fuck. You dong. You shit. You turd prick . . . cock-sucking fair whore pimp, you ass-kisser, you fuck . . . You weakling. You puke. You suck-off. You snatch." Dick, *A Scanner Darkly* (New York: Houghton Mifflin Harcourt, 2011), 260.

3. Ibid., 274–75.

4. Ibid., 285.

5. See Karl Marx, *Capital: A Critique of Political Economy,* vol. 1, ed. Frederick Engels and trans. Samuel Moore and Edward Aveling (Moscow: Progress Publishers, [1867] 2015), 405, 404.

6. While farm labor is distinct from the forms of slavery he studies in *Slavery and Social Death,* Orlando Patterson's analysis is suggestive for understanding the construction of farm worker abjection, as the quotations I have incorporated in this sentence suggest. See Patterson, *Slavery and Social Death: A Comparative Study* (Cambridge, Mass.: Harvard University Press, 1982), 3, 5, 7 10, 13.

7. For photography, see the two massive volumes by Richard Steven Street, *Photographing Farm Workers in California* (Stanford, Calif.: Stanford University Press, 2004), and *Everyone Had Cameras: Photography and Farm Workers in California, 1850–2000* (Minneapolis: University of Minnesota Press, 2008). While there is a vast amount of film and video depicting California farm workers, and in particular the UFW, large collections have not been gathered together and made readily accessible. For samples of relevant film and video clips, see the Farm Worker Movement Documentation Project, https://libraries.ucsd.edu/farmworkermovement/medias/videos/. The largest collection of UFW-related film and video is at the Walter P. Reuther Library at Wayne State University in Detroit. More generally, the most iconic footage of the march to Sacramento, for

example, and of Chavez and Robert Kennedy, has been used repeatedly in documentaries and on television, so that anyone with even a passing familiarity with the UFW has probably seen some of the images.

8. *The Big Land* (1967), David L. Wolper Collection, Cinema Library, University of Southern California; Mark Arax and Rick Wartzman, *The King of California: J. G. Boswell and the Making of a Secret American Empire* (New York: Public Affairs, 2003), 344–45. For similar photographic images and related text see *DiGiorgio Corporation 1965 Annual Report,* Ernesto Galarza Papers, Special Collections M0224, Stanford University Libraries, Department of Special Collections and University Archives, Box 35, Folder 1.

9. Sigmund Freud, quoted in Elizabeth Cowie, *Representing the Woman: Cinema and Psychoanalysis* (Minneapolis: University of Minnesota Press, 1996), 172.

10. Sarah S. Lochlann Jain, *Injury: The Politics of Product Design and Safety Law in the United States* (Princeton, N.J.: Princeton University Press, 2006), 81–82.

11. See https://libraries.ucsd.edu/farmworkermovement/gallery/thumbnails .php?album=277.

12. John Gregory Dunne, *Delano: The Story of the California Grape Strike* (Berkeley: University of California Press, [1967/1971] 2008), 17.

13. Griswold del Castillo and Garcia, *César Chávez: A Triumph of the Spirit* (Norman: University of Oklahoma Press, 1995), 42–44, 49–51.

14. Other early films about the new farm worker movement include *Decision at Delano* (1967), an educational film released with a study guide; *Forbidden Fruit* (1969), by William Daniels, a short color film made to support of the UFW grape boycott; and *Nosotros Venceremos / We Shall Overcome* (1971), an edited compilation of photos set to a sound track by photographer and union volunteer Jon Lewis and originally intended solely for farm worker audiences.

15. Mark Harris, "On Making *Huelga,*" Farm Worker Documentation Project; Harris, e-mail.

16. The details in this paragraph, along with the quotations, are from Dunne, *Delano,* 24–27.

17. Ibid., 28.

18. Street, *Everyone Had Cameras,* 427–28.

19. Quoted in ibid., 432–33.

20. Cesar Chavez, Dolores Huerta, and Luis Valdez, "The Plan of Delano," *El Malcriado,* March 17, 1966, reprinted in *Cesar Chavez, an Organizer's Tale: Speeches,* ed. Ilan Stavans (New York: Penguin, 2008), 11–14.

21. *Huelga* and *Nosotros Venceremos / We Shall Overcome* can be viewed at the Farmworker Movement Documentation Project, https://libraries.ucsd.edu/ farmworkermovement/medias/videos/.

22. Lauren Araiza, "'In Common Struggle against a Common Oppression': The United Farm Workers and the Black Panther Party, 1968–1973," *Journal of African American History* 94, no. 2 (2008): 200–223.

23. Miriam Pawel, *The Crusades of Cesar Chavez: A Biography* (New York: Bloomsbury, 2014), 125.

24. Cesar Chavez, "An Organizer's Tale," in *Cesar Chavez, an Organizer's Tale,* ed. Stavans, 20–21.

25. Cesar Chavez, in *The Words of Cesar Chavez, ed. Richard J. Jensen and John C. Hammerback (College Station: Texas A&M University Press, 2002),* 64.

26. The Walter P. Reuther Labor Library, Wayne State University, Detroit, archives the UFW's papers. See the documents from the UFW Office of the President Collection: "Films" (Box 32, Folder 17); "Media, 1970–71" (Box 43, Folder 20); "Delano Movie Scripts" (Box 28, Folder 11); and "Films about Farmworkers, 1971" (Box 30, Folders 17–19). In the UFW Information and Research Department Records Collection, see "Fighting for Our Lives; film; premiere, 1975" (Box 49, Folder 1–4); "Fighting for Our Lives; film; premiere notices, 1975" (Box 49, Folder 5–6); "Fighting for Our Lives; film; premiere itinerary, 1975" (Box 49, Folder 7); and the files about the film's premiere in Baltimore, Boston, Chicago, Colorado, Connecticut, Grand Rapids, Houston, Milwaukee, Minnesota, Ohio, Pennsylvania, Portland, San Diego, and Seattle (Box 49, Folders 8, 20, 11, 17, 10, 16, 15, 13, 14, 19, 12, 18, 9, 21). Also in the UFW Information and Research Department Records Collection, see "Film Projects, 1970–71" (Box 49, Folder 23). In the UFW Administration Department Files Collection, see "Pesticides Correspondence for 'Forbidden Fruit'" (Box 21, Folder 2); "Fighting for Our Lives College Showings, 1977" (Box Create, Folder 45); and "Film Department, 1974–75" (Box 29, Folder 43).

27. Matthew Garcia, *From the Jaws of Victory: The Triumph and Tragedy of Cesar Chavez and the Farm Worker Movement* (Berkeley: University of California Press, 2014), 157, 283; Pawel, *Crusades of Cesar Chavez,* 311, 313, 315.

28. Frantz Fanon, *Black Skin, White Masks* (New York: Grove Press, 2008), 90–91.

29. Julio García Espinosa, "For an Imperfect Cinema," trans. Julianne Burton, *Jump Cut* 20 (May 1979): 24–26; Fernando Solanas and Octavio Getino, "Towards a Third Cinema," *Documentary Is Never Neutral,* 1969, http:// documentaryisneverneutral.com/words/camasgun.html.

30. See Garcia, *From the Jaws of Victory;* Pawel, *Crusades of Cesar Chavez,;* Pawel, *The Union of Their Dreams: Power, Hope and Struggle in Cesar Chavez's Farm Worker Movement* (New York: Bloomsbury, 2012); and Randy Shaw, *Beyond the Fields: Cesar Chavez, the UFW, and Struggle for Justice in the 21st Century* (Berkeley: University of California Press, 2010).

31. Cesar Chavez, quoted by Daniel Chasen in "Marcher," *New Yorker,* May 27, 1967, 28.

32. John W. Roberts, *Putting Foreign Policy to Work: The Role of Organized Labor in American Foreign Relations, 1932–1941* (New York: Garland, 1995).

33. Peter Linebaugh and Bruno Ramirez, "Crisis in the Auto Sector," in *Midnight Notes Collective, Midnight Oil: Work, Energy, War, 1973–1992* (Brooklyn, N.Y.: Autonomedia, 1992), 157–58.

34. Nelson Lichtenstein, *Walther Reuther: The Most Dangerous Man in Detroit* (New York: Basic Books, 1995).

35. Chavez, Huerta, and Valdez, "Plan of Delano," 12.

36. "*Rerum Novarum,* Encyclical of Pope Leo XIII on Capital and Labor," The Vatican, http://w2.vatican.va/content/leo-xiii/en/encyclicals/documents/hf_l-xiii _enc_15051891_rerum-novarum.html.

37. Ana Raquel Minian, "'Indiscriminate and Shameless Sex': The Strategic Use of Sexuality by the United Farm Workers," *American Quarterly* 65, no. 1 (2013): 78.

38. John D'Emilio and Estelle B. Freedman, *Intimate Matters: A History of Sexuality in America* (Chicago: University of Chicago Press, 1998).

39. Pawel, *Crusades of Cesar Chavez*, 379, 386, 402.

40. See "UFW Position Statements" (Box 28, File 22), in the UFW Administration Department Files Collection, Reuther Labor Library, Wayne State University, Detroit.

41. Bruce Neuburger, *Lettuce Wars: Ten Years of Work and Struggle in the Fields of California* (New York: Monthly Review Press, 2013), 216.

42. Ibid.

43. "Passover at Delano," *El Malcriado*, May 1, 13.

44. *Between the Lines*, Peace and Education Center, University of Michigan, Public Access Television, Lansing, Michigan, November 9, 1987, UFW A-V Collection, Box 10, Walter P. Reuther Library, Archives of Labor and Urban Affairs, Wayne State University.

45. Pawel, *Union of Their Dreams*, 186–89.

46. Ibid., 188–89.

47. Ibid., 249.

48. Chavez, Huerta, and Valdez, "Plan of Delano," 12.

49. "American Jewish Tourists Boycott Mexico Due to 'Zionist Resolution,'" *Lakeland Ledger*, December 22, 1975, 2.

50. See the special forum "From La Frontera to Gaza: Chicano–Palestinian Connections," ed. Laura Pulido and David Lloyd, *American Quarterly* 62, no. 4 (2010): 791–872. Ironically, the forum was based on a Cesar Chavez Day event at the University of Southern California in 2009, and raised questions about the lessons to be learned from UFW boycotts for possible boycotts of Israel (791).

51. Pawel, *Union of Their Dreams*, 132; Shaw, *Beyond the Fields*, 253–54.

52. "Cesar Chavez Hails Philippines' Rule," *Washington Post*, July 29, 1977, A11.

53. See Benedict J. Kerkvliet, "Land Reform in the Philippines: All Show, No Go," *The Nation*, May 11, 1974, 586–89.

54. The photos are archived at the Walter P. Reuther Library of Wayne State University and can be viewed at http://reuther.wayne.edu/search/node/chavez+philippines.

55. Pawel, *Union of Their Dreams*, 234; Shaw, *Beyond the Fields*, 254.

56. Cesar Chavez, "Editorial," *Food and Justice*, January 1988, 2.

57. Octavio Getino and Fernando Solanas, "Toward a Third Cinema," *Tricontinental* 14 (October 1969): 127.

58. See Gladys D. Ganley and Oswald H. Ganley, *Global Political Fallout: The First Decade of the VCR, 1976–1985* (Cambridge, Mass.: Program on Information Resources Policy, Harvard University Center for Information Policy Research, 1987), 98. For more information about video revolutionary movements see especially chapter 9, "Varieties of Global Political Acts Involving VCRs and Videocassettes," 94–119. See also Douglas A. Boyd, Joseph D. Straubhaar, and John A. Lent, *Videocassette Recorders in the Third World* (London: Longman, 1989), 200.

59. Boyd, Straubhaar, and Lent, *Videocassette Recorders in the Third World*, 198.

60. Sacvan Bercovitch, *The American Jeremiad* (Madison: University of Wisconsin Press, 1980).

61. Cesar Chavez, "Statement Ending Fast, Delano, California, August 21, 1988," in *The Words of Cesar Chavez*, ed. Richard J. Jensen and John C. Hammerback (College Station: Texas A&M University Press, 2002), 168–69.

62. Video of the event is archived at the Walter P. Reuther Library, Wayne State University.

63. *Food and Justice*, September 1989, back cover.

64. Michael Rogin, *Ronald Reagan, the Movie: And Other Episodes in Political Demonology* (Berkeley: University of California, Berkeley, 1987), 300.

3. Farm Worker Futurisms in Speculative Culture

1. Michael Cieply, "A Film School's New Look Is Historic," *New York Times*, February 8, 2009, http://www.nytimes.com/2009/02/09/movies/09film.html.

2. On the racial politics of Fairbanks's star image, as well as the actor's racism, see Lary May, *Screening Out the Past: The Birth of Mass Culture and the Motion Picture Industry* (Chicago: University of Chicago Press, 1980), 96–146, 216.

3. Carey McWilliams, *Southern California: An Island on the Land* (Salt Lake City, Utah: Peregrine Smith, [1946] 1995); John R. Chávez, *The Lost Land: The Chicano Image of the Southwest* (Albuquerque: University of New Mexico Press, 1984), 85–106; William Deverell, *Whitewashed Adobe: The Rise of Los Angeles and the Remaking of Its Mexican Past* (Berkeley: University of California Press, 2005).

4. Randy Shaw, *Beyond the Fields: Cesar Chavez, the UFW, and Struggle for Justice in the 21st Century* (Berkeley: University of California Press, 2010), 95.

5. Laura Pulido, e-mail.

6. Maria Elena Chavez, interview with Osa Hidalgo de la Riva, "Chicana Spectators and Media Makers," *Spectator* 21, no. 1 (2006): 42.

7. Shaw, *Beyond the Fields*, 94–95.

8. John Steinbeck, *The Harvest Gypsies: On the Road to the Grapes of Wrath* (Berkeley, Calif.: Heyday Books, [1936] 1988); Carey McWilliams, *Factories in the Field: The Story of Migratory Farm Labor in California* (Berkeley: University of California Press, [1935] 1990), 211–29; Vicki Ruiz, *Cannery Women, Cannery Lives: Mexican Women, Unionization, and the California Food Processing Industry, 1930–1950* (Albuquerque: University of New Mexico Press, 1987); Devra Weber, *Dark Sweat, White Gold: California Cotton, Farm Workers, and the New Deal, 1919–1939* (Berkeley: University of California Press, 1996).

9. Walter Goldschmidt, *As You Sow* (Glencoe, Ill.: Free Press, 1946), 117–19.

10. Richard Steven Street, "*Poverty in the Valley of Plenty*: The National Farm Labor Union, DiGiorgio Farms, and Suppression of Documentary Photography in California, 1947–66," *Labor History* 48, no. 1 (2007): 25–48, and *Photographing Farm Workers in California* (Stanford, Calif.: Stanford University Press, 2004).

11. Richard Griswold del Castillo and Richard A. Garcia, *César Chávez: A Triumph of the Spirit* (Norman: University of Oklahoma Press, 1997), 13. Except where otherwise stated, the information in this section about Chavez and the UFW comes from this source.

12. John Baxter, *Mythmaker: The Life and Work of George Lucas* (New York:

Spike Books, 1999), 21–29; Dale Pollack, *Skywalking: The Life and Films of George Lucas* (New York: Da Capo, 1999), 11–40. Unless otherwise noted, all biographical information about Lucas comes from these two biographies.

13. Ernesto Galarza, *Spiders in the House, Workers in the Field* (Notre Dame, Ind.: University of Notre Dame Press, 1970); Street, *"Poverty in the Valley of Plenty."*

14. Steve Silberman, "Life after Darth," *Wired,* May 2005, http://www.wired .com/wired/archive/13.05/lucas.html.

15. George Lucas, *The Emperor,* Cinematic Arts Library, University of Southern California.

16. *American Cinematographer,* October 1971, reprinted in *George Lucas: Interviews,* ed. Sally Kline (Jackson: University Press of Mississippi, 1999), 9.

17. *NBC Evening News,* December 7, 1970, Vanderbilt Television News Archive, http://tvnews.vanderbilt.edu/?SID=20090918509796142; *KPIX Eyewitness News,* December 6, 1970, https://diva.sfsu.edu/collections/sfbatv/bundles/206821; Mike Davis, "Beating the UFW," in *No One Is Illegal: Fighting Racism and State Violence on the U.S.–Mexico Border,* ed. Justin Akers Chacón (Chicago: Haymarket Books, 2006), 79.

18. According to the records of the Vanderbilt Television News Archive, news of Chavez's imprisonment and his statement to supporters was broadcast nationally by *CBS Evening News* and *NBC Evening News* on December 4, 1970. His release from jail and press conference was again covered by CBS and NBC on December 24, 1970. On the same day similar scenes were broadcast locally in California by San Francisco's CBS affiliate, KPIX. For the latter see the San Francisco Bay Area Television Archive, https://diva.sfsu.edu/collections/sfbatv/bundles/190205.

19. Quoted by Judy Stone, "George Lucas," *San Francisco Chronicle,* May 23, 1971, reproduced in *George Lucas,* ed. Kline, 5.

20. See http://www.chavezfoundation.org/uploads/Si_Se_Puede_History.pdf.

21. *CBS Evening News,* February 28, 1975, Vanderbilt Television News Archive.

22. My reading of *THX 1138* is indebted to Janani Subramanian, who analyzes racial representation in the film in the context of theories of the avant-garde. See her "The Fantastic Avant-Garde," in "Riddles of Representation in Fantastic Cinema" (Ph.D. diss., University of Southern California, 2009). See also her essay "Alienating Identification: Black Identity in *The Brother from Another Planet* and *I Am Legend," Science Fiction Film and Television* 3, no. 1 (2010): 37–56.

23. David James, *The Most Typical Avant-Garde: History and Geography of Minor Cinemas in Los Angeles* (Berkeley: University of California Press, 2005), 208–12.

24. *Bald* is included on *THX 1138: The George Lucas Director's Cut Special Edition* DVD (Burbank, Calif.: Warner Home Video, 2005).

25. Walter Murch, commentary track, ibid.

26. See Lucas quoted by Stephen Farber in *George Lucas,* ed. Kline, 38, and by Michael Pye and Linda Miels in "George Lucas," in *The Movie Brats* (New York: Holt Rinehart and Winston, 1979), reprinted in ibid., 68.

27. Judy Stone, "George Lucas," in *George Lucas,* ed. Kline, 5–7.

28. See Farber in ibid., 38.

29. David Harvey, *A Brief History of Neoliberalism* (New York: Oxford University Press, 2005), 42.

30. As a teen in Modesto, Lucas was on the margins of a car club called the Faros (Spanish for lights, as in headlights), and the name was changed to "Pharaohs" for the film. Pollock, *Skywalking*, 27–28.

31. "Opposition Propaganda" (Box 31, File 15) and "Anti-union Propaganda" (Box 34, File 40), UFW Administration Papers, Walter P. Reuther Library, Wayne State University.

32. "The Little Strike That Grew to La Causa," *Time*, July 4, 1969, http://www.time.com/time/magazine/article/0,9171,840167-2,00.html; *Bitter Harvest: Chavez Fights On* (1976), BBC Video, UFW VHS Collection, Box 1, Walter P. Reuther Library, Wayne State University.

33. Laura Flanders, *Bushwomen: Tales of a Cynical Species* (New York: Verso Press, 2004), 113.

34. Victor Hanson, *An Autumn of War: What America Learned from September 11 and the War on Terrorism* (New York: Anchor Books, 2002), xvi. See also Hanson, *Field without Dreams: Defending the Agrarian Ideal* (New York: Free Press, 1997), and *Mexifornia: A State of Becoming* (New York: Encounter Books, 2004).

35. Hanson, *Field without Dreams*, xxi, 17, xx.

36. Hanson, *Mexifornia*, 97–98.

37. Interview with Alex Rivera, *SF 360*, May 14, 2008, http://www.sf360.org/page/11194; Alex Rivera, director's commentary, *Sleep Dealer* DVD (Los Angeles: Maya Entertainment, 2009).

38. Silberman, "Life after Darth."

39. Michael Omi and Howard Winant, *Racial Formations in the United States: From the 1960s to the 1990s* (New York: Routledge, 1994), 116.

40. Clyde R. Taylor, *The Mask of Art: Breaking the Aesthetic Contract—Film and Literature* (Bloomington: Indiana University Press, 1998), 148–50; Martin Kevorkian, *Color Monitors: The Black Face of Technology in America* (Ithaca, N.Y.: Cornell University Press, 2006), 123–26.

41. George Mariscal, *Brown-Eyed Children of the Sun: Lessons of the Chicano Movement* (Albuquerque: University of New Mexico Press, 2005), 156–59.

42. Michael Rogin, Ronald Reagan, *the Movie: And Other Episodes in Political Demonology* (Berkeley: University of California Press, 1987), xiii, 10, 39–40.

43. Quoted in Silberman, "Life after Darth."

44. James, *Most Typical Avant-Garde*, 213. James was a member of a USC faculty organization in solidarity with the striking service workers discussed at the start of this chapter.

45. Skywalker Sound, http://skysound.com/qtvr/qtvr_tour_front_porch.html (accessed September 17, 2009).

46. See http://skywalkervineyards.com/history/index.html (accessed August 30, 2012).

47. The one exception here is *American Graffiti*, which has been released on DVD with a digitally remastered sound track but apparently no other changes or additions.

48. YouTube user "Videosteni" has produced a useful comparison of the two versions of the film. See http://www.youtube.com/watch?v=kIfTT8EGj3A.

49. Rachael Ida Buff, "The Deportation Terror," *American Quarterly* 60, no. 3 (2008): 523–51.

50. See, for example, Patricia J. Williams, "Racial Ventriloquism," *The Nation,* July 5, 1999, http://www.thenation.com/article/racial-ventriloquism/.

51. See Michele Pierson's *Special Effects: Still in Search of Wonder* (New York: Columbia University Press, 2002), for a critique of understandings of CGI solely in realist terms.

52. See Henry Jenkins, "Quentin Tarantino's Star Wars? Grassroots Creativity Meets the Media Industry," in *Convergence Culture: Where Old and New Media Collide* (New York: New York University Press, 2006), which makes claims for a new participatory digital culture that reduces democracy to market freedoms and affirms forms of corporate capitalism.

53. Ester Hernandez, keynote address, National Association of Latino Artists Conference, September 26, 1992, San Antonio. See the Ester Hernandez Papers, Box 37, Folder 6, Cecil H. Green Library, Stanford University Libraries.

54. Ibid.

55. Hernandez, quoted by Theresa Harlan in "A Conversation with Ester Hernandez," in the exhibit catalog *The Art of Provocation: Ester Hernandez, a Retrospective,* October 10–November 17, 1995, Gorman Museum, Native American Studies, University of California, Davis, Hernandez Papers, Box 93, Folder 1.

56. Ibid.

57. Hernandez, keynote address, National Association of Latino Artists Conference.

58. *La Virgen de Guadalupe defendiendo los derechos de los Chicanos (The Virgin of Guadalupe Defending the Rights of Chicanos)* (1975), etching, 16 × 14 inches, http://www.esterhernandez.com/.

59. Ibid.

60. Ester Hernandez, *Heroes and Saints* (1992), print, 59 × 76.5 cm, Hernandez Papers, Map Folder 12.

61. Ester Hernandez, *The Beating of Dolores Huerta by the San Francisco Police* (1988), charcoal on pastel paper, 71 × 55 cm, Hernandez Papers, Map Folder 2.

62. Michael Doyle, "Grapes Squeezed for Votes by GOP, Demos," *Fresno Bee,* September 21, 1988, A1.

63. Jim Boren, "Sour Grape at Bush Rally: Dancing Raisin Arrested," *Fresno Bee,* September 16, 1988, B1.

64. *San Francisco Examiner,* November 7, 1988, A10; Marcelo Rodriguez, "Sorrows of the Orchard," *San Francisco Weekly,* May 9, 1990, 9; "Huerta Survives Near-Fatal Beating," *Food and Justice* 5 (October 1988): 4, clipping, Hernandez Papers, Box 93, Folder 1.

65. Maureen Dowd, "'I'm President,' So No More Broccoli!" *New York Times,* March 23, 1990, http://www.nytimes.com/1990/03/23/us/i-m-president-so-no-more-broccoli.html.

66. Jim Boren, "Students Ready Bush Welcome, Signs of Support Take Shape for Valley Campaign," *Fresno Bee,* September 14, 1988, B1.

67. Doyle, "Grapes Squeezed for Votes by GOP, Demos."

68. Rodriguez, "Sorrows of the Orchard," 9.

69. Dolores Huerta, UFW press release, "Union Responds to Bush Attack on Grape Boycott," September 14, 1988, Hernandez Papers, Box 91, Folder 2.

70. *Sun Mad* (1982), print 10/100, 56 × 43 cm, Hernandez Papers, Flat Box 10.

71. See the YouTube video "The Story of the Real Sun-Maid Girl," http://www.youtube.com/watch?v=1GpiDqhArE0&feature=player_embedded#!.

72. Hernandez, quoted in Harlan, *Art of Provocation*.

73. Amalia Mesa-Bains, "The Art of Provocation: Works by Ester Hernandez," in ibid.

74. Huerta, quoted on the cover of ibid.

Afterword

1. See http://lowdrone.com/.

2. Rosaura Sánchez and Beatrice Pita, *Lunar Braceros, 2125–2148* (National City, Calif.: Calaca Press, 2009), 7.

3. Ibid., 14.

4. Ibid., 120.

5. Victor Hanson, *Mexifornia: A State of Becoming* (New York: Encounter Books, 2004), 10, 45, 56, 131–32.

6. Ron and Kay Rivoli, "Press One for English," https://www.youtube.com/watch?v=sEJfS1v-fU0.

7. Rob Sebastian and Tim Chambers, *Mobile Media in 21st Century Politics* (New York: New Politics Institute, 2006), 25. See also K. Wayne Yang, "Organizing MySpace: Youth Walkouts, Pleasure, Politics, and New Media," *Journal of Educational Foundations* 21, nos. 1–2 (2007): 9–28.

8. Sebastian and Chambers, *Mobile Media in 21st Century Politics,* 26.

9. Jill Lane, "Digital Zapatistas," *Drama Review* 47, no. 2 (2003): 130.

10. Christopher Knight, "A Past That Still Resonates," *Los Angeles Times,* July 25, 2008, http://articles.latimes.com/2008/jul/25/entertainment/et-galleries25; Mark Tribe, "The Port Huron Project," http://www.marktribe.net/port-huron-project/; Ricardo Dominguez, "We Are Also Responsible: Cesar Chavez, 1971/2008," https://www.youtube.com/watch?v=-bkYfLMlGNY.

11. Ricardo Dominguez, "The Art of Crossing Borders: Migrant Rights and Academic Freedom," *Boom: A Journal of California* 1, no. 4 (2001): http://www.boomcalifornia.com/2012/03/the-art-of-crossing-borders-migrant-rights-and-academic-freedom/.

12. "Boycott Booming," *Food and Justice,* September 1989, 7; "Cesar Chavez's Video Collection," *American Literature* 85, no. 4 (2013), http://scalar.usc.edu/nehvectors/curtis-marez/ufw-computer-animation-1?path=farm-worker-futurism-introduction.

13. Christopher Gray, "Streetscapes: Douglas Leigh, Sign Maker: The Man behind Times Square's Smoke Rings," *New York Times,* October 24, 1998, http://www.nytimes.com/1998/10/24/realestate/streetscapes-douglas-leigh-sign-maker-the-man-behind-times-square-s-smoke-rings.html?src=pm.

14. The information and quotation in this paragraph are from the online Intel Museum and Corporate Archives as the site appeared in 2009. The Intel webpage has subsequently been substantially revised.

15. See David Naguib Pellow and Lisa Sun-Hee Park, *The Silicon Valley of Dreams: Environmental Injustice, Immigrant Workers, and the High-Tech Global Economy* (New York: New York University Press, 2002); and "Tech's Diversity Problem: More Than Meets the Eye," Working Partnerships USA, 2014, http://wpusa.org/WPUSA_TechsDiversityProblem.pdf.

16. See the website for the Intel Museum and Intel Corporate Archives. Similarly, a keyword search for "Intel" at http://www.siliconvalleyhistory.org/ yields numerous such photos of bunny-suited workers in clean rooms.

17. Interview with Steve Allen, Lawrence Bender, and Richard Steinheimer, "Silicon Genesis: An Oral History of Semiconductor Technology," Special Collections, Stanford University, http://silicongenesis.stanford.edu/complete_listing .html#semi.

18. *A Revolution in Progress . . . A History of Intel to Date* (Santa Clara, Calif: Intel Corporation, 1984), http://www.intel.com/Assets/PDF/General/15yrs.pdf.

19. Michael Kanellos, "Silicon Valley's Misplaced *Star Wars* Lust," *CNET News,* May 10, 1999, http://www.cnet.com/news/silicon-valleys-misplaced-star-wars-lust/.

20. Manuel Castells, *The Internet Galaxy: Reflections on the Internet, Business, and Society* (New York: Oxford University Press, 2001), 36–63.

21. David Bacon, "The New Face of Union Busting," http://dbacon.igc.org/ Unions/02ubust0.htm; Pellow and Park, *Silicon Valley of Dreams*; Curtis Marez, "The Homies in Silicon Valley: Figuring Styles of Life and Work in the Information Age," *Aztlán: A Journal of Chicano Studies* 31, no. 2 (2006): 134–48.

22. See Pellow and Park, *Silicon Valley of Dreams,* 112–92.

23. Ibid., 18.

24. See http://www.homies.tv/homies.htm.

25. Michelle Levander, "Janitors Launch Hunger Strike, Apple Throws Its Support to Contractor," *San Jose Mercury News,* November 13, 1991.

26. Brandon Bailey, "Chavez Calls for an Apple Boycott," *San Jose Mercury News,* November 18, 1991.

27. K. Oanh Ha, "iMac Powers Apple to Profit, Led by Sales of New Computer, It Posts First Year in Black since '95," *San Jose Mercury News,* October 15, 1998.

28. For Intel, see the website for the group "FACE Intel," http://www.faceintel .com/. For Foxconn, the Chinese company that supplies Apple, see Students and Scholars against Corporate Misbehavior, "Workers as Machines: Military Management in Foxconn," October 12, 2010, http://sacom.hk/wp-content/uploads/ 2010/11/report-on-foxconn-workers-as-machines_sacom.pdf; Jenny Chan and Ngai Pun, "Suicide as Protest for the New Generation of Chinese Migrant Workers: Foxconn, Global Capital, and the State," *Asia-Pacific Journal: Japan Focus* 8, no. 37 (2010), http://japanfocus.org/-Jenny-Chan/3408/article.html.

29. "East Porterville CDP, California," U.S. Census Bureau, http://quickfacts .census.gov/qfd/states/06/0621012.html.

30. "East Porterville Residents without Water as Wells Go Dry during California Drought," *CBS News Sacramento,* August 27, 2014, http://sacramento .cbslocal.com/2014/08/27/porterville-residents-without-water-as-wells-go-dry -during-california-drought/.

31. Lisa M. Krieger, "California Drought: San Joaquin Valley Sinking as Farmers Race to Tap Aquifer," *San Jose Mercury News*, March 29, 2014, http://www.mercurynews.com/drought/ci_25447586/california-drought-san-joaquin-valley-sinking-farmers-race.

32. "These Are the Top 10 Most Polluted Cities in the U.S.," *Time*, April 30, 2014, http://time.com/82505/most-polluted-cities-in-america/.

33. "Too Young to Die," *SFGate*, October 3, 2004, http://www.sfgate.com/bayarea/article/TOO-YOUNG-TO-DIE-California-has-one-of-the-2720287.php; "Infant Mortality," Healthy Kern County, April 2014, http://www.healthykern.org/modules.php?op=modload&name=NS-Indicator&file=indicator&iid=3012.

34. "Life Expectancy Male" and "Life Expectancy Female," California Life Expectancy, http://www.worldlifeexpectancy.com/usa/california-life-expectancy-by-county-male and http://www.worldlifeexpectancy.com/usa/california-life-expectancy-by-county-female; Julia Wong, "California Draught Leaves Farmworkers Hung Out to Dry," *In These Times*, August 8, 2014, http://inthesetimes.com/working/entry/17060/california_drought_hangs_farmworkers_out_to_dry.

35. Ritchie Bernardo, "2014's Most and Least Educated Cities," *WalletHub*, http://wallethub.com/edu/most-and-least-educated-cities/6656/.

36. Ruth Wilson Gilmore, *Golden Gulag: Prisons, Surplus, Crisis, and Opposition in Globalizing California* (Berkeley: University of California Press, 2007), 156.

37. Ibid., 155.

38. Ibid., 130.

39. Ibid., 148.

40. Ibid., 173.

41. Ibid., 177.

Index

CURTIS MAREZ is associate professor and chair in the ethnic studies department of the University of California, San Diego. He is the author of *Drug Wars: The Political Economy of Narcotics* (Minnesota, 2004), the former editor of *American Quarterly,* and past president of the American Studies Association.